Major General Thomas Mifflin

ALSO BY ROBERT ERNEST HUBBARD
AND FROM McFARLAND

*General Rufus Putnam:
George Washington's Chief Military Engineer
and the "Father of Ohio"* (2020)

*Major General Israel Putnam:
Hero of the American Revolution* (2017)

Major General Thomas Mifflin

The Army's First Quartermaster General and the First Governor of Pennsylvania

ROBERT ERNEST HUBBARD

McFarland & Company, Inc., Publishers
Jefferson, North Carolina

LIBRARY OF CONGRESS CATALOGING-IN-PUBLICATION DATA

Names: Hubbard, Robert Ernest author
Title: Major General Thomas Mifflin : the army's first quartermaster general and the first governor of Pennsylvania / Robert Ernest Hubbard.
Other titles: Army's first quartermaster general and the first governor of Pennsylvania
Description: Jefferson, North Carolina : McFarland & Company, Inc., Publishers, 2025 | Includes bibliographical references and index.
Identifiers: LCCN 2025007401 | ISBN 9781476692029 print ∞
    ISBN 9781476654461 ebook
Subjects: LCSH: Mifflin, Thomas, 1744–1800 | Generals—United States—Biography | Quartermasters—United States—Biography | United States. Continental Army—Biography | United States—History—Revolution, 1775–1783—Biography | United States. Continental Congress—Presidents—Biography | United States. Constitution—Signers—Biography | Governors—Pennsylvania—Biography | Pennsylvania—Politics and government—1775–1865 | United States—Politics and government—1775–1783 | BISAC: BIOGRAPHY & AUTOBIOGRAPHY / Military | HISTORY / United States / Revolutionary Period (1775–1800) | LCGFT: Biographies
Classification: LCC E207.M6 H83 2025 | DDC 973.3092 $a B—dc23/eng/20250320
LC record available at https://lccn.loc.gov/2025007401

ISBN (print) 978-1-4766-9202-9
ISBN (ebook) 978-1-4766-5446-1

© 2025 Robert Ernest Hubbard. All rights reserved

No part of this book may be reproduced or transmitted in any form or by any means, electronic or mechanical, including photocopying or recording, or by any information storage and retrieval system, without permission in writing from the publisher.

Front cover image: Edward Wellmore's engraving of Gilbert Stuart's portrait of Thomas Mifflin, which was painted when Mifflin was in his fifties (Smithsonian American Art Museum).

Printed in the United States of America

McFarland & Company, Inc., Publishers
  Box 611, Jefferson, North Carolina 28640
    www.mcfarlandpub.com

Acknowledgments

At the top of the list, I wish to acknowledge my wife, Kathleen Hubbard, who has been at my side throughout the entire process of this book—from its conception to its final stages of copyediting. Thank you for your encouragement, advice, and support!

I would like to thank the staffs of Philadelphia's National Constitution Center, Independence Hall, National Historic Landmark Fort Mifflin, Boston National Historical Park, Morristown National Historical Park, Stony Point Battlefield State Historic Site, and the Major General Nathanael Greene Homestead.

Thanks also to the New Haven Free Public Library, the Wallingford (Connecticut) Public Library, the Hamden (Connecticut) Public Library, and Yale University's Sterling Memorial Library.

The staff at the Yale University Art Gallery, the Yale Beinecke Rare Book and Manuscript Library, and the Metropolitan Museum of Art were especially helpful. Among the other institutions that have assisted me are: Juniata County Historical Society (in Mifflintown, Pennsylvania), the Michael E. Busch Annapolis Library, and the East Falls Historical Society.

I would like to thank the dedicated and professional editors at McFarland. I am especially grateful to Sophia Lyons for her valuable advice and support.

Table of Contents

Acknowledgments   v
Preface   1
Introduction   3

ONE. Founding Fathers   9
TWO. Early Years   11
THREE. Before the War   21
FOUR. National Politics   26
FIVE. The War Begins   40
SIX. Quartermaster General of the Continental Army   47
SEVEN. The Siege of Boston   51
EIGHT. The Battle of Long Island   56
NINE. After New York   71
TEN. New Jersey Command   84
ELEVEN. British Occupation of Philadelphia   98
TWELVE. Valley Forge   105
THIRTEEN. Conway Cabal   114
FOURTEEN. Mifflin's Properties   133
FIFTEEN. The Continental Congress   137
SIXTEEN. The Constitutional Convention   149
SEVENTEEN. President of the Supreme Executive Council of Pennsylvania   156

Eighteen.	Governor of Pennsylvania	162
Nineteen.	Mifflin's Last Years	187
Twenty.	Mifflin's Legacy	191

Chapter Notes   197
Bibliography   219
Index   223

Preface

I became interested in Thomas Mifflin's career while doing research for a biography of Major General Israel Putnam. In 1776, Mifflin accompanied Putnam to the Continental Congress to complain about wanton acts of violence in New York City against civilian supporters of the King of England.[1]

Several years later, while working on a biography of Israel's distant cousin, Rufus Putnam, I uncovered details about a spying mission by Mifflin and Rufus (then a colonel). This mission provided crucial information to General Washington about enemy troops, leading to the decision to withdraw the American army from New York City.[2]

In these instances, Mifflin demonstrated a compassion for the underdog, along with courage and patriotism. Impressed by these qualities, I became intrigued by this relatively unknown and unrecognized Founding Father. The opportunity to delve deeper into the life of Thomas Mifflin arose when McFarland accepted my proposal for a book on this often-overlooked patriot and his remarkable career that helped secure America's independence.

Author note: In some quotations I have corrected archaic spelling and punctuation, while I have usually retained the original capitalization.

Introduction

Thomas Mifflin achieved the highest military rank in Washington's Continental Army—major general. Several years later, he ascended to the highest federal government civilian leadership position of pre–U.S. Constitution America—president of the Continental Congress. Yet, in the 222 years following Mifflin's passing, only one full-sized biography has been written: Nebraska college professor Kenneth R. Rossman's 1952 work, *Thomas Mifflin and the Politics of the American Revolution*.[1] Besides Rossman's work, the only other biographical piece on Mifflin was the 20-page "A Sketch of the Life of Thomas Mifflin," by attorney William Rawle, which was printed in 1826.

Why hasn't anything else been published other than these two works by Rossman and Rawle? After all, Mifflin, among his other accomplishments, was a member of the First and Second Continental Congresses, the first quartermaster general in the history of the United States, and a major general in the Continental Army. He served as president of the Congress when that was the only federal governing body, he signed the U.S. Constitution, and he was the first governor of Pennsylvania. The list goes on.

One reason for the paucity of biographical attempts is likely the lack of personal papers—private letters, diaries, etc. One reviewer of Rossman's biography asked the following question in 1952:

> The appearance of a biography on Thomas Mifflin raises an immediate and anxious question: Has the author found the "Mifflin Papers"? That such "papers" did in fact exist and would eventually come to light has been the ardent wish of those interested in the career of this remarkable man. He has long been an enigma—still is, for that matter—and his potential biographers, awaiting the discovery of enough evidence to make a study of his life worthwhile, must have been many. That Mr. Rossman has not found the "papers," or much evidence not known for some time, will be a source of keen disappointment.[2]

Given that another 70 years have passed since this review of Rossman's book, we are led to the inevitable conclusion that those "Mifflin Papers"—to what extent there were ever many at all—were destroyed. The circumstances of Mifflin's life and death also lead to this conclusion. His relatively young age at his passing—and the fact that he worked long and hard in public office almost to the end—is a good reason to think that he never had the time, not to mention the desire, to write his memoirs. In addition, the fact that the state of Pennsylvania had to pay his funeral expenses makes it easy to imagine that what private papers he did have were discarded by the workers charged with cleaning out his meager possessions.

Edward Wellmore's engraving of Gilbert Stuart's portrait of Thomas Mifflin, which was painted when Mifflin was in his fifties (Smithsonian American Art Museum).

As decades—and now centuries—have passed, it is increasingly likely that a trove of private papers, diaries, or a memoir may never surface. In addition to workers discarding his papers, it is plausible that Mifflin intentionally destroyed personal letters, documents, and notes prior to his death. Many times, it is only after one's death that historical writings become valuable as an important glimpse into the past, when at the time they were thought to be not worth keeping.[3]

If Mifflin intentionally disposed of his writings and other documents, it could mirror the situation of his colleague, Charles Thomson (1729–1824), who served as secretary for the Continental Congress throughout its existence (1774 through 1787). Thomson wrote a lengthy account of the inner workings of the Congress and its delegates but chose to destroy it to prevent potential harm to reputations resulting from its revelations (Harley, Lewis Reifsneider. *The Life of Charles Thomson*. Philadelphia, George W. Jacobs & Co., 1900, link, accessed 13 Dec. 2023, p. 159).

Introduction

Many historians have hesitated to embark on writing a Mifflin biography. Many may have preferred crafting a comprehensive narrative of another person from whose life a wealth of documents has been meticulously preserved.[4]

Regardless of the existence of personal papers, I believe that Thomas Mifflin's life was so notable, so influential—and most significantly, so critical to the founding of the United States—that Mifflin and students of history deserve a comprehensive, up-to-date, and accessible modern biography. It is my goal to provide just that.

It is not my intention to exhaustively comb archives in an endless pursuit of every tidbit of information about Mifflin and his life. I leave that task for other researchers who may choose a specific incident or time period in Mifflin's life to delve into more deeply. There are numerous subtopics that merit such dedicated research. I hope that the unanswered questions in this volume will inspire those individuals to explore further. Should they uncover significant information, I eagerly await the opportunity to read it.

In addition to Rossman's comprehensive biography, I have relied on William Rawle's short "A Sketch of the Life of Thomas Mifflin." Unlike Rossman, William Rawle personally knew Thomas Mifflin. Rawle served as U.S. district attorney for Pennsylvania during the same years that Mifflin held the position of governor of Pennsylvania in the 1790s. So, he writes this short biography with credible, first-hand knowledge of a colleague that he had known for many years.

Some of Rawle's comments are very insightful, such as that Mifflin's "natural disposition and confirmed habits were of an ardent and active kind: he was unaccustomed to and perhaps unqualified for slow deliberation and patient investigation." Although his work is short, we are indebted to the important information about Mifflin's life and career that would have been lost, but for Rawle.[5]

William Rawle (1759–1836) was raised as a Quaker in Philadelphia similar to Thomas Mifflin, who was fifteen years his senior. However, unlike Mifflin and Mifflin's father, Rawle's father supported the British during the American Revolution. Mifflin began his career as a merchant, while Rawle studied law. Like many well-to-do young men of the time, both men traveled to Europe after completing their schooling, and in later life, both were, for a time, considered Federalists (the party of Washington and John Adams). However, Rawle only served one term in the Pennsylvania Assembly and left for a private law practice, while Mifflin made public service his career.

On September 15, 1783, William Rawle founded a law firm in Philadelphia. Now named Rawle & Henderson, LLP, it is, in the 21st century, the oldest law firm in the United States. Rawle was also a delegate to the Pennsylvania Constitutional Assembly of 1789, the first U.S. Attorney for the District of Pennsylvania (1791), and president of the Pennsylvania Abolition Society.

During his life, Mifflin worked closely with almost every one of the greatest founding fathers of the United States. He served as a fellow member of the Pennsylvania government, as well as the federal Continental Congress and at both the state and federal levels worked alongside a man that many believe was the greatest genius of the thirteen colonies and later the United States of America—Benjamin Franklin.

Both Benjamin Franklin and George Washington were beloved public figures, and were well known to Thomas Mifflin. After George Washington was appointed commander of the Continental Army, he needed a military aide. He had known and worked with numerous people back home in Virginia and in the Continental Congress. Of all the men he had known in civilian or military capacities, he chose one—Thomas Mifflin—to be his first military aide. That was the start of Mifflin's military career—one that would become remarkable and unique.

Why is Mifflin considered an American founding father? Unless we confine the definition of "founding father" to only a few most famous creators of the nation, Mifflin was in every sense one of the country's founding fathers. When Thomas Mifflin was born in Philadelphia, Pennsylvania, in 1744, the city had a population of about 10,000 residents. That's one-half the capacity of, for instance, New York City's Empire State building—one 1931 building! Yet Philadelphia was destined, within three decades, to triple its population and become the birthplace of the United States of America. Mifflin would play a large part in making this birth a reality.[6]

Thomas Mifflin can be considered an heir apparent, born into wealth and privilege; yet he did not rest on his father's achievements, rather he took a more challenging path that was demanded by his high moral convictions. He did not believe in the enslavement of other people. He looked to the future and exerted himself to meet its needs. Let's place Mifflin in a more recent setting to see how to understand this man.

If someone in 1943 was the son of John D. Rockefeller, had as a neighbor and mentor an Albert Einstein, graduated from Harvard or Oxford, and toured the most developed countries of the world as a graduation present, one might say he's "born with a silver spoon in his mouth." If, further, at age 31, he had been chosen by Supreme Allied Commander in Europe Dwight Eisenhower to have responsibility to supply all American forces in Europe that would be fighting Hitler's

Introduction

Germany, and be raised to the rank of general nine months after that, he would be the 20th century's equivalent to Thomas Mifflin.

Son of a wealthy and prominent Philadelphia, Pennsylvania, merchant, Thomas went to the best college of his day, and had as a neighbor arguably the most famous and brilliant American in the world—Benjamin Franklin. In 1775, at age 31, Mifflin was chosen by the commander in chief of the Continental Army, George Washington, to be his first military aide, and was given the responsibility to supply the Continental Army with all of its supplies. Mifflin successfully executed these duties with diligence and hard work and was raised to the rank of brigadier general after nine months.

But that's only part of the story. Mifflin used his education; his practical, business knowledge, acquired as a merchant; his organizational skills; and his ability to work with all types of people and made an incredible career that rivaled any of the American Founding Fathers—except those that are household names today. Yet Thomas Mifflin is anything but a household name. Why is that? That is a question that I will address with this book.

> "[I] never saw a greater display of personal bravery, than was exhibited on this occasion in the cool and intrepid conduct of Colonel Mifflin."
> —Militia General Thomas Craig, one of the last surviving officers of the American Revolutionary War, remembering Mifflin leading militia troops against British regulars in 1775.[7]

> "In *patriotic principles* never changing—in *public action* never faltering—in *personal friendship* sincerely warm—in *relieving the distressed* always active and humane—in his own affairs improvident—in the business of others scrupulously just."
> —William Rawle, the first U.S. district attorney for Pennsylvania (1791–1799), and the president of the Pennsylvania Abolition Society.[8]

> "[Thomas Mifflin] was in early life '*the beloved man*' of Pennsylvania, ... her confidence and affection in respect to him, were *never* diminished."
> —William Rawle.[9]

Chapter One

Founding Fathers

The Founding Fathers shared a belief in liberty, self-governance, and the rights and freedoms of individual people: freedom of speech, freedom of religion, and freedom to assemble. This was perhaps the major reason they were willing—and able—to work together to achieve something no other nation up to that point had accomplished. The freedoms found a permanent place in the first ten amendments to the U.S. Constitution.

Most of the Founding Fathers were already leaders before the American Revolution. George Washington played a prominent role in the French and Indian War a decade and a half earlier. When hostilities with British troops began, Benjamin Franklin was nearly 60 years of age and an internationally-celebrated scientist. The Founders were also a diverse group—including lawyers, military leaders, medical doctors, farmers, merchants, businessmen, and other occupations.

Who is considered a Founding Father of the United States? The *Encyclopædia Britannica* lists ten "greats" who have "stood the test of time." Four went on to become the first four presidents of the United States: George Washington, John Adams, Thomas Jefferson, and James Madison. Three were primarily known as early and vocal supporters of American independence: George Mason, Samuel Adams, and Patrick Henry. Two played important roles in the establishment and development of the new nation: Alexander Hamilton (the first secretary of the treasury) and John Marshall (the chief justice of the U.S. Supreme Court for 34 of the first 45 years of the country's existence). The last founder of the ten, Benjamin Franklin, was likely the most brilliant and accomplished North American man of the 18th century.

Renaissance man Franklin was a successful inventor, scientist, statesman, diplomat, politician, writer, businessman, publisher, printer, and philanthropist. He transformed lives: first with his published writings—which had a broad reach in teaching, informing, and persuading the general masses—and second with his practical inventions like lightning rods, the Franklin Stove, and bifocals.

Three of these men—Thomas Jefferson of Virginia, John Adams of Massachusetts, and Benjamin Franklin of Pennsylvania—would go on to serve on the five-person committee that drafted the Declaration of Independence.[1]

Most of the major founding fathers played important roles in forming the new national government and its relationship with state governments. Two of them—Washington and Hamilton—served as general officers in the American Revolutionary War.

If the term "founding father" was limited to these men, the library sections devoted to biographies of the American Revolution would be very sparse indeed. But there is no reason they should be so restrictive—the successful split with Great Britain and the formation of a new nation would probably have occurred if any one of these men had been taken out of the picture. The one possible exception is Washington—and that only because of his role as commander of the American armed forces during the Revolutionary War. It is not without reason that James Thomas Flexner gave his 1974 biography of Washington the title *Washington: The Indispensable Man*.[2] If he had not been in charge of the military forces throughout the entire seven years of the war, the British might well have been victorious and independence might have been delayed for another century.[3]

There were other founding fathers, sometimes referred to as the second tier. Many say the 39 delegates at the Constitutional Convention who signed the U.S. Constitution should be considered founding fathers. One half of *Encyclopædia Britannica's* "greats" were also signers of that document: George Washington, Benjamin Franklin, James Madison, Alexander Hamilton, and George Mason. Thomas Mifflin was one of these 39 signers, too, and, as we will see, he served in high military and civilian positions during the Revolutionary War.

In addition to founding fathers, we have "founding mothers"—women who played an especially important role in the founding of the United States of America. Some of the most prominent were: Abigail Adams, who advised her husband John Adams throughout his long career; Dolley Madison, who more than anyone else established the role of an active first lady; and dramatist, poet, and historian Mercy Otis Warren. Warren has been called "the leading female intellectual of the Revolution and early republic."[4]

CHAPTER TWO

Early Years

Mifflin's Birth

Thomas Mifflin was born in Philadelphia, Pennsylvania, on January 10, 1744, according to today's calendar. (At the time of his birth, the thirteen American colonies were using the Julian calendar. Under that calendar, his birthday was December 30, 1743.)[1]

Less than three months before Thomas Mifflin was born, a 37-year-old Philadelphia man, who was destined to serve as one of his future mentors, made news: he discovered that storm systems move from west to east. It had been assumed by scientists that storms moved in the same direction as wind on the earth's surface. However, in early November 1743, Benjamin Franklin was unable to view a lunar eclipse because the Philadelphia sky was overcast. However, he had earlier written to his brother in Boston, Massachusetts, to tell him about the event. When the later responded, he mentioned he saw the eclipse, but that a storm moved in shortly afterward. Putting two and two together—and interviewing other people—Franklin came to the conclusion that the weather systems moved from west to east. A fact that makes 21st century weather predictions possible!

On the international stage, the years of Mifflin's life saw conflict after conflict between Great Britain and France. One of the most significant naval battles of the 18th century occurred in the month following Mifflin's birth—a joint French-Spanish fleet defeated the British fleet at the Battle of Toulon (February 22–23, 1744). As a young man, Mifflin would visit both countries, and in his official capacity both during and after the American Revolution, he would interact with both in the most profound ways.

At the time of Mifflin's youth, the British empire was expanding, but not nearly as extensively is it would in the following century. Still, it controlled, in addition to Canada and the thirteen American colonies,

11

islands in the Atlantic and Pacific Oceans (with its Caribbean islands being especially valuable), and tiny parts of South America and Africa. Although some of these land holdings were small, they were geographically diverse and very important in terms of world trade. The political structure at each location was different—Britain ruled using direct military control, royal charters, proprietary colonies, etc. The American colonies were relatively self-governing, but when troubles developed in the 1770s, Britain took a heavy-handed approach—one that included taxation and military occupation as major ways to retain control.

Life in Philadelphia

When Thomas Mifflin was growing up in Philadelphia, the population of the city was about 13,000 people. Around that time, the population of the New York City was about the same, while the population of Boston was in the neighborhood of 16,000.[2]

When Mifflin was six years old (1750), the population of the 13 colonies is estimated to have been about 1.2 million people. About 47 percent of these were in the Southern colonies, 29 percent in New England, and 24 percent in the Middle colonies.[3]

According to the U.S. Census Bureau, the total United States population in 1776 was 2.5 million people, which is less than the population of Chicago today. (It's also only one-half of today's population of Ireland. According to the World Bank, Ireland as of 2022 had five million people.)[4]

Thomas Mifflin came from a well-to-do fourth-generation Philadelphia Quaker family. (Quakers were also known as the Religious Society of Friends.) Thomas Mifflin's Quaker ancestors came to Pennsylvania before Province of Pennsylvania founder William Penn.[5]

Thomas Mifflin's father, John Mifflin, and his mother, Elizabeth (Bagnell) Mifflin (1715–1737), were both about 29 years old when Thomas was born. Born on January 18, 1715, John Mifflin became a member of the Philadelphia Common Council. After four years, he was elected an alderman, serving with Benjamin Franklin. On November 2, 1755, John Mifflin joined the Philadelphia Provincial Council.[6]

In a position of substantial authority, John was one of the commissioners charged with using a 60,000 pound grant for the defense of the province. When he died in February 1759 at age 44, he was buried in the "Friends' Burying Ground."[7]

Of the ten directors of the Library Company who voted to admit Thomas' father John as a member on August 27, 1734, are the names of

Benjamin Franklin, merchant William Coleman (who years later would employ Thomas), and merchant and judge Thomas Hopkinson (1709–1751) whose grandson Joseph Hopkinson would one day marry Thomas Mifflin's daughter Emily.[8]

Thomas Mifflin had a half-brother—lawyer John Fishbourne Mifflin (April 21, 1759, to May 13, 1813)—who was 15 years his junior. John Fishbourne's mother was Sarah Fishbourne (1733–1816). John also graduated from the Academy of Pennsylvania (in 1775) and became one of its trustees (in 1802). Like Thomas, John Fishbourne Mifflin was elected to the most respected scholarly society of the time—the American Philosophical Society (1796).[9]

Thomas Mifflin, Quaker

Thomas Mifflin was educated at a Quaker school in Philadelphia on 4th Street between Chestnut and Walnut. That stretch of 4th street is also the site of Carpenter's Hall, which was the location of the First Continental Congress in 1774. It was also the location of Benjamin Franklin's Library Company, the American Philosophical Society, and the First and Second Banks of the United States, with Independence Hall located only a block to the west of Carpenter's Hall. This part of Philadelphia was a bustling place filled with culture and business.

Mifflin's first biographer William Rawle states:

> The general course of education at *that* time was calculated for the *utilities* of *domestic* life, or the limited calls of *provincial employment*; and it would have been deemed *absurd and dangerous* to hold up the *heroes* of Greece and Rome for the imitation of the youth of Philadelphia. Intended for the mercantile profession, the education of Mifflin, although *carefully* superintended by his respectable father, was not protracted by a close *study of ancient languages*, and his knowledge of them was, consequently, moderate; yet he passed with reputation through the *usual collegiate* course....[10]

Most members of the Quakers in the North American British colonies did not participate in the American Revolution because of their pacifist beliefs. The most notable exceptions were two men who achieved the highest rank in the Continental Army: Major General Nathanial Greene and Major General Thomas Mifflin. Another American who was also raised in a Quaker family was writer and activist Thomas Paine (1737–1809). His most famous work, the pamphlet *Common Sense* (1776), was incredibly influential in persuading people of the need to be independent of Great Britain.

It's helpful to understand the environment that young Mifflin was growing up in. Philadelphia was founded by Quaker leader William Penn in 1662 (82 years before Mifflin's birth), and the city was one of the British colonies' most important centers of commerce and culture.

Penn chose Philadelphia as the name for the city. The word is a combination of the Greek words for love (phileo) and brother (adelphos). Thus, the city's nickname: the City of Brotherly Love. The Bible's Book of Revelation mentions a city of that name as one of the seven cities of Asia Minor to which that book was addressed. Today, the Turkish city Alaşehir is located on the site of the ancient Philadelphia.

Because of Penn's influence, the colony of Pennsylvania, of which Philadelphia was a part, became a haven of religious freedom. For this reason, in addition to Quakers, it attracted many religious groups, including Anglicans, Baptists, Roman Catholics, and Jews.[11]

Inspired by his Quaker faith, William Penn was also an early proponent of the abolition of slavery, and his colony set an example of freedom, that while not perfect, influenced the attitudes and policies of the other colonies. The Quakers' "1688 Petition Against Slavery" was the first protest against slavery in the thirteen colonies.

Located on the Delaware River, Philadelphia naturally became an important trading center. In addition to commerce with other Eastern seaboard colonies, it engaged in a robust import and export trade with Europe and the Caribbean. This led to a complex mixture of residents—English, German, Swedish, Dutch, African, etc., as well as various occupational groups from merchants and tradesmen, to day-laborers and indentured servants. The Mifflin family—most notable Thomas and his father—benefited financially as part of this merchant class.

Thomas Mifflin also profited from the rich cultural and intellectual life of the city, which was the home of the College of Philadelphia and the American Philosophical Society. He was a graduate of the former and an active member of the latter.

The influence of the Quaker faith was strong in both the city as a whole and in the Mifflin family in particular. Thomas's Quaker education shaped him in many ways. Notably, he was firmly opposed to slavery. Although his city included enslaved people, the Quaker population was gradually able to eliminate legal slavery. On a state level, on March 1, 1780, the Pennsylvania General Assembly passed the Gradual Abolition Act of 1780, which was the first extensive abolition of slavery legislation not only Pennsylvania, but in the entire the Western hemisphere. This would set a precedent for other settlements, colonies and countries to discuss the morality of enslavement and to enact laws to outlaw and prevent it.

College of Philadelphia

The Academy and College of Philadelphia, known today as the University of Pennsylvania, has a long, interesting history, and many students graduated before carving their way into their chosen careers. Many important leaders claim it as their alma mater. Thomas Mifflin was one of them. He received his A.B. degree from it in 1760. This was only three years after the institution's first graduating class. To get a perspective of the city's size at the time of his graduation, the city's 2,960 houses served as homes for 18,756 people. Only 23 years later, the number of houses in Philadelphia had doubled to 6,000.[12]

One of Mifflin's fellow students at the commencement of 1760 was Patrick Alison, who was destined to become chaplain to the Continental Congress in 1776.[13]

The *Pennsylvania Gazette* of May 15, 1760, reports on the Academy and College of Philadelphia's graduation ceremonies:

> The Orations Disputations, and other Academical Exercises were agreeably intermixed with sundry Anthems and Pieces of Psalmody, sung by the Charity Boys, [The Charity School of Philadelphia was a charity school for the children of the poor.] attended with an organ, which the Liberality of the Town lately bestowed. At the close of the whole, the Audience was most delightfully entertained with two Anthems sung by several Ladies and Gentlemen, who have not been ashamed to employ their Leisure Hours in learning to celebrate their Master's Praises with Grace and Elegance. And we have already noted how [Francis] Hopkinson 'conducted the organ with that bold masterly Hand for which he is celebrated.[14]

Five years after Mifflin's graduation, the Academy and College of Philadelphia established the first medical school in the thirteen American colonies. In the middle of the Revolutionary War (1779), it became the first American college to be designated a university.

Two men who earned degrees from this University later signed the U.S. Constitution—Thomas Mifflin and Hugh Williamson.[15]

Williamson received his degree three years before Mifflin. Mifflin later served as a trustee of the University. On June 18, 1773, Thomas Mifflin replaced Doctor Phineas Bond as a trustee of the Academy and College of Philadelphia after the latter's death.[16]

Three other signers of the Constitution were awarded honorary degrees from this educational institution: future U.S. Supreme Court Justice James Wilson in 1766, George Washington in 1783, and U.S. Senator Rufus King in 1815.[17]

The students often graduated from the Academy and College of Philadelphia at age 16; however, only the wealthy could afford to attend. In 1740, plans were made to begin a charity school in Philadelphia. Because of costs, the project languished until 1749 when Benjamin Franklin (founder of America's first subscription library [1731] and first hospital [1751]), published the essay "Proposals Relating to the Education of Youth," He organized a group of 24 trustees that would put his proposals into action. They purchased a building and opened the Academy and Charitable School in the Province of Pennsylvania in 1751. Franklin became its first president, serving for a few years, and then became a trustee for the rest of his life.[18]

As of the 21st century, the University of Pennsylvania is a member of the prestigious Ivy League of colleges. Most of its approximately 25,000 students are enrolled in graduate or professional degree programs. Notable alumni of the university include billionaires Elon Musk and Warren Buffett, 36 Nobel laureates (including faculty), and gunfighter Doc Holliday.

After graduating from college in 1760, 16-year-old Thomas spent four years working for merchant William Coleman. In his *Autobiography*, Benjamin Franklin describes Coleman, whom he had known since their early years (Coleman was a year or two older than Franklin): "William Coleman, then a merchant's clerk, about my age, who had the coolest, clearest head, the best heart, and the exactest morals of almost any man I ever met with. He became afterwards a merchant of great note, and one of our provincial judges. Our friendship continued without interruption to his death, upwards of forty years...."[19]

One can understand an 18th-century American merchant's job from Erna Risch, who wrote in *Supplying Washington's Army* how vitally important and necessary it was to the military to have a competent and reliable one: "The merchant's role involved the functions of shipper, banker, wholesaler, retailer, warehouseman, and insurer.... The individual merchant did not have to perform all of them in order to sell his goods. He could, for example, ship his merchandise in a vessel of another shipowner, consigning it to an agent for sale."[20]

Thomas Mifflin would soon put the knowledge he learned working with merchant William Coleman to good use. He would expand on this knowledge and become a valuable asset to the military during the Revolutionary War.

The European Trip

In the 18th century, it was common for wealthy young men in Great Britain to go on a "Grand Tour" of other European countries to

Two. Early Years

supplement their education. The experience and knowledge gained of various cultures and languages, and the manners they would acquire, was meant as a way to prepare them for future careers as leaders in business, government, the arts, medicine, etc.

Some of Colonial America's richest young men followed their British predecessors and crossed the Atlantic to make the European Grand Tour. It wasn't until the 19th century that young women began going on the Grand Tour as well. This European trip was thought to be beneficial for Thomas Mifflin after he graduated from college. The year-long hiatus would assist him in acquiring the refined manners of the European elite. For him, the trip would be especially worthwhile, since he would have an opportunity to acquire a priceless knowledge of international trade that would assist him in his import and export business activities.

Famous leaders of the American Revolution era who took a European tour include future U.S. presidents Thomas Jefferson, James Madison, and John Quincy Adams, as well as John Jay, who became the first chief justice of the U.S. Supreme Court.

One of the most famous of the Grand Tour personages was a fellow Philadelphian, portrait painter Benjamin West, who in 1760 (which by the way was the year Mifflin graduated from college) toured Europe. He ultimately made England his permanent home, became an official painter for King George III, and—decades later—served as President of the Royal Academy. When West was in his twenties, he painted a portrait of a teenage Thomas Mifflin.[21]

On February 15, 1764, Mifflin left New York for England, arriving in Falmouth on the southwest tip of England on March 16.[22] He soon continued on another 300 miles to London.

Mifflin didn't have an easy time on his first (and only) long-distance trip. He wrote to his uncle Jacob Lewis (the brother of his father's second wife) that he was seasick on one-third of the trip, and the ship was "a little leaky especially the first Part of our Voyage in which we had two Gales of Wind that loosened our Rudder."[23]

The year Mifflin traveled to Great Britain, King George III had reigned as its monarch for four years and would continue to do so for another 56 years. It was also the year that English painter William Hogarth (October 26) died in London.

With a population of about three-quarters of a million people, the city of London dwarfed Philadelphia in size. Its main buildings were incredibly impressive—the Tower of London's central White Tower was almost 700 years old, and the main part of Westminster Abbey was over 500 years old. However, the Abbey's western towers had just been completed only 19 years before Mifflin's visit. Still, despite all the impressive architecture, the city was a mixture of wealth and poverty.

In London, Mifflin was able to learn firsthand about the trade practices between Britain and its North American colonies. In the three-way trade among the 13 North American colonies, Great Britain and the West Indies, Mifflin was able to study up close the British connections. How the British Isles would receive raw materials, such as furs, lumber, indigo and tobacco, from the colonies and send back textiles, manufactured products, and other processed items. Also, how Great Britain received molasses, sugar and other food items from the Caribbean islands. Mifflin was able to observe English shipping and personally discuss business practices with some of the most important people in Britain. Although only 20 years old, he was a member of arguably the wealthiest family in the largest city of the British Empire outside of the British Isles.

In France, Louis XV was king. He had reigned since he was five years old, and then was in the 49th year of a 59-year reign. It was also the year that Madame de Pompadour, mistress of King Louis, died.

Rossman comments that Mifflin's time in France "no doubt had some influence upon his pro–French sympathies of later life," and of his time was spent learning the French language and taking riding lessons "four times a week, proper training for a country gentleman, and, as it turned out, valuable for his future military service."[24]

Mifflin's experience on the European trip also served him well in later years when he needed to speak as an equal with the most important people in the business world, in the government, and in the military.

During his time in Europe, Mifflin wrote back home, but most of his correspondence has not been preserved. One that did survive was a May 26, 1764, letter from Paris to his uncle, Jacob Lewis. In it, Mifflin tells of his efforts to learn French and to learn to ride.[25]

In November 1764, Mifflin left France and returned to London via Falmouth. At the time, Mifflin was still only 20 years old. Back home, a friend of his family, Benjamin Franklin, was 58.

In 1765, with his schooling, four years of work with Coleman, and most of a year traveling in Europe under his belt, Thomas Mifflin was ready to start his career: he established a Philadelphia business with his brother George. Its offices were located near the intersection of Front and Chestnut Streets. Unfortunately, like most places associated with the life of Thomas Mifflin, the building no longer exists.

Mifflin's riding classes in France came in handy at age 22 when he became a member of the exclusive Gloucester Fox Hunting Club. Other members included: John Dickinson, a future president of Pennsylvania, Robert Morris (1734–1806) later known as the "Financier of the American Revolution," and future Revolutionary War Brigadier General John Cadwalader (1742–1786).

Schuylkill Fishing Company

On May 1, 1769, at age 25, Mifflin was elected a member of the exclusive Schuylkill Fishing Company. Later renamed the State in Schuylkill, the club was appropriately located along the Schuylkill River.[26] Famously involved in partying more than fishing, the club was founded in 1732 and included the most wealthy and powerful members of Philadelphia society among its membership. Famous for its Fish House Punch, it is believed by many to be the oldest social club in the United States.[27]

A recent book on mixology states that George Washington enjoyed his drink and "it's said that after he partook of Fish House Punch at Philadelphia's State in Schuylkill ... he couldn't bring himself to make an entry in his diary for the following three days."[28] A history of the club, published in 1889, began with: "If you look to its antiquity, it is the most ancient, if to its dignity, it is the most honorable—if to its jurisdiction, it is the most extensive."

As has always been true, many social clubs can provide networking opportunities. Participation in local social events or club meetings could provide a merchant like Mifflin with many opportunities to establish business connections.

Shortly after his 24th birthday in 1768, Thomas Mifflin was elected to the American Philosophical Society. Founded the year before Mifflin was born by Benjamin Franklin and other accomplished persons of Philadelphia, it was composed of prominent men who shared an interest in science.[29]

It included among its membership many prominent citizens. They came from various occupations: medical doctors, members of the clergy, lawyers, merchants, tradesmen, etc. In the 21st century, it is the oldest active scholarly society in the United States.

The American Philosophical Society's first president was Thomas Hopkinson and Benjamin Franklin was its first secretary. In 1769, Franklin was elected president and held that office until his death in 1790. Among its earliest members were U.S. presidents George Washington, John Adams, Thomas Jefferson, and James Madison. Other members included Lafayette, Alexander Hamilton, John Marshall,

Louis Pasteur, Thomas Edison, Marie Curie, Albert Einstein, and Margaret Mead.

As of the 21st century, the Society—still based in Philadelphia—has about 1,000 members. Less than 6,000 individuals have been accepted as members over the course of its nearly three-centuries-long existence, with more than 250 of them being Nobel Prize winners.[30]

Chapter Three

Before the War

By the 1770s, Mifflin was ready for another career. Although a highly successful merchant, he longed for something more. Something that would contribute to the community and utilize his obvious talents. William Rawle, who worked with Mifflin when the latter was in his 40s and 50s, described him as "remarkably handsome, though his stature did not exceed five feet eight inches. His frame was *athletic*, and seemed *capable* of bearing much fatigue. His manners were cheerful and affable. His elocution open, fluent, and distinct."[1]

In the late 18th century, Philadelphia had grown to become one of the most important centers of trade in the British Empire. Only London and Liverpool were more significant. Many of the most successful individuals in the city's business world were adherents to the Quaker faith. Two of the most important of these were John Mifflin and his son Thomas.

Philadelphia's location at the point where the Delaware and Schuylkill rivers meet allowed inland businesses to bring food and other products to this area for shipment. Coal and ore producers similarly benefited from this access—successfully allowing them the profitable means of long-distance shipping. From Philadelphia, goods were often shipped to the Caribbean Sea, where they were traded for sugar, rum, etc. These items were then sent to England where they were traded for manufactured goods that were shipped back to Philadelphia. This triangular trade route was extremely profitable.

However, the city's prosperity didn't depend entirely on trade—some of the country's earliest industry sprang up in eastern Pennsylvania and Philadelphia became a magnet for art and culture. None of these distinctions was nearly as important as the part Philadelphia played in the evolution of government—on the local, state and national levels. And it was for his role in each of these institutions of government that Thomas Mifflin became one of the most famous public figures in the city of Philadelphia, the Commonwealth of Pennsylvania, and the new United States of America.

Warden

Thomas Mifflin's life of public service began on March 9, 1771, when at age 27 he was appointed a warden of Philadelphia. As Rossman explains, there were six Philadelphia wardens at the time, who "regulated the nightly watch, provided for 'enlightening the streets, lanes, and alleys,' and had charge of the pumps of the city, the only water supply."[2]

Elected to the Pennsylvania Provincial Assembly

In 1772, Thomas made his first foray into the colony's government with his election to the Pennsylvania Provincial Assembly. Eventually, he would stay in the position for three additional terms. These sessions were held from October 14 through the 16th of 1772; January 4, 1773, through February 26, 1773; and September 20 through the 30th, 1773. He served on the committee of public accounts and the committee of grievances. In the autumn of 1773, he was reelected, and went on to serve in the assembly during 1774 and 1775. Mifflin biographer Rawle writes of him at this time:

> In 1772, when he had attained only 28 years of age, Thomas Mifflin was chosen one of those burgesses. His conduct gave so much satisfaction to his constituents, that in the ensuing year he again received the same distinction, which was rendered the more flattering from his having a colleague in the illustrious Benjamin Franklin, who was then on his return from Europe.[3]
>
> [Mifflin's] opening talents rendered him an *early favorite* with his fellow citizens. In the *provincial legislature*, the city of Philadelphia was then represented by two burgesses annually elected, and to be one of those two burgesses was reckoned no inconsiderable honor, even in quiet times; but when clouds began to gather round us; when the blind desire to draw a forced revenue from the colonies, led the British ministry to put in jeopardy the immense national profit derived from our trade, and when a severity of restriction on our internal transactions was openly menaced and partly enforced, it became important that the metropolis of the central province should select for its *counsellors* and *agents*, men of the *purest principles* and the *best abilities*.[4]

Recreation

In the 1760s and 1770s, not all was business for the young Mifflin. As Rossman relates in his biography:

As to skating, it was a recreation in which Mifflin, by all accounts, was "very expert." He was mentioned by William McKay in *Lang Syne Reminiscences* as being "decidedly superior to the rest for dexterity, power, and grace." Skaters used the Delaware River mostly, and again here was occasion for much sociability and eating. The Philadelphia Dancing Assembly, organized in the forties, gathered in the exclusive set too. By the mid-sixties even good Quaker names began to appear on the Assembly lists, and among them Mifflin's.[5]

The Philadelphia Dancing Assemblies was founded in 1748. In its early years members met every Thursday evening from January through May. They would start at 6:00 p.m. and end at 12 midnight.[6] One memorable meeting was on February 21, 1792, when the dancing assembly hosted a ball to honor President George Washington on his 60th birthday. Present were George and Martha Washington; Vice President John Adams; foreign ministers; Speaker of the House of Representatives Jonathan Trumbull, Jr.;[7] most members of Congress; and Governor of Pennsylvania Thomas Mifflin.[8]

Thomas Mifflin married distant cousin Sarah Morris at the Quaker "Fair Hill Meeting" on March 4, 1767.[9] Sarah Morris Mifflin (1747–1790) was the daughter of Morris Morris and Elizabeth Morris of Philadelphia.[10]

A portrait of Mifflin with his wife Sarah was painted by Boston-born artist John Singleton Copley (1738–1815) probably around 1771 to 1773. Mifflin would have been in his late twenties at the time and Sarah in her mid-twenties. It was common in 18th-century America for married couples to have separate portraits painted. However, apparently Thomas and Sarah wanted to be shown together in this painting. It would not have been to save money—at this point of his life, merchant Thomas Mifflin was one of the wealthiest men in Philadelphia.

Art historian Charles Henry Hart (1847–1918)[11] wrote that the Mifflin painting is the best large painting by Copley of which he was aware. He describes the work as: "Nothing can be more simple, or sound more monotonous, than the color scheme." General Mifflin is in a drab cloth suit and "his Lady" in a gray silk gown[12] relieved only by the white neckerchief and under sleeves, the single ornament being what was possibly an artistic license, a small white rose and pink bud with green leaves, at the throat. His hair is powdered and her hair is natural. The table top upon which is her fringe frame, is of polished mahogany and the chairs are dark green. An anomaly in the picture is the outdoor effect of the blue sky of twilight in the background to the right, while the composition is illumined by broad daylight from the front. "The reproduction shows how faultless is the modeling; solid yet mobile."

Hart relates a well-known story that Sarah Mifflin "sat twenty times

Early 1770s oil painting of Thomas Mifflin and his wife, Sarah Morris Mifflin, by John Singleton Copley. At the time, Thomas was about 29 years old, and Sarah was about 26 years old. This is considered one of Copley's finest works (Philadelphia Museum of Art, public domain, via Wikimedia Commons).

for the painting of the hands alone, which are rendered with rare skill. As can be seen, the canvas is very luminous, the figures being placed in a strong light coming from the right and no part of the picture is slighted, the utmost 'attention' having been bestowed upon every detail, but with such consummate artistry has this been done that all labor has been concealed, which is not always true of Copley's work."[13]

Family

Thomas and Sarah's two daughters Frances and Emily were born, respectively, in 1770 and 1774 in Philadelphia, Pennsylvania. Frances married Jonathan Mifflin (a distant relation) on April 23, 1795. They were the parents of Thomas Mifflin and John Mifflin. Frances died in 1796 at approximately age 26.

Emily married Joseph Hopkinson on February 27, 1794. They had 13 children, four of which were born during Thomas Mifflin's lifetime. Their first-born child was named after Emily's father. Thomas Mifflin Hopkinson was born on December 18, 1794, and passed away on May 9, 1871. One son was born 23 days after Alexander Hamilton was killed in a duel with Aaron Burr. Thomas Mifflin's grandson Alexander Hamilton Hopkinson (August 4, 1804–August 11, 1827) died while in U.S. Navy service on board the USS *Lexington* off the island of Malta.

Emily died over half a century after her sister—on December 11, 1850, at about age 76. Her husband Joseph had died in 1842 at approximately age 72. Emily is buried in Christ Church Episcopal Cemetery in Bordentown, New Jersey.[14]

The last surviving grandson of Thomas Mifflin, Oliver Hopkinson, served as a colonel of the 51st Pennsylvania Emergency Troops during the American Civil War. He was wounded at the Battle of Antietam. Hopkinson was a student at the University of Pennsylvania, graduating 72 years after his grandfather (Class of 1832). He married Elisa Swaim in 1845 and they had 11 children. When he died at age 92 in 1905, he was the oldest living graduate of the University of Pennsylvania.[15]

CHAPTER FOUR

National Politics

Visits to Other Colonies

During 1773, 29-year-old Thomas and 26-year-old Sarah visited Newport, Rhode Island. They stayed in the 130-year-old city from June until September 1773. More than anywhere else in the 13 colonies, Rhode Island was a haven for two groups who sought relief from the intolerance they experienced in Europe: Quakers and Jews. Immigrants from both groups first came to the city in the 1650s. As the Newport Historical Society states, the presence of Quakers and Jews in the mid–18th century "along with their international trade connections, helped transform the town from a small agricultural outpost to one of colonial America's five leading seaports (along with Boston, New York, Philadelphia, and Charleston)."[1] It was only natural that a young, wealthy Quaker couple would be comfortable vacationing in such a city.

As one of British North America's main shipping centers, Newport provided the perfect professional opportunity for Thomas, a merchant by trade. It's likely that he and his wife spent many enjoyable—and educational—days visiting a harbor that was filled with sailing ships from around the world.

Little did the Mifflins know at the time that within three short years, Newport would be occupied by British military forces and would remain so for three years. During this period, more than one-half of Newport's population would desert the city.[2] What the Mifflins did witness during their vacation in 1773 was the unrest and discontent of the Rhode Island colonists. The oppressive policies of the British government were not resulting in compliant residents.

In July 1773, Thomas Mifflin's maternal grandfather died, and he and his wife attended his funeral in Boston. The city was, and had been for several years, a hotbed of discontent. While in Boston, they met with some of the key figures of the independence movement: John and

Four. National Politics

Abigail Adams, Samuel Adams, and John Hancock. Mifflin was eager to learn what the Massachusetts rebel leaders had planned for the future, while they were just as eager to connect with allies to their cause that resided in other colonies. (It is believed that it was on this visit to Boston in July 1773 that Thomas and Sarah Mifflin had their portrait painted by the noted artist John Singleton Copley.)

At the time, John and Abigail Adams were probably the most influential couple in Colonial America. After the Mifflin visit,

John Adams, who many years later was elected the first Vice President of the United States and later the second President of the United States (1797–1801). Adams was an early supporter of Thomas Mifflin in the Continental Congress (Library of Congress).

Portrait of Abigail Adams by Benjamin Blyth. Adams was the first woman to serve as Second Lady of United States and the second woman to serve as First Lady of the United States. She was arguably the most influential woman during the early years of the nation (Library of Congress).

John Adams wrote in his diary (in an entry dated July 16, 1773):

Drank Tea at Dr. Coopers with Mr. Adams, Mr. S. Elliot, Mr. T. Chase, and with Mr. Mifflin of Philadelphia, and a French Gentleman. Mr. Mifflin is a Grandson, his Mother was the Daughter, of Mr. Bagnall of this Town, who was buried the day before Yesterday. Mr. Mifflin is a Representative of the City of Philadelphia—a very sensible and agreeable Man. Their Academy emits from 9 to 14 Graduates annually. Their Grammar School has from 90 to 100 scholars in all. Mr. Mifflin is an easy Speaker—and a very correct Speaker.[3]

What did the conversations of the two couples involve? Surely there was much talk of politics. There was growing discontent among the people of Pennsylvania, and especially Massachusetts, over "taxation without representation"—the fact the 13 colonies were governed by an authority an ocean away and they had no say on what—and how much—taxes they would be required to pay. Also, their consent was not required before Parliament in London passed other laws that directly or indirectly affected them. Over the past century and a half since the first English settlements had been established in the Northern colonies, residents had in so many ways governed themselves—in everything from settling disputes between farmers to protecting their colonies from attack. By the 1770s, they began to seriously question why they couldn't write their own laws and control all government functions. Three years prior to the Mifflins' visit, one major event had occurred to turn up the heat on the movement for independence from British. It was called the Boston Massacre, where five colonists were fired upon—and killed—by British soldiers.

To get a good idea of what was on John Adams' mind at the time, we can look decades into the future and read his memories of this time. In an 1818 letter to a magazine editor, Adams offered his definition of the American Revolution:

> "But what do We mean by the American Revolution? Do We mean the American War? The Revolution was effected before the War commenced. The Revolution was in the Minds and Hearts of the People. A Change in their Religious Sentiments of their Duties and Obligations. While the King, and all in Authority under him, were believed to govern, in Justice and Mercy according to the Laws and Constitutions derived to them from the God of Nature, and transmitted to them by their Ancestors—they thought themselves bound to pray for the King and Queen and all the Royal Family, and all the Authority under them, as Ministers ordained of God for their good. But when they Saw those Powers renouncing all the Principles of Authority, and bent up on the destruction of all the Securities of their Lives, Liberties and Properties, they thought it their Duty to pray for the Continental Congress and all the thirteen State Congresses, &c."[4]

It would only be five months after the meeting of the Mifflins with the Adamses that Boston would experience the dumping of a shipload of British tea into its harbor by American colonists. A protest against a new tax on tea, the December 16, 1773, event would go down in history as the Boston Tea Party. And, the following year, Massachusetts and Pennsylvania would join together with most of the other colonies to form the first large-scale organized reaction to British rule: the First Continental Congress, whereby representatives of each of the colonies met in Mifflin's city of Philadelphia to discuss their grievances and plan their resistance.

University Trustee and Election to the Pennsylvania Provincial Assembly

The year 1773 was also when Mifflin became a trustee of the Academy and College of Philadelphia. It was 13 years since he graduated from the institution and moved into the business world. From 1773 to 1775, Mifflin served as treasurer of the institution's Board of Trustees.

The following year—1774—while Mifflin was still a member Philadelphia's Colonial Assembly, the British Parliament passed the Intolerable Acts, which included the closing of the Port of Boston. As a prosperous merchant as well as a government official in the city which had the Northern colonies' other major port, Mifflin was very concerned that the British would resort to extreme measures. If the British soldiers could be ordered to shut down Massachusetts's major port, what could stop them from doing the same to Pennsylvania's premier port?

At this time there were various political factions in Pennsylvania. Many did not want to see a break from Great Britain. They included many Episcopalians (the American version of the church of England), some people of German descent, many Quakers, and some Presbyterians. The most activist factions that pushed for independence from Great Britain were the Whigs. Of them, some worked for moderation; others pushed for violent confrontation. Those at the other end of the spectrum—those who still held allegiance to the King of England and wanted to remain part of the Mother County—were the Tories.

Philadelphia and the eastern counties of Pennsylvania pretty much controlled the state legislature. And the delegates from the city represented the wealthier class since most residents could not vote because they did not have enough money or land to qualify them to be voters.

Elected to the First Continental Congress

During the 17th and 18th centuries, Great Britain established colonies from the present-day U.S. state of Massachusetts in the north to the state of Georgia in the south.

The French and Indian War (called the Seven Years' War in Europe), resulted in Britain's defeating France and her allies. However, Britain also incurred huge war debts. The British government's solution was to pass along the costs—as well as the costs of stationing troops to protect colonist territories to the west—to the 13 colonies along North American's Atlantic coast.

In 1765, the British parliament passed the Stamp Act, which imposed taxes on printed paper items, including legal documents, newspapers, and even playing cards. Colonist resentment flared up and the phrase "taxation without representation" was the cry of the day. A colonial rights organization, The Sons of Liberty, spearheaded the protests. In other colonies, similar groups were organized. Early leaders of the resistance included future American Revolution figures Samuel Adams, Paul Revere, John Hancock, Benedict Arnold, and Patrick Henry.

After a widespread colonial boycott of British goods, Parliament relented and repealed the Stamp Act. In 1768, Parliament passed the Townshend Acts, and colonists saw it as another unreasonable tax on a people who had no representation in the government.

On March 5, 1770, the first violence broke out: five people in Boston, Massachusetts, were killed in a confrontation between British troops and a mob of activists. History knows it as the Boston Massacre.

As mentioned, in December 1773, the American colonists dumped a shipment of British tea into Boston harbor in response to Parliament's tax on imported tea. This was followed by Parliament's passing what were called the Intolerable Acts the following year.

In 1774, the British government's trade-restricting Coercive Acts (also known as the Intolerable Acts) incited anger among the colonists. Soon, other colonies joined with Massachusetts to create a new government body in late 1774—the First Continental Congress. In Philadelphia, 56 delegates represented 12 of the 13 colonies. Only Georgia didn't send delegates.

Pennsylvania's delegates were elected by its legislature, the members of which knew 30-year-old Thomas Mifflin well, as he had been one of them. He was elected and attended the First Continental Congress session of September 5 to October 26, 1774.

According to Rawle: *All* the colleagues of Mifflin [representing Pennsylvania at the First Continental Congress] were his seniors. Joseph Galloway[5] was a gentleman of the bar, of great talents, and considerable property. He had been an active opponent of the Proprietaries, and possessed the confidence of great numbers of the people, though many suspected that he was not sincerely attached to the American cause, and their suspicions were confirmed by his subsequently joining the army of Sir William Howe. Edward Biddle[6] also was a lawyer. He resided at Reading, in the county of Berks: he was a man of ready elocution, sound principles, and correct judgment. "*Samuel Rhoads*[7] a respectable merchant of Philadelphia, belonged to the Society of Friends—without the talent of speaking in public, he possessed much *acuteness of mind*, his judgment was *sound*, and his practical information *extensive*. The other two gentlemen, *Messrs. Morton*[8] *and Humphreys*[9] resided in the country, and were respectable, though not prominent men."[10] In addition, 44-year-old George Ross[11] and 41-year-old John Dickinson represented Pennsylvania.[12]

One person who interacted with Mifflin throughout his career was medical doctor Benjamin Rush. He was an influential colonist during this period, playing a major role in the American Revolution, and in the development of the new country. Rush started as a close friend of Thomas Mifflin, and later grew to become one of his fiercest critics.

George Reeser Prowell's 1914 *Continental Congress at York, Pennsylvania, and York County in the Revolution* points out that Dr. Rush "took occasion to speak of Washington in the most scathing terms. He often dealt in vituperation in making remarks about others." Prowell relates an anonymous letter Rush sent to Patrick Henry "containing bitter sarcasm and scathing reflections on Washington's character and ability as a soldier." The letter was given to Washington who recognized the handwriting as Rush's and commented, "We have caught the sly fox at last."[13]

In a letter to Thomas Jefferson on January 4, 1792, Rush displays his anger at Mifflin as he asks Jefferson to ask President Washington to consider his brother Jacob Rush for the open position of District Judge of Pennsylvania:

> Soon after the accession of Mr. Mifflin to the Government of Pennsylvania, he gratified his resentment against me for opposing his election, by removing my brother from a Seat on the bench of the supreme Court of Pennsylvania. The public clamor against this cruel and arbitrary measure, and the numerous testimonies which rose up in favor of my brother's integrity and Abilities in the execution of his office, induced Mr. Mifflin to appoint him a district Judge for four of the frontier Counties of the State.[14]

An additional reason for Dr. Rush to become an enemy of Mifflin was that Rush opposed Mifflin in the 1790 gubernatorial election. After Mifflin became governor, he did not renew Rush's position as an "Inspector of Sickly Vessels" for the port of Philadelphia. The part-time job had paid Rush about 20 pounds a year.

A man known to hold a grudge, Rush wrote in his autobiography that Mifflin was known to be a "very immoral character" and accused him of adultery and addiction to "swearing and obscene conversation." However, Rush reveals the reason for his hatred of Mifflin when he writes: "His [Mifflin's] political character was as bad as his moral. He had deserted his friends and joined with the men who slandered them. He was wholly dissipated and given to low company. His popularity was acquired by the basest acts of familiarity with the meanest of the people. He avoided the society of gentlemen and cherished that of the mechanicks." [In the latter part of the 18th century, the term *mechanicks* usually meant unskilled workers.][15]

Massachusetts Asks for Help

On May 19, 1774, the Massachusetts patriot leaders—including Samuel Adams and John Hancock—kept Mifflin appraised of what they were doing and encouraged Pennsylvania's support. Mifflin's Pennsylvania confederates in the endeavor were Joseph Reed and Charles Thomson.

The importance of young Mifflin's influence in Philadelphia politics is seen by the actions of Paul Revere. Thomas Mifflin's grand-niece, Martha J. Mifflin, wrote in 1899, "At the time of the closing of the port of Boston, on account of the opposition to the duty on tea, Paul Revere was sent with letters to Joseph Reed and Thomas Mifflin, asking Pennsylvania to support the cause."[16] Revere arrived in Philadelphia on May 19 with the letters and Boston resolutions.[17] Apparently, an individual letter or letters were sent to Charles Thomson as well.[18] Thomas Mifflin was in favor of sending the strongest messages of sympathy and aid.[19]

Meeting at City Tavern

Mifflin, Reed, and Thomson scheduled a meeting of a few hundred people at the City Tavern on May 20, 1774—the day after Revere's arrival. As Thomson wrote years later, the objective of the activists was "to return a friendly and affectionate answer to the people of Boston, to forward the news of their distress to the southern colonies, and to consult them and the eastern colonies on the propriety of calling a congress to consult on measures necessary to be taken."[20]

The three men needed to meet with John Dickinson, who was very influential with the powerful Quaker residents of the city. They wanted to convince him to work with them. Mifflin, Reed, and Thomson met with Dickinson the day of the meeting, and he agreed to be present that evening. An account of the meeting follows:

Four. National Politics

The letter received from Boston was read, after which Reed addressed the assembly with temper, moderation, but in pathetic terms. Mifflin spoke next and with more warmth and fire. Thomson succeeded, and pressed for an immediate declaration in favor of Boston, and making common cause with her; but being overcome with the heat of the room and fatigue (for he had scarce slept an hour two nights past), he fainted and was carried into an adjoining room.

Great clamor was raised against the violence of the measures proposed. Dickinson then addressed the company.... After he had finished the clamor was renewed; voices were heard in different parts of the room, and all was in confusion; a chairman was called for to moderate the meeting and regulate debates; still the confusion continued. As soon as Thomson recovered, he returned into the room. The tumult and disorder was past description. He had not strength to attempt opposing the gust of passion or to allay the heat by anything he could say. He therefore simply moved a question that an answer should be returned to the letter from Boston; this was put and carried. He then moved for a committee to write the answer; this was agreed to and two lists were immediately made out and handed to the chair. The clamor was then renewed on which list a vote should be taken. At length it was proposed that both lists should be considered as one, and compose the committee. This was agreed to, and the company broke up in tolerable good humor, both thinking they had in part carried their point.[21]

The meeting resulted in a milder outcome than the most activist individuals might have wanted, i.e., termination of trade with Great Britain until demands were met. Mifflin thought the best reaction to Britain's injustice would be done through a continental congress—not a boycott. Most other Pennsylvania leaders agreed. The May 20 meeting resulted in the formation of a "committee of correspondence," which was composed of Mifflin and 18 other members.

The committee met the next day. It wrote an answer to the Boston patriots and petitioned the governor of Pennsylvania, asking him to convene the Assembly. It contained almost one thousand signatures. The governor refused. The mood of the people in Philadelphia was dark. At the time Boston Harbor would be blocked, the mood of the people was somber; Philadelphia shops were closed and church services were held. Ships in Philadelphia harbor lowered flags to half-mast.

As an alternative to the meeting of the Assembly, supporters of Boston gathered with 8,000 people on June 18. Resolutions passed that they owed allegiance to the King of England, but the North American colonists were "entitled to the same rights and liberties within the colonies that subjects born in England were entitled to within that realm." They also called for the immediate convening of a congress of all the American colonies.[22]

To secure the support of the public for a continental congress, it was decided that Dickinson, Thomson and Mifflin should make a tour of the frontier counties. They succeeded in that mission, and Mifflin was one of the delegates chosen to be a delegate to the First Congress.[23]

Pennsylvania Home of the First Continental Congress

Pennsylvania, and its major city of Philadelphia in particular, played a unique role in the American Revolution. Geographically, the state occupied a central location among the 13 colonies. It was a natural choice for a national headquarters since it could be reached by horse in a reasonable amount of time from most of the other colonies. Also, in the 1770s, Philadelphia (including its the greater metropolitan area) was the second most populous city in the English-speaking world. London, England was, of course, the first.[24]

The First Continental Congress in 1774 was the first time there was a permanent federal government body in the colonies.[25] The first series of Continental Congress meetings occurred from September 5, 1774, to October 24, 1774, and met in the City Tavern and Carpenter's Hall, a recently built four-story-high Georgian Colonial brick building. Attending members included George Washington, early revolutionaries Patrick Henry and Samuel Adams, future second president of the U.S. John Adams, and—representing Pennsylvania—businessman Thomas Mifflin.

You might say that Mifflin got in on the ground floor of the Revolution—and he was only 30 years old. It wouldn't be until the following year that many of the greatest names of the Revolution would attend, including Benjamin Franklin (Second Continental Congress), and future U.S. presidents: Thomas Jefferson (Second Continental Congress and the Confederation Congress), James Madison (Second Continental Congress and the Confederation Congress), and James Monroe (Confederation Congress). This Second Continental Congress would meet from 1775 through 1781, and the Confederation Congress met from 1781 to 1789.

Historian Paul Johnson described the situation at the time: "Congress had no legitimacy, the army was a band of rebels, and Americans, however organized, could never be more than subjects, with no more collective rights than Indians."[26]

From the Continental Congress, John Adams wrote to his wife Abigail:

> I shall be killed with kindness in this place. We go to Congress at nine, and there we stay, most earnestly engaged in debates upon the most abstruse mysteries of state, until three in the afternoon; then we adjourn, and go to dine with some of the nobles of Pennsylvania at four o'clock, and feast upon ten

thousand delicacies, and sit drinking Madeira, Claret, and Burgundy, till six or seven, and then go home fatigued to death with business, company, and care. Yet I hold out surprisingly.[27]

Often the delegates met at the Mifflin home. The diaries of Adams and George Washington mention these gatherings. As the delegates got to know one another personally, there were disagreements. One important issue was whether the colonies should boycott British goods. Mifflin, and the other delegates who were merchants, in general opposed boycotts—at least at this stage of the independence movement.

On September 12, 1774, John Adams wrote in his diary: "Attended my Duty on the Committee, until one O Clock, and then went with my Colleagues and Messrs. Thompson and Mifflin to the Falls of Schuylkill, and viewed the Museum at Fort St. Davids, a great Collection of Curiosities. Returned and dined with Mr. Dickinson."

In his biography of George Washington, U.S. President Woodrow Wilson mentions Thomas Mifflin:

> There was no assurance that even the best leaders of a colony could rise to the statesman's view and concert measures to insure the peace of an empire. Rising lawyers like John Adams, brusque planters like Colonel Harrison, well-to-do merchants like Thomas Mifflin, might bring all honesty and good intention to the task and yet miserably fail. A provincial law practice, the easy ascendency of a provincial country gentleman, the narrow round of provincial trade, might afford capable men opportunity to become enlightened citizens, but hardly fitted them to be statesmen.[28]

On October 7, 1774, as delegates began assembling in Philadelphia, delegate John Adams wrote to his wife Abigail:

> The Elections of the last Week in this City, prove this. Mr. Dickenson was chosen almost unanimously a Representative of the County. The Broadbrims began an opposition to your Friend Mr. Mifflin, because he was too warm in the Cause.[29] This instantly alarmed the Friends of Liberty and ended in the Election of Mr. Mifflin, by Eleven hundred Votes out of Thirteen, and in the Election of our Secretary Mr. Charles Thompson to be a Burgess with him. This is considered here as a most complete and decisive Victory in favor of the American Cause. And it [is] said it will change the Ballance in the Legislature here against Mr. Galloway who has been supposed to sit on the Skirts of the American Advocates.
>
> [Adams added:] Mrs. Mifflin who is a charming Quaker Girl, often enquires kindly after your Health. Adieu my dear Wife—God bless you and yours. So wishes and prays, without ceasing, John Adams.[30]

The next day, Adams wrote the following in his diary; as can be seen, he doesn't pull any punches in his descriptions of his fellow delegates:

The Deliberations of the Congress, are spun out to an immeasurable Length. There is so much Wit, Sense, Learning, Acuteness, Subtilty, Eloquence, &c. among fifty Gentlemen, each of whom has been habituated to lead and guide in his own Province, that an immensity of Time, is spent unnecessarily.

Johnson of Maryland has a clear and a cool Head, an extensive Knowledge of Trade, as well as Law. He is a deliberating Man, but not a shining orator—His Passions and Imagination don't appear enough for an orator. His Reason and Penetration appear, but not his Rhetoric.

Galloway, Duane, and Johnson, are sensible and learned but cold Speakers. Lee, Henry, and Hooper are the orators. Paca is a deliberator too. Chase speaks warmly. Mifflin is a sprightly and spirited Speaker. John Rutledge dont exceed in Learning or oratory, though he is a rapid Speaker. Young Edward Rutledge is young, and zealous—a little unsteady, and injudicious, but very unnatural and affected as a Speaker. Dyer and Sherman speak often and long, but very heavily and clumsily.[31]

When the Congress needed to choose a secretary—who was not also a delegate—Thomas Mifflin nominated fellow Philadelphian Charles Thomson, who in another month would, along with Mifflin, be voted in as a Philadelphia burgess. Thomson served as secretary for the next 14 years. He died in 1824 at age 94. In his role as secretary of the Congress, Thomson knew most delegates very well, and he was in a position to be aware of many secrets. After writing hundreds of pages of his memoirs, he realized that many reputations would be seriously damaged by his revelations. Consequently, he destroyed his entire work.

Interestingly, Thomson had recently married and had just arrived in Philadelphia with his bride, Hannah Harrison, on the morning of the first session of the Congress. In compensation for the abrupt disruption to their honeymoon, Congress voted a gift for Mrs. Thomson—a silver urn, which became a family heirloom.

Articles of Association

A fruit of this first Continental Congress was the Articles of Association, which were approved by representatives of the American colonies about nine months before the Declaration of Independence. Written in response to the British government's 1774 Intolerable Acts, it called for the American colonies to boycott the import and export of goods to and from Great Britain, Ireland, and the East Indies.

The Articles stated that to be economically free of the mother country, the 13 colonies will "encourage frugality, economy, and industry, and promote agriculture, arts and the manufactures of this country." The hope was that economic independence would directly lead to political independence. That, of course, is exactly what it did. The only thing that most colonists did not predict was that a long and bloody war would also be necessary.

The Articles of Association was signed by 53 delegates including George Washington of Virginia, John and Samuel Adams of Massachusetts, and Thomas Mifflin of Pennsylvania. It is often considered one of the four most important documents of the American Revolution, with the others being the Declaration of Independence, the Articles of Confederation, and the U.S. Constitution.[32]

The Philadelphia Associators

The Philadelphia Associators was established in 1747 by Benjamin Franklin as an all-volunteer force of citizen-soldiers whose mission was to defend the colony of Pennsylvania. (Thomas Mifflin was only three years old at the time.) Very active during the French and Indian War, the Associators were pretty much dormant until the fighting broke out at Lexington and Concord in 1775. Mifflin was one of the local leaders who helped the most to revive the organization.

These local Philadelphia militia units helped protect the city, and fought with the other American troops to defeat the British in the American Revolutionary War. The Philadelphia Associators played an especially important role during the first years of the war—before the

Painting of Thomas Mifflin by American artist Charles Willson Peale (1741–1827). This work was most likely created at the time Mifflin was serving as President of the Continental Congress (National Park Service Museum Collections, Second Bank of the United States, Philadelphia).

Continental Army was fully staffed and trained. Today, they are considered to be the "Foundation of the Pennsylvania National Guard."[33]

An article in *Techniques & Tech* does a good job of describing the Associators:

> Typically, the Associators at the time of the Revolution "were not under the authority of the state, but more directly the Committee of Safety, under the arm of the Continental Congress. Perhaps the best analogy for this type of soldier would be the United States Volunteer regiments of the Civil War; they weren't quite 'regular' infantry, as the Continental Line, but they also weren't militia.... Incidentally, most Associator companies were led by an officer or group of officers wealthy enough to supply and outfit an entire unit. This is why Associator companies were so well equipped." Many companies flew their own flags and designed their own uniforms.[34]

Approximately three-quarters of the 6,000 soldiers that Pennsylvania contributed to the fight for independence were members of the Associators. Their infantry and artillery were especially praised for their role in winning the battles of Trenton (December 1776) and Princeton (January 1777). In the latter battle, the Philadelphia Associator battalions were part of the force that General Washington personally led in his famous counterattack.

Elected to the Second Continental Congress

Delegate Mifflin's fervor and close ties with the Massachusetts delegation insured his re-election to the Second Continental Congress in the spring of 1775.[35]

It met from September 5, 1774, to March 3, 1789. Then Congress adopted the Articles of Confederation on November 15, 1777. It was finally ratified by all of the American colonies on March 1, 1781. It, in effect, served as the country's first constitution, remaining active from then until 1789. During those years, the Second Continental Congress was called the Congress of the Confederation.

Unfortunately, the Articles of Confederation established a weak national government vis-à-vis the 13 state governments. Issues such as the inability of Congress to levy taxes, the requirement that all treaties with other countries be ratified by individual states, and the lack of power by Congress to regulate interstate commerce all added up to an unworkable situation. Mifflin was one of the strongest proponents of changes to the Articles, or its replacement by a new national constitution. After 1775, he would see the problems that a loose confederation of states caused him in his role as quartermaster general of the

Continental Army, and he was convinced that something needed to be done if the new government—and the new nation—were to survive.

In 1787, a Constitutional Convention voted for a new constitution, which superseded the Articles of Confederation on March 4, 1789, and today it is still in effect as the U.S. Constitution.

Expelled from Quakers—March 1775

In 1775, Pennsylvania Quakers faced a serious dilemma, as many of their young men longed to join their peers and fight for independence from Great Britain—even to the point of participating in military drills. Thomas Mifflin became a senior major in Philadelphia's 3rd Battalion.

The March 1775 monthly meeting of Philadelphia Quakers took up the case of Thomas Mifflin and resolved:

> Thomas Mifflin, of this city, merchant, who hath professed to be a member of our religious Society, having for a considerable time past been active in the promotion of military measures, it became our concern and care to endeavor to convince him of the inconsistency of his conduct with our peaceable principles, but he declaring himself not convinced of our Christian testimony against wars and fightings, and persisting therein, whereby he hath separated himself from religious fellowship with us, we are under a necessity to declare that we cannot esteem him to be a member of our religious society until by the illumination of Divine Grace he is further convinced and becomes desirous of being truly united in religious fellowship with us, to which state we desire he may attain.[36]

Four months after Mifflin's expulsion, another wealthy young man, Nathanael Greene, was rejected by his Quaker chapter in Rhode Island for about the same reasons. Within the next half-a-dozen years, both men would be instrumental in training their respective state military organizations, and become, respectively, the first and third quartermaster generals of the Continental Army. Both would rise to the highest possible military rank at the time—major general, and both would be tagged with the nickname "The Fighting Quaker."[37]

However, Mifflin would become estranged from Washington just as Greene rose in the commander in chief's estimation. The rivalry between the two men became well known throughout the Army.

Greene's ascendancy was primarily due to his brilliant military strategy, which ultimately led to American successes in the Southern colonies. However, it probably didn't help Mifflin much when Greene and his wife Catherine named their first two children George Washington Greene and Martha Washington Greene. These children were born in 1775 and 1777 respectively.

Chapter Five

The War Begins

On March 23, 1775: Patrick Henry gave arguably the most famous—and significant—speech of the Revolution in which he cried "Give me liberty or give me death."

On the evening of April 18–19, 1775, silversmith Paul Revere rode through the eastern Massachusetts's countryside to warn that British troops were heading west from Boston to take over the colonist's armory at Concord. Hours later the battles of Lexington and Concord occurred.[1]

The battles of Lexington and Concord are usually considered the beginning of the American Revolutionary War. They started on April 19, 1775, with a battle on Lexington town green, in which British soldiers confronted about 80 militiamen and shot eight of them to death. After regrouping, the British troops continued on to their intended destination—the town of Concord. There at its North Bridge another fight ensued, but this time about 500 colonial militiamen outnumbered the British troops. They came from New Hampshire, Connecticut, and Rhode Island, as well as Massachusetts. The British light infantry suffered a severe loss with almost 50 killed. On their retreat back to Boston the British casualty figures rose as they were ambushed all the way back through the woods and fields. When news of the fighting spread, militias and volunteers organized. In the following weeks, almost 20,000 militiamen surrounded Boston, laying siege to it … a siege that lasted for another nine months.

The battles of Lexington and Concord also demonstrated to the people of the 13 colonies that the British army—the most powerful armed force in the world—could be beaten by farmers and tradesmen when they were fighting on their home turf.

Great Britain responded to the battles by closing the port of Boston and dissolved the Massachusetts Assembly. They also had Major General Thomas Gage (1721–April 2, 1787) in America to establish law and order. In office since 1763, he carried the title Commander in Chief, North America.²

Thomas Mifflin's first biographer, Rawle, wrote that when Philadelphians heard of the Battle at Lexington, a town meeting was called. At it:

> "...the fellow citizens of Mifflin were delighted by his *animated* oratory." Other addresses were delivered on this solemn occasion, *all of* which partook of the same feeling; but, although the *youngest* of these speakers, Mifflin had the exclusive merit of suggesting the necessity of a *steady adherence* to the resolutions that were adopted. The language with which he concluded was long remembered. "Let us not," he said, "be *bold in* declarations, and afterwards *cold in action*. Let not the patriotic feelings of *to-day be forgotten* to-morrow, nor have it said of Philadelphia, that she passed *noble resolutions, slept upon* them, and afterwards *neglected* them."³

At that time, Mifflin expressed opinions on freedom and independence that he would hold for the rest of his life. After Lexington and Concord, Militia units gathered around Boston. The Continental Congress began to organize them into an army and appoint leaders. Both the Northern and the Southern colonies wanted one of their own in the position of overall commander. Virginia was especially insistent that its soldiers not be under the command of a Northerner. Massachusetts and the other colonies of the north pushed it no further and supported a southerner to command the army—Virginian George Washington. He was already known to the delegates from his role in the French and Indian War. It also didn't hurt that in prior sessions of the Continental Congress, Washington made a habit of wearing his military uniform. It was a perfect example of the saying "clothes make the man."⁴

Commissioned a Major in the Continental Army

As for many young men in April 1775, news of British troops firing on Americans in Massachusetts towns was a game changer for them—and that included Mifflin. Although he was already firmly in support of independence from Great Britain, Mifflin had not actively pushed for military action. As a Quaker, in a city with a large Quaker population, his position wasn't an easy one.

Rawle mentions the town meeting called in Philadelphia after Lexington, and states:

> What he recommended to others, he practiced himself. The formation of military companies and regiments, the acquisition of as great a portion of military knowledge as there could be obtained, and the exercises of daily drill and discipline soon became general. Of one of these regiments, he was appointed

the *major*, and no efforts on *his part* were wanting to improve this species of domestic defense. But his active spirit could not long be confined to *mere measures* of preparation; he panted for opportunities of coming into *action* and he flew to the camp then formed before Boston.[5]

On May 29, 1775, John Adams sent a letter from Philadelphia to his wife, Abigail Adams. In it he stated: "The military Spirit which runs through the Continent is truly amazing" and Philadelphia "turns out 2,000 Men every day." Adams notes that John Dickinson (1732–1808) is a colonel, Joseph Reed is a lieutenant colonel, and Thomas Mifflin is a major. He adds that Mifflin *"ought to have been a Genl. for he has been the animating Soul of the whole."*[6]

On July 8, 1775, the Connecticut delegate to the Second Continental Congress, Silas Deane, mentioned Thomas Mifflin in a letter to his wife Elizabeth Deane. He wrote that Mifflin was "greatly missed in this city [Philadelphia], as he was the soul of everything either civil or military here; not that the military fails, but it does not increase as it would under his animating and indefatigable endeavors."[7] A couple of months later, Deane, wrote to his wife: "I met Mrs. Mifflin, this morning, bound for the Camp. If she pass thro' Wethersfield, wish you to be acquainted with her. She is a most agreeable lady, and worthy your notice on every account, but more particularly as you propose visiting Philadelphia."[8]

Within the next few years, Deane would play a key part in convincing France to join the American efforts against Britain in North America. "He also played a role in attracting foreign soldiers to the American Revolution—Baron Johann de Kalb, Thomas Conway, Casimir Pulaski, and Baron von Steuben."

Lechmere's Point

Rawle describes the situation outside of Boston:

Destitute of materials for besieging a place even *slightly* fortified, the occupations of the American army were *chiefly confined* to restraining the excursions of General Gage, and intercepting his supplies. A small affair of this kind afforded [Mifflin] the first opportunity of displaying both his *courage* and his *judgment*. A detachment had been sent from the British army to a place called *Lechmire's Point*, for the purpose of collecting cattle; Mifflin solicited and obtained the command of a party to oppose them, and succeeded, with half disciplined militia, in repelling the regular soldiery. An eye witness, the aged and venerable General *Craig*, declared to the writer, that he "never saw a greater display of personal bravery, than was exhibited on this occasion in the *cool* and *intrepid* conduct of Colonel Mifflin."[9]

Appointed a Major in the Continental Army (May 1775)

According to Rawle: "With no *other* opportunity to distinguish himself, Mifflin in common with his brother officers, was obliged to remain in a state of inactivity, while the enemy were confined in Boston. Hopes were entertained that some effort would be made to capture the town, but Congress had laid general Washington under a restriction of previously obtaining the approbation of a council of war."[10]

On June 16, 1775, two days after it established the Continental Army, the Continental Congress passed a resolution calling for the creation of a Quartermaster General position for the Continental Army. It would be a staff officer who would be in charge of supplies for the entire army. The resolution read: "*Resolved, That there be one Quartermaster General for the grand army, and one deputy under him for the separate army. * * * That the pay of the Quartermaster General be $80 per month, and that of the deputy $40 per month.*" In another resolution the following month,[11] Congress stated: "*Resolved, That the appointment of a Quartermaster General * * * be left to General Washington.*"[12]

Commander-in-Chief George Washington. Mifflin served under Washington as a military aide in 1775, as quartermaster general of the Continental Army, and as a field commander. They also worked together as delegates in the Continental Congress and in the years when Washington was President of the United States and Mifflin was the governor of the Commonwealth of Pennsylvania. This work was painted and engraved by Charles Willson Peale in 1787 (Library of Congress).

Bunker Hill— June 17, 1775

Two months after Lexington and Concord, the first major battle of the Revolutionary War occurred on a peninsula north of the city of

Boston. Fought on Breed's Hill, it has gone down in history with the name of an adjacent hill—Bunker Hill. On June 17, 1775, Colonial militia fought off seasoned British troops for most of the afternoon, afflicting heavy casualties. Although the British won the battle, 70 percent of the men killed or wounded were British—while 226 British men were killed, the Americans lost only 140. The number of wounded was even more lopsided: 828 British to 271 American. Especially disconcerting for the British was the fact that many British Army officers were killed in action that day. It seems the colonials did not follow the traditional "honorable" practice of only killing the ordinary soldiers and leaving the officers alone.

Washington's First Aide-de-Camp

Two days after the Battle of Bunker Hill, Congress commissioned George Washington as Commander in Chief of the Continental Army (June 19, 1775). Two weeks after that, Washington appointed Thomas Mifflin as his first aide-de-camp and Mifflin's fellow Philadelphian Joseph Reed as Washington's military secretary.[13]

The day after Washington left for Boston, the Philadelphia correspondent of the *Maryland Gazette* wrote: "Major Thomas Mifflin (3d Batt.) is appointed aid-de-Camp to General Washington, and accompanies the General to the camp near Boston. The active and successful part which this gentleman has taken in the civil and military affairs of the Province of Pennsylvania has endeared him so much to his fellow citizens, that few men have ever left us more universally beloved or regretted."[14]

The following month—on August 14, 1775—Washington appointed Mifflin, then a major, as the Army's first Quartermaster General.[15]

In the preceding years, both Washington and Mifflin had served as delegates to the First Continental Congress. Washington was undoubtedly aware of Mifflin's lack of experience in military matters, but this was not uncommon for a 31-year-old man in the first year of the Revolutionary War. Unless he had participated in battles like Lexington, Concord, or Bunker Hill a few months earlier, a native-born man of Mifflin's age would have had no way to acquire substantial military experience. Furthermore, Mifflin could not have been professionally trained, as there were no military academies in Pennsylvania at the time. While many men in the colonies were members of militia units, any action they might have seen would likely have been limited to skirmishes with local Native American tribes.

Five. The War Begins   45

Even the officers of the new Continental Army were generally inexperienced at this stage of the war, given that the last conflict involving the 13 colonies was the French and Indian War, which had ended 12 years earlier.

However, the Continental Army was not solely composed of very young officers. Veterans of the French and Indian War played a crucial role in the eventual victory of the colonial forces over the well-trained professional British Army.

A notable example occurred at the Battle of Bunker Hill, where three outstanding colonels from the French and Indian War—Massachusetts' William Prescott, New Hampshire's John Stark, and Connecticut's Israel Putnam—led an inexperienced force against the British on a peninsula north of Boston and fought valiantly. These men set an example that would inspire troops for the remainder of the war and throughout history. Putnam, in particular, was already a "legend in his own time," for his experiences fighting the French, their Native

The William Brattle House in Cambridge, Massachusetts, served as Quartermaster Thomas Mifflin's headquarters during the Siege of Boston (1775–1776). The building was formerly home to William Brattle, a loyalist who left the Boston area shortly before the Revolutionary War broke out (Library of Congress).

American allies, and the Spanish on the island of Cuba. He acquired invaluable practical lessons on the strategy and tactics of these old enemies, as well as from the professional British soldiers he fought alongside in the French and Indian War.[16]

One other man continued to be greatly impressed with the 31-year-old Mifflin: Founding Father John Adams. On June 21, 1775, which was two days after Congress commissioned George Washington as Commander in Chief of the Continental Army, Adams wrote to Massachusetts' legislature member James Warren[17]: "Major Mifflin goes in the Character of Aid de Camp to General Washington. I wish You to be acquainted with him, because, he has great Spirit Activity, and Abilities, both in civil and military Life. He is a gentleman of Education, Family and Fortune."[18]

CHAPTER SIX

Quartermaster General of the Continental Army

On August 14, 1775, Washington choose Mifflin, his aide-de-camp for only about six weeks, to fill the newly-created position of quartermaster-general of the Continental Army. Mifflin's extensive business experience in Philadelphia no doubt played a large part in this selection.

By the following winter, the quartermaster general's office numbered 28 people. Mifflin also employed merchants to purchase whatever they might need—tents, lumber, tools, etc. These merchants usually received a two to two-and-one-half percent commission.[1]

However, Mifflin's tenure in this crucial role was marked by challenges, including a lack of supplies and a shortage of funds to cover expenses. The nature of the work, coupled with these obstacles, left Mifflin dissatisfied and eager to transition into a position more aligned with his talents and ambitions.

Despite these challenges, Mifflin persevered in the role for nine months, resigning as Quartermaster General in May 1776. His initial replacement served for only four months, leading to Mifflin's being persuaded to return to the position on October 1, 1776. This time, he remained in the role for over a year, resigning for a second time on November 17, 1777, citing ill health as the reason for his departure.

On August 29, 1775, Washington wrote to Virginia Continental Congress delegate Richard Henry Lee from his headquarters in Cambridge, Massachusetts:

> Mr. Mifflin who I have appointed Quarter Master Genel from a thorough persuasion of his Integrity—my own experience of his activity—and finally, because he stands unconnected with either of these Governments; or with this, that, or t'other Man; for between you and I, there is more in this than you can easily imagine.[2]

Richard Henry Lee's reply to Washington on September 26 contained this text:

> I think you could not possible have appointed a better Man to his present Office than Mr. Mifflin. He is a singular Man, and you certainly will meet with the applause and support of all good men by promoting and countenancing real merit and public virtue, in opposition to all private interests, and partial affections.[3]

Virginia's Richard Henry Lee, who had an opportunity to develop a close acquaintance with Mifflin during their service in the First Continental Congress, not only was one of the most eloquent and influential delegates at the First and Second Continental Congresses but had also introduced one of Congress's most renowned resolutions the previous year. This resolution boldly declared: "that these United Colonies are, and of right ought to be, free and independent States, that they are absolved from all allegiance to the British Crown, and that all political connection between them and the State of Great Britain is, and ought to be, totally dissolved."

Mifflin would come to recognize a major disadvantage of holding the position of quartermaster general. Since a great deal of money passed through his hands, it opened the door to charges of dishonesty. Mifflin's biographer Kenneth Rossman addressed the problem: "Much money and many contracts were to pass through his [Mifflin's] hands. Thoroughly honest himself, he must nonetheless exercise great caution so as not to alarm the suspicious."[4]

In October 1775, the ever-popular Mifflin was elected to the Pennsylvania Assembly for the fourth time. As he was serving in Boston, he resigned from his Assembly seat and a few months later Joseph Reed replaced him.

When Mifflin began working as quartermaster general, Washington's army had three divisions: one was at Roxbury, Massachusetts; another at Prospect and Winter Hills; and a third at Cambridge. Each division was composed of two brigades and each brigade had about six regiments.[5]

A good example of the duties Mifflin needed to perform as quartermaster general is this estimate of expenses from October 5, 1775. It was for a barracks building 96 feet by 16 feet, which is to house 100 men in a total of six rooms.[6]

Boards	30 pounds
Joist, Slit work	6 pounds
Timber for the Frame	12 pounds 6 shillings

Six. Quartermaster General of the Continental Army

Shingles	10 pounds 16 shillings
Nails	9 pounds
Bricks	12 pounds 6 shillings
Additional Wages to 16 soldiers to build the barracks	16 pounds
The total cost of a barracks	96 pounds 8 shillings

The construction cost for each barracks building was approximately 20,000 pounds in today's British pound or approximately 25,000 21st century U.S. dollars. Mifflin estimated the need for 120 barracks, with 90 to be constructed in the Cambridge, Massachusetts, encampment and 30 in the Roxbury, Massachusetts, encampment. He calculated the total cost at 12,000 pounds (100 pounds per barracks multiplied by 120 barracks) and added an additional 8,000 pounds for firewood for the soldiers at both camps. Therefore, in terms of today's currency, the overall cost to build the two camps outside of Boston was approximately three million dollars.

Recruiting Officer

Mifflin comprehended the motivations that would draw young men to support the cause of independence. His inclusive vision extended beyond specific social classes, encompassing not just the upper class, unskilled workers, or the middle class, but all segments of the population. This broad appeal contributed significantly to his ability to secure substantial voter support in subsequent elections.

In addition, witnesses to his speeches attest that Mifflin was among the most compelling orators of his time. His exceptional ability to inspire both his troops and potential recruits was noteworthy, underscoring his effectiveness as a communicator and leader.

In September 1775, a major change in the British high command took place: William Howe[7] took over as commander in chief of British land forces in America. He would remain in charge until May 1778.

In November 1775, one of Washington's schooners captured the British transport *Nancy*. On November 30, General Heath wrote: "Intelligence was received from Cape-Ann, that a vessel from England, laden with warlike stores, had been taken and brought into that place. There was on board one 13 inch brass mortar, 2,000 stand of arms, 100,000 flints, 32 tons of leaden ball, &c. &c. A fortunate capture for the Americans!"[8]

It was by far the largest prize won by the Americans so far in the war. Upon hearing of the loss of the brass mortar and its addition to the Colonial artillery, General William Howe warned his superiors back in Britain of the danger it posed to the troops in Boston.[9]

When the mortar was being added to the Patriot army, Major General Israel Putnam, with the assistance of Thomas Mifflin, engaged in a comic ceremony on Cambridge Common. Putnam mounted the mortar while holding a bottle of rum, while he and Mifflin gave it the name "Congress."[10]

Promoted to Continental Army Colonel

On December 22, 1775, Mifflin was promoted to the rank of colonel in the Continental Army when Congress passed the following resolution: "*Resolved,* That the Quartermaster General have the rank of a colonel in the Army of the United Colonies."[11]

At the end of the year 1775, Patriots took Fort Ticonderoga in New York, but failed to invade Canada.

Battle of Moores Creek Bridge, February 1776

Two months after Mifflin's appointment to the rank of colonel, the Patriot forces received some rare good news. On February 27, 1776, patriot militia defeated British-aligned Loyalist troops at the Battle of Moores Creek Bridge in North Carolina. After less than ten minutes of fighting, they took 850 Loyalist prisoners. This battle is often referred to as "The Lexington and Concord of the South," both because it began the shooting war in the Southern American colonies, and because it boosted patriot morale. The approximately 1,000 Scottish Highlanders armed with broadswords attacked about 1,000 patriots who were at the bridge that spanned Moores Creek. About 50 of the British-aligned troops were killed or wounded. Only one patriot was killed in the battle; one other was wounded.

The Battle of Moores Creek Bridge was the first unquestionable victory of the war for the patriots, prompting the British to withdraw from North Carolina. That allowed the dismantling of the British-aligned government, the establishment of a patriot state government, and the declaration of the state's independence from the mother country.

Chapter Seven

The Siege of Boston

Dorchester Heights

The following month, and hundreds of miles north of Moores Creek Bridge, the patriot forces in Massachusetts achieved an even more significant victory. Washington had his army set up fortifications on Dorchester Heights south of the city of Boston, Massachusetts. He used cannon Henry Knox's troops had taken from New York's Fort Ticonderoga, as well as a prefabricated fortification device that was recommended to him by Colonel Rufus Putnam to protect the American soldiers.[1]

The overnight placement of artillery on hills that overlooked the City of Boston left British General William Howe with little choice but to evacuate the city. On St. Patrick's Day—March 17—an estimated 10,000 British troops, along with hundreds of their loyalist allies, left Boston on awaiting ships. The siege had lasted nine months. The British fleet sailed for Halifax, Nova Scotia.

It was the first major success of the war for the patriot forces. Since 1901, residents of South Boston and surrounding areas have celebrated "Evacuation Day"—along with St. Patrick's Day—as an official holiday.

Despite this departure, George Washington anticipated that the British were not finished with the thirteen colonies. Correctly guessing that New York City might be a future target, he made preparations to move troops south and west. As part of these preparations, he dispatched Colonel Thomas Mifflin to meet up with Brigadier Generals Heath and Sullivan at Norwich, Connecticut.

Sent to New York City

A week after the British forces left Boston, Washington, while at his quarters in Cambridge, Massachusetts, wrote the following orders to Quartermaster General Mifflin:

> As the Motions of The Enemy, & the Operations of the Ensuing Campaign, renders it indispensably necessary that a very large Body of Troops should be immediately assembled at, or near New York; You will immediately proceed to Norwich in Connecticut where you will, in Concert with the Brigadiers General Heath, & Sullivan, regulate the Embarkation of The Brigades under their Command: & settle all such Matters with the Commissary General of Provisions, and Contractors for the Transports, as may be further necessary for expediting the March of the rest of Army: with The Stores, Artillery, Camp Equipage, &c. &c.[2]

Not one for being unconcerned about details, the Commander in Chief continued with exact instructions for Mifflin:

> This being done you will proceed without Delay to New York where your first Care will be to provide Barracks for the Troops; Firing, Forage, Quarters for the General Officers. Fix upon a proper House, or Houses for a General Hospital, Stabling for the Continental draught Horses, &c., Intrenching Tools, must also be immediately provided, with a Sufficient Quantity of Joist, & Plank, for Platforms; & Timber for Gun Carriages. in short every necessary Article for the public Service and which your Experience the last Campaign convinces you will be wanted for that now approaching.[3]

Washington in a March 24, 1776, letter to Mifflin wrote: "I shall at present only recommend that the same Integrity, Zeal, diligence & Activity, which has hitherto animated your past Services"[4]

Five days later,[5] Washington sent the following orders to Major General Israel Putnam:

> As there are the best reasons to believe that the Enemy's Fleet & Army which left Nantasket Road last Wednesday Evening are bound to N.Y. to endeavor to Possess that Important Post & if Possible Secure the Communication by Hudsons River to Canada. it must be Our Care to prevent them their Designs. To that End, I have Detached B.G. Heath with the whole Body of Rifle Men & five Battalions of the Conl Army by the Way of Norwich in Connect to New Y.

In this letter, Washington mentions Mifflin:

> You will meet the Q.M.G. Col. M[ifflin] & Com[missary] G[eneral] at N.Y. as they are both men of Excellent Talents in their different Departments you will do well to give them all the Authority & Assistance they require, and Should a Council of War be necessary it is my direction they Assist at it.
> ...Devoutly Praying that the Power which has hitherto sustained the American Arms may continue to Bless them with his Divine Protection, I bid You Farewell.

Washington then arranged to consult with the Congress in Philadelphia and directed General Horatio Gates and Colonel Mifflin to meet him there. Mifflin arrived first, on May 13, along with his wife and "attendants"; Gates came on May 21; and Washington on May 23.

Seven. The Siege of Boston

Statue of Major General Israel Putnam in Hartford, Connecticut's Bushnell Park. A legendary hero of the French and Indian War and the American Revolutionary War's Battle of Bunker Hill, Putnam was Thomas Mifflin's commanding officer during part of the Revolutionary War (photograph by author).

Three days after his arrival in Philadelphia, Mifflin was promoted to the rank of brigadier general in the Continental Army.

Five days after Washington sent the March 29 letter, General Israel Putnam arrived in New York City. Tensions were not at their peak, and the relative inaction gave the top leadership a chance to unwind. One letter by General Anthony Wayne mentions his fox hunt with General Nathanael Greene. He also speaks of a planned future hunt with generals Israel Putnam and Thomas Mifflin.[6]

After this point in the War, a major player in Mifflin's military career would be Horatio Gates. Born in England 16 years before Mifflin, Horatio Gates had his share of military experiences. Wounded during the French and Indian War, he returned to England but later chose to settle in the Virginia colony three years before the outbreak of the American Revolution. Due to his reputation and prominent position, Gates was appointed one of the first brigadier generals in the Continental Army. The following year, he earned a promotion to major general and assumed command of colonial troops in New York. In October 1776, Gates successfully impeded a British invasion from Canada, preventing the takeover of northern New York.

Gates reached the pinnacle of his military career during the Battles of Saratoga in New York. His army defeated British General Burgoyne in two crucial encounters on September 19, 1777, and October 7, 1777, marking a critical turning point in the war.

However, the lowest point of Gates' career occurred nearly three years later, on August 16, 1780, at the Battle of Camden in South Carolina. His decision to hastily leave the battlefield as his men were in retreat tarnished his reputation. Born in 1727, Horatio Gates died in 1806 at the age of 78.

Weeks later, on May 15, 1776, famed Massachusetts patriot leader Samuel Adams wrote to Washington asking for protection for the city of Boston: "As two General

Miniature portrait of Thomas Mifflin by John Trumbull. This was probably painted in 1790, which was the year Mifflin, at age 46, won his first election for Pennsylvania governor. This 3⅝-inch × 3-inch oil painting is located in the Yale University Art Gallery (courtesy Yale University Art Gallery).

Officers will be sent thither, it would, I am persuaded, give great Satisfaction to the People, if Generals Gates and Mifflin might be fixed upon. This however, I cheerfully submit to your Excellency's Judgment and Determination; being well assured, that the Safety of that distressed City will have as full a Share of your Attention as shall be consistent with the good of the whole."[7]

Chapter Eight

The Battle of Long Island

Promotion to Continental Army Brigadier General

June 12, 1776, was a significant day in American history. It was the day that statesman George Mason's Virginia Declaration of Rights, a model for the U.S. Constitution's Bill of Rights, was adopted by the Virginia Constitutional Convention, and it was one day after the Continental Congress appointed a Committee of Five to draft the Declaration of Independence. The 12th was also the day that the Continental Congress took up a complaint by Major General Israel Putnam and Brigadier General Thomas Mifflin.

General Israel Putnam, a prisoner of war of the French during the French and Indian War, had a reputation for treating enemy soldiers humanely when they were his prisoners—both in that war and in the Revolutionary War. So, when he witnessed a case of the humiliation and abuse of a loyalist by a mob in New York City, he was disgusted.

Putnam complained directly to his commander, General Washington. Washington refused to do anything about it, but apparently approved Putnam's going to Congress. Brigadier General Thomas Mifflin joined him in lodging the complaint. Mifflin, having served with many members of the Continental Congress in the First and Second Congresses, shared Putnam's belief that everyone, even enemies, deserved humane treatment.

The Continental Congress minutes of Wednesday afternoon, June 12, 1776, record the proceedings:

> Generals Putnam and Mifflin having complained to this Congress of the riotous and disorderly conduct of numbers of the inhabitants of this city, which had led this day to acts of violence towards some disaffected persons: It was therefore, *Resolved*, That this Congress by no means approve of the riots that have happened this day; they flatter themselves, however, that they have

proceeded from a real regard to liberty, and a detestation of those persons who, by their language and conduct, have discovered themselves to be inimical to the cause of America. To urge the warm friends of liberty to decency and good order, this Congress assures the publick that effectual measures shall be taken to secure the enemies of American liberty in this Colony; and do require the good people of this city and Colony to desist from all riots, and leave the offenders against so good a cause to be dealt with by the constitutional representatives of the Colony.[1]

Stephen Moylan Becomes the Army's Quartermaster General

Mifflin served in the quartermaster general position until he was commissioned a brigadier general in the Continental Army, which was on May 16, 1776. On June 5, 1776, Mifflin and his staff left for New York with Washington and the other officers. Mifflin was replaced as quartermaster general by Colonel Stephen Moylan.[2]

A Catholic immigrant from Ireland, Moylan had the type of background that appeared to prepare him for the quartermaster general position—he had extensive experience with his family's shipping company. However, Moylan served less than four months, and resigned on October 1, 1776.

It does not appear that Moylan's relationship with Washington was adversely affected by the resignation, as a few months later, on January 22, 1777, the commander in chief, in a letter to Continental Congress President John Hancock, stated: "Colo. Baylor, Colo. Moylan (who as [a] Volunteer has remained constantly with the Army since his discontinuance in the Quarter Masters department) and Colo. Sheldon, command[s] the three new Regiments of light Dragoons."[3]

Stephen Moylan's time as quartermaster general was uneventful. Perhaps most notable about Moylan was the fact that he was apparently the first person to use the term "United States of America." On January 2, 1776, he wrote a letter to Joseph Reed in which he expressed a desire to be the first ambassador to Spain from the thirteen colonies. Moylan wrote: "I should like vastly to go with full and ample powers from the United States of America to Spain."[4]

The U.S. Navy's Naval History and Heritage Command mentions a small vessel named after Thomas Mifflin by Washington in 1776: "*General Mifflin* was a small sloop [schooner] procured by General Washington in the spring of 1776. Upon arrival in New York in April, the general fitted out a small fleet of vessels for the protection of the local waters, *General Mifflin* among them. She cruised in the neighborhood of Long

Island, often in company with sloop *Montgomery*, and captured several vessels, before her final disposition."[5] It was around the same time as the *General Mifflin* was christened that the fort at Philadelphia was unofficially also named after Thomas Mifflin.[6]

On June 28, 1776, 22,000 British troops attempted to take Charleston, South Carolina. Fort Sullivan, standing at the entrance to the city's harbor on Sullivan's Island, stood in the way. Met with heavy artillery fire from the fort, the British couldn't land their troops, and turned back to New York. It would be almost another four years before the British would take Charleston, South Carolina.

Given a Command

The next day, June 29, 1776, several hundreds of miles to the north, Thomas Mifflin was given Colonel John Shee's and Colonel Robert Magaw's Pennsylvania battalions with respectively 496 and 480 men. Mifflin's Brigade also consisted of Colonel Israel Hutchinson's 27th Continental Regiment (with 513 men), Colonel Paul Sargent's 16th Continental Regiment (527 men), and Colonel Andrew Ward's Connecticut Regiment (437 men).

A veteran of the French and Indian War,[7] Israel Hutchinson was almost 50 years old at the time he commanded his 27th Continental regiment at the Battle of Long Island. At the beginning of the Revolution, he was a captain at the Battle of Lexington (1775), and a colonel at the Siege of Boston. Along with John Glover's troops, he and his 27th Continental Regiment manned boats in retreat from Long Island, thus helping to save Washington's army. Later in the year 1776, he was with Washington at the crossing of the Delaware and at the Battle of Trenton. Israel Hutchinson was born and died in Danvers, Massachusetts (1727–1811).

In the months after Colonel Paul Sargent and his 16th Continental Regiment was assigned to Mifflin, he would go on in 1776 to fight at the battles of Harlem, White Plains, Trenton, and Princeton. Born in Salem, Massachusetts, in 1745, Sargent was a merchant by trade and had investments in shipping that were decimated during the American Revolutionary War by captures and shipwrecks. In his later years, he was supported by his pension. He died in Maine in 1828 at age 83.[8]

During the American Revolution, a significant number of Jewish colonists, around 100 out of the estimated 2,500 living in the thirteen colonies, served in the Continental Army or colonial militias. A substantial portion of the Jewish colonists resided in Philadelphia. Today, the city's Mikveh Israel Synagogue is the oldest continuous synagogue in the United States.[9]

Among the Jewish colonists, Haym Salomon (1740–1785) played an especially crucial role in supporting the cause of independence. An immigrant from Poland, Salomon joined the Sons of Liberty and collaborated closely with financier Robert Morris to provide financial backing for the American war effort. His expertise in trading Continental currency for more stable Dutch and French currencies played a vital role in financing both the war and the emerging American government.

In addition to his financial contributions, Salomon offered interest-free loans to prominent figures in the new nation, including Thomas Jefferson, James Madison, and generals Thomas Mifflin and Baron von Steuben.

However, despite their significant contributions, many Jewish individuals faced financial struggles after the war. Historian Howard M. Sachar notes in *A History of Jews in America* that "nearly every Jewish contractor, privateer, and financier of note came out of the Revolution with his fortune either gone or painfully diminished."[10]

After the American Revolutionary War, both Haym Salomon and Robert Morris found themselves in debtors' prison. As we will see, although he never similarly suffered, Thomas Mifflin died a pauper as well.

Before the Battle of Long Island

On July 2, 1776, which was less than two months before what would be the largest battle of the Revolutionary War, Mifflin wrote to Washington from New York City:

> I find the Works well advanced but not in a State of Defense—The Teems allotted to them have been taken off—some of them sent to Town for Materials & there detained—others necessarily employed in hauling up the powder (which is now stored in the best place I could find) and provisions from the Landing.
> From the Colonels Reports the Mens Arms are in a most alarming Situation—Col. Magaw has not more than 125 in his Regiment fit for Service—Col. Shee about 300 including all the Carbines which they received lately by your Order. If the Enemy pay us a Visit we will do our best and endeavor to make up in Zeal what we want in Appointment. Should sufficient Reinforcements arrive at New York may we not expect a Share? You are best acquainted with the Importance of this post my dear General and I flatter myself will put it into our power to do something more than mere Defensive Work within our Lines.
> I think the Enemy may divert our Attention to the Heights above Kings Bridge—if so, is it expected that We can detach a party to oppose them—I shall

be happy in your Orders how to act if a Landing should be attempted above or below us at the same Time that we may have Reason to believe our present post to be one of their Objects. Were the Works in good Order & the Men well equipped I could easily determine those points but circumstanced as we are I do not see how we can permit even a small party to leave the Environs of this Camp without exposing it to imminent danger; & yet I might be tempted.[11]

Washington aide Richard Cary wrote Mifflin later that day: "I am orderd by his Excellency General Washington to return you for answer ... that it is not in his power to supply you with any arms, as there is a great want of them in the Camp here, which he supposes you are not insensible of—There is a number of Rifle Guns which are retaind for the Recruits, and which the General will lend you for the present, if there are any Men in Cols. Magaw's or Shee's Regts who know how to use them, otherwise he thinks they will be sent to no purpose—Colo. Moylan has this day dispatched some Armourers & Tools agreeable to your direction—You may depend on receiving a reinforcement as soon as any considerable number of Militia arrives; as yet so few have reached this that none can possibly be spared—The General has not the least expectation that in your present situation you will be able to do more than defend your own Lines, tho he is fully persuaded your most vigorous Exertions will be manifested in every respect—He also much approves of your intentions to exercise with the Artillery those men who are not Armed."[12]

Declaration of Independence Is Signed

In July 1776, the Declaration of Independence was signed, marking for history the date, July 4, most often given as the birthdate of the new country. Contrary to some sources, Thomas Mifflin did not sign the Declaration of Independence. The confusion may have resulted from the fact that Mifflin did sign the U.S. Constitution over a decade later. When the Declaration of Independence was signed in the summer of 1776, Mifflin was serving as a brigadier general in the Continental Army. Nine other men signed for Pennsylvania: George Clymer, Benjamin Franklin, Robert Morris, John Morton, George Ross, Benjamin Rush, James Smith, George Taylor, and James Wilson. Pennsylvania was the third largest English colony in the 13 colonies. The second largest, Virginia, had seven signers.[13]

Mifflin had been a member of the First Continental Congress in 1774. The year prior to the Declaration of Independence, Mifflin left the Second Continental Congress (June 1775) to become a military aide to George Washington and the first Quartermaster General in the

Continental Army. He was promoted to brigadier general on May 16, 1776, and was serving as such in July 1776. After the war, Mifflin was elected to the Confederation Congress and represented Pennsylvania there from 1782 to 1784.

It was said that the soldiers of the Continental Army were not especially excited about the Declaration of Independence being signed. One source states that "on an occasion of the reading of the document to the soldiers at [New York's] Fort Washington, they received it in perfect silence." General Mifflin, knowing this was no time for hesitation, sprang upon a cannon, and, in a clear voice, exclaimed: "My Lads, the Rubicon is crossed.[14] Let us give three cheers for the Declaration!" The effect was electric.[15]

On July 14, 1776, Mifflin wrote the following to his commander in chief. It gives a good idea of the work Mifflin was engaged in two months after he had left the quartermaster general position. Little did he know at the time, but his successor, Stephen Moylan, would quit the job in a couple of months and Mifflin would again be saddled with the job.

> The party opposite to us on the Jersey Side are at Work on the Mountain and will soon have the Ground prepared for Cannon—I was obliged to call the party of 150 Men from our point and set them to work on two Traverses which the Enemy's Fire on Friday convinced me were necessary in the Fort.
>
> I have removed the small Building, which was placed near the Bastion on the Right entering the Sally port, behind one of the Traverses; and have thought Necessity made Use of it as a Magazine. When the Carpenters have finished the proper Magazine I will take Care to settle it as low as possible and render it as secure as the Ground will permit. At present we have no Security for our powder.
>
> A Battery on the Height, above our point, of 18 pounders would render the passage of the River very difficult although our late Experiments may have taught us that it is not easy to prevent it. The Ships were obliged to pass very near to it. Our Rifles reached them. The Men having worked all Friday Night & being much fatigued I have released them from Fatigue this day. I want much your Excellency's Orders respecting the places next to be secured—Bulwarks connected with our Fort are certainly necessary—We are weak without them. I shall therefore, unless otherwise directed, order the party of 150 from N. York to finish the Battery on the point and then erect another on the Rock above it— Our own Men to finish the Traverses and proceed with some Outworks and a strong Abbatis—As to a Ditch it is very difficult & will require much Time to complete one. That I must leave until more essential Works are completed.
>
> Last Night I sent an alert and prudent Officer to watch the Motions of the Ships & Tories—He is properly equipped & well qualified for the Business. The Ships lay in Sight of us all Yesterday about 4 or 5 Miles above Dobbs Ferry: I have sent out to know where they are this Morning: the Weather prevents our seeing them at their Station of Yesterday.
>
> I beg Leave to mention the Necessity of securing the Communications

Opposite to us with New Jersey. A small part of the Flying Camp as the Ground is strong would answer the purpose.

The Heights over the Bridge and South of Kings Bridge near the three Trees well known by your Excellency are in my opinion of immense Importance to us—especially if the Enemy attempt an Impression, or determine to throw up a Line of Contravallation, against our posts on this Island, and try to shut us in.[16]

The Board of War

On June 12, 1776, the Continental Congress established the Board of War and Ordinance [sic], a Congressional committee charged with the task of supervising the activities of the Continental Army, and offering guidance to Congress on military matters. This decision came a year after the Battle of Bunker Hill and the appointment of George Washington as commander in chief of the Continental Army. Most delegates felt that a civilian board was needed.

The first Board of War and Ordinance was composed of five members of Congress, with Massachusetts' John Adams serving as the chair. The other committee members were: Roger Sherman [Connecticut], Benjamin Harrison [Virginia], James Wilson [Pennsylvania], and Edward Rutledge [South Carolina]. This representation ensured that major states from different regions were included, employing a similar approach used a year earlier when appointing Commander in Chief Washington's first four major generals—Artemas Ward of Massachusetts, Charles Lee of Virginia, Philip Schuyler of New York, and Israel Putnam of Connecticut.

One of the driving forces behind the creation of the Board of War was the debate over the most effective strategy for conducting the war. Some Americans believed that each state should have its own armed forces, while others argued for a robust national army. With the first Board of War composed of members from two northern states, one Middle Atlantic state, and two southern states, most people were satisfied they were fairly represented.

The Board would act as an interface between the commander in chief of the Continental Army, General Washington. and the national civilian government, i.e., the Continental Congress, on matters of military strategy, operations, etc. As a committee of Congress, it was charged with the responsibility to make reports to Congress as a whole so that it could make better informed decisions on issues of a military nature. Thomas Mifflin, as a past member of the Continental Congress, could understand well the value of a board composed of civilian leaders who were elected by their respective states. Also, he had worked closely with Continental Army officers ever since he took on the role of military aide to commander-in-chief Washington. In that capacity, he could predict how military officers might react to such a board.

The June 12, 1776, Congressional resolution that created this Board of War and Ordinance stated:

> Resolved, That a Committee of Congress be appointed by the Name of "A Board of War and Ordinance"—to consist of five Members—
> That a Secretary and one or more Clerks be appointed by Congress with competent Salaries to assist the said Board in executing the Business of their department.
> That it shall be the duty of the said Board to obtain and keep an alphabetical and accurate Register for the Names of all officers of the land forces in the Service of the united Colonies with their Ranks and the date of their respective Commissions; and also regular Accounts of the State and disposition of the Troops in the respective Colonies; for which purpose the Generals and Officers commanding in the different departments & posts are to cause regular Returns to be made into the said War Office—
> That they shall obtain and keep exact Accounts of the Artillery, Arms, Ammunition and Warlike Stores belonging to the United Colonies and of the manner in which and the places where the same shall from time to time be lodged and employed and that they shall have the immediate Care of all such Artillery, Arms, Ammunition and Warlike Stores as shall not be employed in actual Service, for preserving whereof they shall have power to hire proper Magazines at the public Expense.[17]

Nine days later, the five members of the new board wrote to the Commander in Chief[18]:

> The Congress having thought proper to appoint us to the Board of War and Ordinance, ... it will be necessary for you forthwith to furnish the Board with an exact State of the Army under your Command and everything relative thereto. You will therefore be pleased, as speedily as possible, to give the necessary Directions for true and accurate Returns to be made to you, so as to enable you to give the Board the proper Information. As much depends on reducing into Method the Business recommended to our Notice, we beg you will forward all Measures conducive to this desirable Purpose by every Means in your Power. It is expected that in future monthly Returns be regularly transmitted to the War Office that Congress may frequently have a full and general Knowledge of the true Situation of their military Affairs without which it will be impossible to conduct them with Propriety and Success. We must farther request that you will keep up a constant and regular Correspondence with us that we may cooperate with you in such Measures as may tend to advance the Interest of America in general and the particular Department committed to your Care. You will be pleased in the Returns of the several Regiments to mention the Colonies in which they were raised, the Times when and the Periods for which the Men were enlisted as it will be necessary for us to have sufficient

Notice of these Matters that Congress may keep up the Army to its full Compliment. We are your Excellency's most obedient and most humble Servants,

John Adams
Roger Sherman
Benj Harrison
James Wilson
Edward Rutledge

A day after his appointment to the Board of War, John Adams wrote to General Nathanael Greene:

> I will enclose to you, a Copy of the Resolution establishing, a Board of War and Ordinance; and as you may well imagine, We are all, inexperienced in this Business. I Should be extremely obliged to you for, any Hints for the Improvement of the Plan, which may occur to you, and for any Assistance or Advice you may give me, as a private Correspondent in the Execution of it. It is a great Mortification to me I confess, and I fear it will too often be a Misfortune to our Country, that I am called to the Discharge of Trusts to which I feel myself So unequal, and in the Execution of which I can derive no Assistance from my Education, or former Course of Life. But my Country must command me, and wherever she shall order me, there I will go, without Dismay.[19]

Four days later, John Adams wrote to his wife Abigail:

> The Congress have been pleased to give me more Business than I am qualified for, and more than I fear, I can go through, with safety to my Health. They have established a Board of War and Ordinance and made me President of it, an Honor to which I never aspired, a Trust to which I feel myself vastly unequal. But I am determined to do as well as I can and make Industry supply, in some degree the Place of Abilities and Experience. The Board sits, every Morning and every Evening. This, with Constant Attendance in Congress, will so entirely engross my Time, that I fear, I shall not be able to write you, so often as I have. But I will steal Time to write to you.[20]

One might guess that the establishment of the Board of War would be a huge disappointment to Commander in Chief Washington, but on the contrary, he considered it an excellent idea. Just before he was informed of Congress' action, he had written to John Hancock: "the more I reflect upon the Subject, the more I am convinced of its' Necessity, and that Affairs can never be properly conducted without it."[21]

Washington's opinion of the Board of War was destined to change. Often, relations between them were strained. After all, both were under the pressure of an ongoing war on home soil with enemy troops continually presenting a threat. Congressional delegates had to deal with their respective state governments back home on matters of financing, troop recruitment, supplies procurement, coordination with state militias, etc. Meanwhile, Washington faced the challenge of leading a non-professional army against the most highly-trained military force in the world.

Bernard D. Haas, in his thesis on Maryland delegate Charles Carroll as a member of the Board of War, discusses problems with the Board as it was first constructed:

> The Board of War persisted in executing tactics of war down to the last detail, even to minor military movements for the smallest contingent of men. Little did it leave to its generals.
> A striking example of this, while Carroll was on the Board, was the organization of a regiment of Rangers from South Carolina on July 24, 1776. On this occasion the Board reported to Congress that the regiment of Rangers be incorporated into the Confederated Army, and in its plans for the organization of this force the Board listed the finest details, ordering a lieutenant colonel as commandant for the regiment, a major, ten captains, twenty lieutenants, a surgeon, a paymaster, twenty sergeants, and five hundred privates, carefully specifying what pay was to be given to each man, determining how the contingent would fight, whether on horseback or foot.[22]

Brigadier General Promotion

Rawle addresses Mifflin's brigadier general promotion:

> Very soon after this great event [the evacuation of the British troops from Boston on March 17, 1776], Col. Mifflin received from Congress the commission of Brigadier General, which at so *early* an age [Mifflin was 32 years old] was no *inconsiderable honor*. He had before this time performed the laborious duties of *Quarter-Master General*; which were afterwards undertaken by Stephen Moylan, an accomplished Irish gentleman resident among us, but of habits and manners not exactly suited to the difficulties of the times: he therefore soon abandoned the office, and Mifflin was requested by Congress to *resume* it.
> Military men know this to be a post of the first necessity, and of severe responsibility; but it is one which tends to subtract the occupant from the chance of distinction in actual warfare; and therefore, as well in this respect, as in regard to the nature of the employment itself, Mifflin's acceptance of the office was somewhat of an act of *self-denial*. The country was in a state of *disorder*—its *commerce* was suspended—and, of the articles most in demand, some could not be procured at *all*, and others were *reluctantly* parted with. In the organization of the department, everything was new and unsettled; and, in its operations, almost every measure either *offended* the people, or *disappointed* the government. In all his share of public life, Gen. Mifflin found *this* the most obnoxious to his *feelings*, and, for a time, the most prejudicial to his *character*.[23]

On August 4, 1776, John Adams listed reasons for Mifflin's promotion to brigadier general by Congress in a letter to General Nathanael Greene:

Mifflin, was a Gentleman of Family, and Fortune in his Country, of the best Education and Abilities, of great Knowledge of the World, and remarkable Activity. Besides this, the Rank he had held as a Member of the Legislature of this Province, and a Member of Congress, and his great Merit in the civil Department, in Subduing the Quaker and Proprietarian Interests added to the Tory Interests of this Province to the American system of Union, and especially his.... Activity and success in infusing into this Province a martial Spirit and Ambition which it never felt before, were thought Sufficient Causes for his Advancement.[24]

Congress at this juncture entertained a high opinion of Mifflin. In their secret journal, it appears (on May 25, 1776) that a committee was appointed to confer with Gen. Washington, Gen. Gates, and Gen. Mifflin, "touching the frontiers towards Canada."

Talk of Canada's possible role in the Revolution to their south was a subject in May 1776. John Adams' diary entry for May 23 states: "Resolved That a Committee of five be appointed to confer with General Washington, Major General Gates, and Brigadier General Mifflin, upon the most speedy and effectual means of supporting the American Cause in Canada."[25]

Rawles writes: Of the *result* of this particular conference no traces appear; and, as an incident of *general* history, it would scarcely deserve notice, but to the *biographer* [of Mifflin] it is not devoid of interest. The friends of the youthful hero were *gratified* by seeing him associated with *one* on whom the destinies of their country seemed to depend, and with *another*, whose age and experience stamped a value on his opinions.[26]

On June 29, 1776, Brigadier General Mifflin was given a command and his cousin Jonathan was made brigade major to him.

During the American Revolutionary War, both sides recognized the importance of the Hudson River (then commonly called the North River) through New York Colony/New York State. It was literally the divider between the far Northern colonies of New England, and the rest of the country (the Middle Atlantic and Southern Colonies/States from New Jersey south to Georgia). So important was it that General Washington considered the possibility of permanently stationing an army on either side of the Hudson River.

West Point Chain

An interesting anecdote involving Thomas Mifflin and a blacksmith named Samuel Wheeler sheds light on the efforts to secure the river. Apparently, Mifflin overheard Washington say, "I wish I could get a chain made; but that is impossible." Mifflin spoke up: "I know a man that can make such a chain.... Mr. Samuel Wheeler, a friend and townsman of mine." A pleased Washington replied, "I should like to see that man." Mifflin said, "He is here, now, in the army."[27]

Once Wheeler was brought to General Washington, the latter asked him, "I wish a chain made, to put across the North River, to stop the British ships. Can you make it?" "I can," the blacksmith replied. To Washington's exclamation, "I wish you to make it," Wheeler responded that he needed to do it at his shop back in Philadelphia. Washington stated: "I will cheerfully give you dismission from the army. Badly as we want men, we cannot afford to keep such a man as you."[28]

Wheeler made the huge chain and transported its individual links from his shop, up through New Jersey to New York. The chain was eventually hung across the Hudson at West Point. The British could only cut it by heating up a link and using a chisel and sledgehammer to break it.[29]

On August 20, 1776, John Adams wrote to Joseph Ward, Major General Artemas Ward's secretary:

> You Speak of a General Mifflin who was young in Experience, and in the Service. I wish our Massachusetts Colonels, old as they are, had as much Activity, and as extensive Capacities and Accomplishments as that young General. However, he is not so very young. He is old in Merit in the American Cause. He has the utmost Spirit and Activity, and the best Education and Abilities. He is of one of the best Families and has a handsome Future in his Country. He has been long a Member of the Legislature here, and of Congress. He was long the most indefatigable and successful Supporter of the American Cause in this Province, where it has labored more than anywhere else. He was the prime Conductor, and the Center of Motion to that association, which has completed the Reduction of this Province to the American Union, and has infused a martial Spirit into a People who never felt any Thing like it before. You can Scarcely name a Man, anywhere who has more Signal Merit.[30]

On August 27, 1776, British troops attacked American forces who were defending New York City in Brooklyn, on the far western end of Long Island. In what came to be called the Battle of Long Island (or the Battle of Brooklyn), the larger, better-trained British troops decisively defeated the Americans. In the aftermath, Washington's forces retreated to Brooklyn Heights, facing a British force more than twice its size. The situation was critical; the destruction of the Continental Army and the potential end of the rebellion loomed.

Washington decided upon the only course of action that had a chance for success: the evacuation of Long Island. On the night of August 29–August 30, Washington planned a secret retreat of his entire force. Thomas Mifflin's brigade had arrived too late to participate in the battle, but it was allowed to handle the very dangerous task of protecting the rear of the evacuating force.

On August 29, Washington entrusted Mifflin with a crucial message for General Heath, instructing him to dispatch all available boats to New York City for an evacuation. During a council of war, attended by major generals Putnam and Spencer, and brigadier generals Mifflin, Parsons, Wadsworth, McDougall, Scott, and Fellows, the unanimous advice was to recommend a retreat. Washington made the final decision to proceed with the evacuation. On Thursday August 29, orders were circulated to leave campfires burning into the night. The men were instructed to be as silent as possible as they went about their preparations to leave the island. Plans were made to move the wounded. All wagon wheels were muffled.

All did not go perfectly, however. A complication arose involving Washington's aide, Major Alexander Scammell.[31] In the confusion, Scammell misunderstood Washington's orders to move quickly and directed General Mifflin and his men toward the embarkation place. Washington intervened, redirecting Mifflin and explaining the miscommunication.

Once over half of the troops had secretly embarked from Long Island, a thick fog developed, enabling the remaining men to cross even as daylight emerged. As planned, Mifflin and his troops were the last to leave. During this critical operation, the soldiers of Smallwood's "Maryland 400" played a vital role by providing cover for General Washington and his troops, allowing them to escape undetected from pursuing British forces. Their actions that day almost wiped them out, but it's possible that they saved the Continental Army.[32]

Although free from Long Island, Washington and his men were now in a very precarious position on Manhattan Island. A council of war was held on September 12, and the decision was made to evacuate Manhattan. The vote was 10 to 3 with generals Spencer, Clinton and Heath opposing the move. There was nowhere to go except north as they were surrounded by water—water that was totally controlled by the British Navy. The evacuation took on a new urgency due to the findings of Mifflin and Rufus Putnam, who scouted the area near present-day Bronx, New York.

Evacuation of Long Island

Years later, Colonel Rufus Putnam wrote in his Memoirs[33] that in early September 1776, he and Thomas Mifflin, by orders of Washington, were sent to reconnoiter the country between Kingsbridge [today, Kingsbridge is a residential neighborhood in Bronx, New York] & Morrisania [today, it is part of southwestern Bronx] & eastward on our return we met with General Washington near Harlem heights, where we made our report to him in consequence of which a council of general officers was convened, whose advice was the withdrawing the army from the city … this measure was the Salvation of the army, and which probably would not have been but for the discoveries made by Mifflin & myself.[34]

One similarity in the military careers of Rufus Putnam and Thomas Mifflin involved their ambitions. Both longed for positions where they could directly command troops in battle. Rufus as a young man in the French and Indian War was always seeking to see action, but instead was assigned the task of construction sawmills, military fortifications, etc. His prior experience in construction was in such demand that he was often the only soldier with the competence to effectively complete those tasks. Mifflin's background as a successful merchant with a college degree made him the best suited for the position of quartermaster general of the army. Although Washington occasionally gave him an active command, that was the exception rather than the rule. The commander in chief quite simply could not find anyone else who could handle the quartermaster general's duties any better than Mifflin.[35]

When members of a Congressional committee visited Washington's camp, on September 27, they persuaded Quartermaster General Moylan to resign and convinced Mifflin to assume his old role again. Just about everyone was pleased, except for Mifflin who reluctantly—for the sake of the army—agreed to drop his active role as a commander in order to fix the quartermaster-general's department.

On October 11, 1776, John Jay wrote fellow Continental Congress delegate Edward Rutledge: "Let no considerations induce you to excuse General Mifflin from the office of quartermaster-general. Moylan acted wisely and honestly in resigning. Try no new experiments: you have paid for the last. Let me repeat it—keep Mifflin."[36]

Kip's Bay

On September 15, 1776, about 4,000 British and Hessian troops landed at Kip's Bay on the eastern shore of Manhattan Island. (Today, the United Nations headquarters building sits near that site.) Brigadier General Thomas Mifflin was riding toward the landing site with major generals Washington and Putnam.

A month after the Kip's Bay landing, William Smallwood described the events in a letter: "sixty [British] Light Infantry, upon the first fire, put to flight two brigades of the Connecticut troops—wretches who, however strange it may appear, from the Brigadier-General down to the private sentinel, were caned and whipped by the Generals Washington, Putnam, and Mifflin, but even this indignity had no weight, they could not be brought to stand one shot."[37] Major General Putnam, a proud resident of Connecticut and one of the bravest of the Army's general officers, was especially disgusted by the actions of the Connecticut troops.

Immediately, Washington's troops moved north to Harlem. General Israel Putnam, whose 3,000 troops were at the south end of the island, also headed north and met up with Washington's men. After chasing Washington's troops from a landing at Throg's Neck to a fight at the Battle of White Plains, British General Howe proceeded slowly. Too slowly it turns out, and then he turned around and returned to New York City. White Plains was a British victory, but it left Washington's Army intact and able to fight another day.

Things began looking up for Washington's army until, on November 16, 1776, the British captured Fort Washington on the Hudson River and made 2,800 men their prisoners. Two days later, the British captured Fort Lee. Both forts proved to reap a windfall of supplies that helped the British almost as much as it hurt the Americans. Washington regretted that he gave General Greene too much authority—Greene had strongly urged the retention of the fortifications.

On November 21, Mifflin wrote to Robert Morris, lamenting the loss of supplies at Fort Lee, stating: "The unhappy affair of Mount Washington has totally changed the Face of the Campaign and may probably encourage the Enemy to push forward until they are rebuffed."

Mifflin expressed his concern for the safety of Philadelphia. Then he went on: "The bad policy of attempting to make a stand at Mt Washington is now evident. I have talked heretofore about it & about it. I have abus'd the project and was never more surprised or chagrined than when I heard the post was reinforced instead of being dismantled and abandoned. Had we adhered to the Fabian plan we should have been at ... in the seat of Honor this Winter; the Enemy would have come off without Honor & Europe would have given us strong proofs of her affection before the Spring."[38]

After the devastating loss of Forts Washington and Lee, Washington, moved across the Hudson River into New Jersey. With British General Howe's forces following him, Washington reached the Delaware River with about 3,000 troops. Howe returned to New York City for the winter, leaving some soldiers in New Jersey, and in Newport, Rhode Island.

Chapter Nine

After New York

With the Moylan departure, Congress requested that Mifflin return to the quartermaster general position. After he reluctantly agreed, Mifflin began the challenging task of obtaining and stocking supplies for the troops. It was extremely frustrating that two months later, the British now owned them when they captured Fort Washington and Fort Lee.

One can get an idea of how busy Mifflin was at the time by reading such letters as this one from Major General Philip Schuyler to the Richard Peters, the secretary of the Board of War, in October 1776: "I am extremely happy to find that we have a prospect of being in some measure supplied with the articles you mention, and of which we stand in great need. ... General Mifflin has such a variety of business to attend to, that it is a kind of cruelty to burden him with any not immediately in his department."[1]

About five months later, Brigadier General Mifflin was elevated to the rank of major general by the Continental Congress (February 19, 1777). He was the fourteenth of what would be 29 men to achieve the rank of major general in the Continental Army during the Revolutionary War.

The next fall (October 8, 1777), Mifflin once again asked Congress to be relieved of his quartermaster general position, as well as terminate his commission as major general. It accepted his quartermaster general resignation on November 8, but stated that Mifflin: "be desired—notwithstanding his resignation of Quartermaster General was accepted—to continue in the exercise of that office, and that he be invested with full powers to act until another Quartermaster General should be appointed and should enter upon the duties of the office."

Congress also retained Mifflin's rank and commission as a major general. It does not appear that Mifflin "again entered formally upon these duties" of quartermaster general.

Fifty-eight individuals have served as quartermaster general of the United States Army between August 14, 1775, and April 2023. Only two of them—Thomas Mifflin and Montgomery C. Meigs—served two nonconsecutive terms in that position. Both men were in the position during wartime—Mifflin during the American Revolutionary War and Meigs during the American Civil War. However, Mifflin's two stints added up to only about 22 months, while Meigs' two terms added up to more than 20 years![2]

Four men served as quartermaster general of the Continental Army during the American Revolutionary War: major generals Mifflin and Nathanael Greene, and colonels Stephen Moylan and Timothy Pickering. From the creation of the office two months after the Battle of Bunker Hill until the Battle of Yorktown, which effectively ended the war, Greene was in the position for 887 days (41 percent of the war), Mifflin served 688 days (about 32 percent of the war), Pickering 441 days (20 percent of the war), and Moylan 114 days (5 percent of the war).[3]

The Mifflin biographical article on the official website of the U.S. Army Quartermaster Corps and Quartermaster School states:

> His political enemies accused him of embezzlement and a Congressional committee recommended that he be held responsible for the mismanagement caused by subordinates during his tenure as Quartermaster General. General Washington was directed by Congress to order an inquiry on the matter. General Mifflin invited the inquiry, claiming that Congressional interference had prevented him from properly directing the Quartermaster Department, but an inquiry never occurred. Mifflin indignantly resigned his commission as a Major General on August 17, 1778, and it was finally accepted by Congress on February 25, 1779. Despite these difficulties, Congress continued to call upon General Mifflin for advice. The most notable example was in 1780 when he assisted framing recommendations for reorganization of the Army staff departments.[4]

It's interesting to note that Mifflin's reputation was not so affected by accusations by his political enemies that it prevented Mifflin Hall—the Headquarters Building for the Quartermaster School in Fort Lee, Virginia—from being named for him.

Congressional Inquiry

Rawle states: "By one of those strange vacillations to which public bodies are always liable, Congress, after having at different times manifested almost unbounded confidence in [Mifflin], suddenly requested General Washington to make an *inquiry* into his conduct, and if the

Nine. After New York

distresses of the army were owing to his *misconduct,* or that of his inferior officers, to order a court martial."

It should be remembered that Mifflin had served in the First and Second Continental Congresses with most of these delegates and had accumulated political enemies as well as friends. Rawle continues: "We may reasonably suppose that this procedure arose from clamors with which Congress was beset, and which they knew not how otherwise to appease. His particular friends might, indeed, have concurred in the measure from a desire of vindicating his character; and it is not improbable that the commander in chief was *himself* satisfied that no neglect of duty was imputable to him. We may account, for the distresses of the army, as proceeding from a variety of causes not imputable to General Mifflin."

Did General Mifflin himself welcome an inquiry? Rawle has no doubt about it:

> It is certain that he earnestly courted the inquiry, and after waiting some time, and finding that no proceeding took place, he indignantly returned his commission to Congress, and insisted upon being allowed to resign, but this application was not more successful than the former. It was referred to a committee, who *made no report.* Exactly *one month afterwards,* an unequivocal proof that he was not suspected of any *dishonorable peculation* was given, by the advance to him of *one million of dollars,* to be employed in closing the business of the quarter-master general's department. This sum being, of course, in continental bills of credit, was equal in value to *two hundred thousand dollars* in specie. An amount sufficiently large however in the existing embarrassments of the government to evince the return of public confidence to him.
>
> And yet, from the necessity of satisfying the public mind, Congress did not lose sight of the inquiry originally directed. On the 23d of January, 1779, they were informed by one of their committees, that General Washington had done nothing in the business . By another resolve he was directed to proceed. Still, however, no formal inquiry seems to have been instituted, or if any did take place in the course of the year, it was favorable to him, since in January, 1780, he was appointed by Congress a member of a board to retrench the general expenses, and the thanks of Congress were voted to him and Colonel *Pickering,* for " the *wise* and *salutary plans*" they had recommended.[5]

As Mifflin's 20th-century biographer Kenneth Rossman stressed, Washington didn't want to proceed with an inquiry. He wrote to Congress stating that Mifflin had resigned from the army and "as he is no longer an officer, I should not conceive that he can be amenable to a military tribunal."[6] Rossman's opinion was that "Mifflin was not guilty of peculation[7]; at least the charge has never been supported. His utter willingness and desire for the inquiry further bespeak his innocence."

People are apt to speculate that influential and powerful public figures have done something illegal, unethical or inappropriate. It seems this was as frequent in the 18th century as it is today. One insinuation regarding Mifflin was that while serving as quartermaster general of the Continental Army, he profited from transactions with private businesses. It was—and has been—speculated not that he necessarily accepted bribes, but that he granted favors and expected payback in future years. It is true that many of the transactions he initiated and expediated were with former business associates, but that does not necessarily lead to the conclusion that there was any corruption. One must remember that Mifflin was one of the top merchants of the largest city in the 13 colonies—Philadelphia—and as such, had business connections that were second to none. Was he to ignore the influence he had with friends and associates if they would help him not only manage the quartermasters department, but manage it well?

To be quartermaster general of the Army at the beginning of the American Revolutionary War was no mean thing. Rather, it was a continual stream of time-consuming, frustrating, and often impossible tasks. Mifflin, and succeeding quartermaster generals, did not have the luxury to put out three bids for every army purchase and wait for responses. Time was of the essence. A colonel might require additional horses for an upcoming campaign, food supplies might be required at a fortification, or a whole host of items might be needed if the enemy had captured a supply train.

Even when the campaign season was winding down, the quartermaster general's department was responsible for safeguarding a camp's equipment from thieves, the environment, etc. Tents, entrenching tools, arms and munitions, etc., had to be quickly moved and stored appropriately. The men, horses and wagons to do this had to be ready.

An example of the tasks that Mifflin faced is described in the following letter he wrote to George Washington on March 9, 1777. He asks for the commander in chief's help in dealing with the state of Massachusetts. The 33-year-old Mifflin had just been promoted to major general by Congress less than three weeks earlier.

> ...By Order of Congress I have received 450,000 Dollars towards the Purchase of Horses Wagons & Forage; all which Articles are now providing with as much Haste as possible. Agreeable to your Orders I write to Mr. Snickers for 50 Wagons with 4 Horses each but gave him no Direction to purchase Forage as I had some Time before the Receipt of your Excellency's Letter employed a Gentlemen in that Quarter to purchase for me.
>
> I sent, three Days ago, from this place 12 fine Teams & shall dispatch 16 more in a Day or two for your Camp. At Lancaster I find some Difficulty to procure any Horses or Wagons; the purchase of Horses for the Troops by many different

Hands without Limitation or Discretion has almost ruined us. I do not wish to find Fault with any Gentlemen's Conduct nor do I mean to do it: but most certainly there has been very great Mismanagement in the purchase of the Light Horse. Horses have risen near 50 P. Cent in One Month.

I have received many Complaints from Trenton Bordentown & Burlington against Mr. Francis Wade & Co. who received Orders from your Excellency at Morris Town to purchase Forage & provisions in these places. I am well informed that his Conduct is very exceptionable & injurious to the Service; but have had no Opportunity of examining into the several Complaints against him—perhaps a Letter from your Excellency to him directing the most moderate Behavior in future may be of Use—he is an active industrious Man but I fear wants Discretion.

Last Night two of my Clerks arrived here from Morris Town in Order to settle my Accounts which I shall immediately set about—I will lose no Time in finishing them & in completing all my Business & shall wait on you as soon as I possibly can for further Orders.

I have Intrenching Tools already finished Sufficient for the next Campaign— The Tomahawks or Hatchets go on well—20,000 are now ready to be delivered. The Ammunition Wagons come in fast and I hope we may have three Weeks longer to prepare for Mr Howes Reception.[8]

This letter is not the exception. In his time as quartermaster general, Mifflin asked countless times for Washington's assistance in ordering, cajoling, and pleading with local and state officials, military commanders, and the Continental Congress. Mifflin had the knowledge necessary to perform the duties of quartermaster—perhaps better than anyone else; but Washington had the authority to handle successfully the really tough cases.

The quartermaster general position was also viewed by many with suspicion. The opportunities for personal gain at the expense of the taxpayers was great. Mifflin, like anyone in the job, had to contend with libel and slander.

If a trusted dealer back in Philadelphia could and would immediately fulfill an order, neither Mifflin nor any of the other Quartermaster Generals of the American Revolution could afford to quibble about what some naysayers in the future might say about a possible "trade of favors." Their job was to see that the war was not lost because of a lack of supplies. Nothing else took precedence over that. Even if it looked improper.

How "things looked" was even a concern of Washington. Thomas Jefferson would write of Washington: "his integrity was most pure, his justice the most inflexible I have ever known, no motives of interest or consanguinity, of friendship or hatred, being able to bias his decision. he was indeed, in every sense of the words, a wise, a good, & a great man."[9]

Still, Washington, could be concerned with the appearance of impropriety. Days after Mifflin's letter on the purchase of horses and wagons, he wrote to his quartermaster general:

> I very sincerely congratulate you upon your late promotion. The purport of this Letter is private. Your design in restraining the Wagon Master, from buying and selling Horses, I highly approve, because I am well assured, that a contrary practice would be introductory of a great deal of fraud, and imposition upon the public: But as it is more than probable that, in the course of service, many Horses will be so worn down as to render it beneficial to the public to have them sold, I should be glad, in that case, and no other, to come in as a common purchaser of a parcel of Mares, to the number of even fifty or an hundred.
>
> I have many large Farms and am improving a great deal of Land into Meadow and Pasture, which cannot fail of being profited by a number of Brood Mares; the getting of which, may perhaps, come easier and readier, in this way, than any other. I again repeat, that it is upon the presumption the good of the service requires such Sales, that I mean to become (as another person) a purchaser: But could wish, nevertheless, that it might be done without any mention of my Name; well knowing that the most innocent and upright Actions are often misconstrued, & that it would not be surprising, if it should be said, that I was defrauding the public of these Mares by some collusion or other.
>
> I should not care how low in flesh, or even crippled, they are, provided I could get them home; but I should not like to have them Old, and would prefer Bays, though I shall not object to any Color. If such Sales are found necessary, you can, I dare say, easily manage the matter so, in my behalf, as to keep my name out of the Question. My best respects to Mrs. Mifflin. With truth and sincerity, I am, Dr Sir, Your obt & Affectionate. G. Washington.[10]

In the broader context, George Washington Greene, in his 1846 biography of his grandfather Nathanael Greene, noted that Nathanael Greene faced similar challenges in 1780. After serving two years in the quartermaster general position, Nathanael Greene, like Mifflin, encountered "calumny and suspicion." Greene, too, desired to leave the desk job for a more active military command. The challenges and suspicions faced by both Mifflin and Greene highlight the complexities and scrutiny associated with roles like the quartermaster general position during the Revolutionary War. The younger Greene writes of his grandfather:

> But when he perceived that measures were taking, which rendered his department odious in the eyes of the people; that the most laborious devotion to his duties, and the most scrupulous integrity, were insufficient to shield him from calumny and suspicion; that the envenomed breath of slander had reached the ears of his personal friends, and shaken, for a moment, the confidence of his own brother; he resolved that nothing but a radical change in the whole system should induce him to retain an office, in which the sacrifice of the fame he most coveted was attended with the suspicions most painful to a man of honor.[11]

In a letter to Pennsylvania's Supreme Executive Council President Reed on August 29, 1780, General Nathanael Greene wrote:

You know I had got sick of the Department long since, not less from the treatment I met with in Congress, than with the army, and was desirous of resigning; but I should not have ventured upon the measure this campaign, if I could possibly have conceived I could have got through the business upon the new system. But it appeared to me that Congress intended to tie up my hands in such a way that I should either fail in the business or depart from the plan. In either case I should have been ruined.¹²

Nathanael Greene

Born in Rhode Island in 1742, Nathanael Greene was about one and a half years older than Thomas Mifflin. Greene initially worked in his family's iron forging business, catering to the shipping industry. However, his perspective on the struggle of the North American colonists shifted after his family was accused of burning the Royal Navy schooner HMS *Gaspee* in 1772. Despite being a Quaker, Greene developed an interest in military service, earning him the nickname the "Fighting Quaker," a moniker also attached to Thomas Mifflin. Greene was expelled from his church in 1773 after he attended a military parade and voiced his support for armed opposition to Great Britain. However, Greene remained a Quaker for the rest of his life.

Major General Nathanael Greene, like his rival Thomas Mifflin, was a former Quaker, a quartermaster general, and a major general during the Revolutionary War. His greatest success came as the commander of the Continental Army in the southern states (courtesy Yale University Art Gallery).

In 1775, Greene was commissioned a militia brigadier general with three regiments of Rhode Island troops. In 1776, he joined the Continental Army and was promoted to major general. After the Valley Forge encampment, he was made quartermaster general of the Continental Army. In

December 1780, he took over command of the Southern forces and for the following ten months led them to ultimate victory over the British in the Southern colonies. Greene died in 1786 at his house in Georgia, which had been given to him by the people of the state.[13]

Raising an Armed Force in Pennsylvania

In 1776, the British seized control of New York City and threatened to take Philadelphia. Historian George Reeser Prowell relates: "Thomas Wharton, president of Pennsylvania, on December 23, issued an address appealing to every friend of his country." Meantime, General Thomas Mifflin, the "fighting Quaker" of the Revolution, was requested by the State Assembly to make a tour of Pennsylvania. He made speeches in every section of the state, arousing the patriotism of the people by his fascinating eloquence. He came to York and also visited Carlisle. In both of these towns he stirred up so much enthusiasm that an early chronicler was constrained to say "the quota from the back counties was easily raised. In fact, the loyalty to the union of states in the interior counties was much more pronounced than in the city of Philadelphia."[14] Rawle writes:

> In November, 1776, the commander in chief sent him from *Newark* with a *confidential* letter to Congress. Our affairs at that time wore a gloomy aspect; and it required firm hearts to continue in resistance to the apparently overwhelming power of Sir William Howe. There was probably much committed to Mifflin beyond the contents of the letter; and Congress being desirous to avail themselves of his *information* and his *judgment*, he was, in a manner not very usual nor perhaps altogether consistent with military *order*, directed to *remain near them*, of which Gen. Washington was apprised.[15]

On November 10, 1776, Washington, in preparing for his army's winter layover, wrote to Quartermaster General Mifflin:

> As the period is fast approaching when part of this Army will stand released from their Engagements to serve the public, and little prospect remains of prevailing upon them to stay longer, it becomes highly necessary for you, in time, to set about a Collection (at least an Enquiry after) the Tents and other Stores which have been delivered from your Department, and see that they are carefully deposited in some safe Place.[16]

Washington was also concerned that all of the unused "entrenching tools" be moved to a safe place. He stated that "The Uncertainty of the Enemy's Designs, renders it almost impossible to point out places with any Degree of propriety for Magazines of Forage &ca dependent upon your department." He suggested the Peekskills area of New York

Nine. After New York

and "Croton (or Pine's) Bridge." Washington ended by stating that if Mifflin needed further instructions, his own judgment or orders from Major General Lee must apply.[17]

On November 14, 1776, the Board of War (then consisting of Benjamin Harrison, James Wilson, Edward Rutledge, and Francis Lightfoot Lee) wrote to General Washington from Philadelphia. This letter shows well the high esteem in which Thomas Mifflin was held by members of the Board.[18]

> The Congress having received Information that a considerable part of the Enemy's Fleet had sailed from Sandy Hook to the Southward, & judging that immediate Steps were necessary to be taken for the preservation and Defense of this City, were pleased to vest us with all their powers to effect this important Business—As Genl Mifflin has a considerable Influence in this place, the Board judge it for the Interest of the Service that he be immediately ordered to this City, where his Exertions we doubt not will turn out to the Advantage of our Cause. Your Excellency will therefore be pleased to give him Directions upon the Subject as soon as possible; provided you shall be of Opinion that he cannot be more usefully employed in any other place, which we beg Leave to submit to you: If the Enemy should bend their Way to this part of the Continent, we doubt not that your Excellency will yield us every possible Assistance.[19]

On November 26, Mifflin notified Washington that he had arrived in Philadelphia, met with John Hancock, and the next day appeared before Congress. Mifflin appraised its members of the "dangerous & critical Situation of the Jerseys & Pennsylvania & the Necessity of immediate vigorous Exertions to oppose" the British forces.[20]

Congress ordered Mifflin to stay with them until Washington required him to return to the army. They then took up the matter of raising troops. The Congress's Committee of Safety proposed "to call on every Man in the State to turn out; such as refuse are to be find £5 [per] mo. the Fines to be distributed among those who enlist."[21]

From Philadelphia, Mifflin wrote back to General Washington:

> Tomorrow the City militia is to be reviewed. If they appear in such Numbers as we expect I am to give them a Talk well seasoned. The German Battalion move from hence Tomorrow[.] Three Regiments from Delaware & Maryland are to follow them to Brunswick as soon as possible—By which I fear the Shores of Delaware at & near New Castle will be much exposed provided Mr. Howe attempts to disembark in this River. Your Excellency's Opinion on the Designs of the Enemy & the best means to oppose them, should they divert your Attention in Jersey and attempt an Impression on this State by means of their Ships, will be necessary from Time to time. The Light Horse of the State of Virginia are ordered to join your Excellency's Army.

Then, acting in his role as quartermaster general, Mifflin wrote:

> The principal military Stores are to be removed from hence—500,000 Musket Cartridges will be sent to Brunswick[.]" A Prize Ship came in Yesterday— she had on board, when taken by a Congress packet, 20,000 hard [dollars], 9,000 of which were lost by an Attempt [to heave] them on board the packet at Sea. [I] have ordered 1,000 Wagons to be collected if possible near this City; to remove when Occasion requires the most essential Articles belonging to the public.[22]

The first week of December, residents of Philadelphia received word that General Howe's troops were on the move, and were headed toward them. The Continental Congress record of December 10, 1776, shows great concern for the safety of Philadelphia:

> Resolved, That general Mifflin be directed to repair immediately to the neighboring counties, and, by all the means in his power, rouse and bring them in, to the defense of Philadelphia.
> As the Congress deem it of great importance to the general good and safety, that general Mifflin should make a progress through the several counties of the state of Pennsylvania, to rouse the freemen thereof, to the immediate defense of this city and county.
> Resolved, That the assembly be requested to appoint a committee of their body to make the said tour with general Mifflin, in order to assist him in this good and necessary work.
> Resolved, That the president return to Congress the 25,000 dollars received for the use of the marine committee.
> Resolved, That major general Putnam be directed to have the several recruits, and other continental troops in Philadelphia, immediately paraded, and that he proceed, without delay, to make the proper defenses for the protection and security of this city:
> That the council of safety of Pennsylvania be requested to give major general Putnam all the assistance in their power, for the execution of the above necessary business, by calling forth the inhabitants, and by any other means in their judgment proper.[23]

Congress Moves to Maryland

Rawle writes of Mifflin's efforts to raise additional troops at this time: "The spirits of the people were at this period much *depressed*. The contest was considered by some as *desperate*, by all as *doubtful*. Our army, dwindling every day in number, was obliged to seek refuge in defensible positions. New Jersey was overrun, and the safety of Philadelphia was endangered. The inhabitants of this city were necessary for its defense, and it was from the *country* that the recruits for the army, anxiously invoked by Gen. Washington, were to be drawn; but much *torpor* and much dejection seemed to prevail."[24]

Rawle, who years later knew Mifflin well, went on:

> "Something *out of the common course* was necessary to revive the ardor of 1775. *Personal application* was determined on, and one, who *besides sincere and unaffected patriotism*, had already shared the dangers of the field, and who possessed a powerful and impressive eloquence, was to be selected. These qualities were combined in Gen. Mifflin, and he was directed to proceed through the adjacent counties, to exhort and rouse the militia to come forth in defense of their country." The legislature of Pennsylvania, then in session, was requested to appoint a committee to accompany him. On this *honorable* and *extraordinary* mission he set out immediately. He assembled the inhabitants in every convenient place of *public resort*, his *animated eloquence* was heard from the pulpit of the *church*, from the *meeting house*, and the *court house*, and everywhere with the happiest effect.[25]

In December 1776, as the British Army advanced towards Philadelphia and the militia was not strong enough to resist, Major General Israel Putnam and Brigadier General Thomas Mifflin strongly recommended to the Continental Congress the evacuation of the city to conduct the government's business in a safer location.

With Mifflin in the Philadelphia to arrange the movement of supplies out of the city, Major General Israel Putnam arrived on December 12 to take charge. Putnam lost no time in declaring martial law. Putnam, Mifflin, and French engineers planned the movement of military stores to a location outside of the city. Although Mifflin did more to encourage the militia than probably anyone else could have done, the mood of the people was low.

Enlistments and reenlistments suffered outside of Philadelphia's city limits. This prompted Congress to ask Mifflin to visit other counties to rally the people.

The Continental Congress's journal entry for December 12, 1776, contains further details on their deliberations and decisions during this critical period.

> Resolved, That General Putnam be authorized to employ all the private armed vessels in this harbor, for the defense and security of the city. And that he take the most effectual measures for manning them, and putting them in fit condition for the above purpose.
>
> General Putnam and Brigadier General Mifflin being called to a conference, and having, by strong arguments, urged the necessity of the Congress retiring, it was, therefore,
>
> Resolved, That Mr. Wilson be desired to inform the assembly and council of safety of Pennsylvania of the proposed adjournment of Congress, and the place to which they have resolved to adjourn; and to inform them, that Congress will, at all times, on their application, be ready to comply with their requisitions for the security of this city and state against the common enemy.

> Whereas the movements of the enemy have now rendered the neighborhood of this city the seat of war, which will prevent that quiet and uninterrupted attention to the public business, which should ever prevail in the great continental council:

Congress chose to relocate to Baltimore, about 100 miles to the southwest.

> Resolved, That this Congress be, for the present, adjourned to the town of Baltimore, in the state of Maryland, to meet on the 20th instant, unless a sufficient number to make a Congress shall be there sooner assembled; and that, until the Congress shall otherwise order, General Washington be possessed of full power to order and direct all things relative to the department, and to the operations of war. That the several matters to this day referred, be postponed to the day to which Congress is adjourned.[26]

After this meeting with Congress on the 12th, General Putnam wrote the following to General Washington:

> My Dear General
>
> Your Favor of Yesterday I have received—All Things in this City remain in Confusion, for Want of Men to put them into Order—The Citizens are generally with you—The Continental Recruits are clothing & arming as fast as possible, & are employed on Guard & Fatigue Duty, for which there is scarce a Relief—A Party are now going to the Jerseys, to bring off all the Craft out of the Creeks.
>
> The Council of Safety have this Day issued Orders for every able Bodied Man to be enrolled, & put to work on throwing up the Lines—I have reconnoitered the Ground round the City, in Company with General Mifflin, & the French Engineers, who are preparing a Draft of the Lines which we are to begin to morrow—The principal Stores are removed to Christiana Bridge by Orders from Congress to General Mifflin who sets out to Morrow by Directions from that Body with a Committee of the Assembly & Council of Safety to endeavor to animate the Inhabitants of the Province to come in to your Relief which through some unhappy Circumstances has been too long delayed.
>
> The Continental Frigate commanded by Captain Biddle ordered by Congress on a Cruise, since the arrival of the Roebuck & two other Ships in our Bay is countermanded & with four or five Privateers ordered to be stationed in the River.
>
> Major Mifflin remains with me as a Deputy in the Quarter Master General's Department.[27]

Six days later, Virginia delegate Richard Henry Lee wrote the following to Patrick Henry from Baltimore, Maryland:

> The movements of the enemy's army in the Jerseys, by which the neighborhood of Philadelphia had become the seat of war, determined Congress to adjourn from thence to this town, where public business will be entered on the 20

instant, unless a sufficient number of members should be assembled to begin sooner. At this place the public business can be conducted with more deliberation and undisturbed attention, than could be the case in a city subject to perpetual alarm, and that had necessarily been made a place of arms. The propriety of this measure was strongly enforced by the continental Generals Putnam and Mifflin, who commanded in Philadelphia, and who gave it as their opinion, that, although they did not consider the town as liable to fall into the enemy's hands but by surprise, yet that possibility rendered it improper for Congress to continue there.[28]

Chapter Ten

New Jersey Command

Battle of Trenton

U.S. Army historians Robert K. Wright, Jr., and Morris J. MacGregor, Jr., in their *Soldier-Statesmen of the Constitution* write: "As the Army's position in northern New Jersey started to crumble in late November 1776, Washington sent him [Mifflin] to Philadelphia to lay the groundwork for a restoration of American fortunes. Mifflin played a vital, though often overlooked, role in mobilizing the Associators to reinforce the continentals and in orchestrating the complex resupply of the tattered American forces once they reached safety on the Pennsylvania side of the Delaware River. These measures gave Washington the resources to counterattack."[1]

After Fort Washington and Fort Lee on the Hudson River fell to the British forces in November 1776, Washington led 3,000 of his troops across New Jersey and over the Delaware River into Pennsylvania. British commander Howe established his winter encampment in New York City, but left several garrisons in New Jersey. One, at the town of Trenton, was manned by approximately 1,500 Hessian soldiers.

Washington made his famous crossing of the Delaware River on December 26, 1776, to surprise Britain-allied Hessian troops at Trenton. His forces killed 22 of the enemy soldiers and captured 900. Only two Americans were killed. Thomas Mifflin commanded many of the 2,400 American troops at the battle.

Not only did Trenton lead to Mifflin's promotion, but according to biographer Rawle, "The gallant coup de main at Trenton produced a gleam of sunshine, which greatly aided his [Mifflin's] exertions [to raise troops], and he was delighted at the respectable addition which was soon made to the army in New Jersey."[2]

Two days after the Trenton surprise attack, Mifflin wrote the following letter to General Washington from Bristol, Pennsylvania, which

Ten. New Jersey Command

lies on the west bank of the Delaware River between Trenton and Philadelphia:

> My dear general.... I came here at 4 o'clock this Afternoon. 500 Men sent from Philadelphia. Yesterday crossed to Burlington this Morning. this Evening I sent over near 300 more—To Morrow 7 or 800 shall follow—I will cross in the Morning and will endeavor to form them into Regiments & a Brigade—they consist of many different Corps & want much Regulation. If your Excellency has any Orders for me, other than to join General Cadwalader as soon as possible, please to favor me with such as are necessary and I will punctually obey them. Pennsylvania is at length roused & coming in great Numbers to your Excellency's Aid—Mr. Hall will return with your Orders—I am informed that we cannot cross at Bordentown nor at any Place between that Place & this. I have no Doubt of effecting it here having sent from Philadelphia in the Morning several fine Boats which are now here.[3]

Mifflin concludes the letter with mention of Washington's surprise attack: "I most heartily congratulate your Excellency on your late capital Stroke & wish most ardently a Repetition." The next day, December 29, Washington aide Tench Tilghman wrote back to Mifflin in a letter that refers to both Mifflin's duties: a commander and as a quartermaster general.

> Yours to his Excellency came to hand a few Minutes ago, we awoke him to give you an Answer which he desires may be as follows—He will not undertake to give you any particular Orders, but leaves it to your Judgment, either to join General Cadwallader or proceed up towards Trenton, as, from Circumstances, you may think most proper. He would cross over with the Continental Troops tomorrow, if there was any provision made for them in Jersey, but as there is not, neither is there enough here to enable them to draw four days [per] Man, he does not think it prudent to do it till some Magazines are established. He begs you will have all the provision you can get or hear of forwarded on towards Trenton and procure as many Wagons as possible. Flour is particularly wanted, please to make Enquiry what Quantity is at the Mills of Bordentown, Allen Town and Croswix [Crosswicks, New Jersey]. Get every Intelligence in your Power and communicate it to the General. Caution Cadwallader not to suffer the Enemy to turn too quick upon his young Troops, he may play the devil by waiting properly upon Flank and Rear. I am led from my own feelings on the Occasion to suppose what yours are, that is, if there is a possibility of overtaking them to be at them yourself. You see you have full Powers and I am sure you will use them to the best Effect.

Mifflin's force at the time consisted of:

> Detachments from regiments of the Pennsylvania Continental Line:
> - Second Regiment, Colonel John Philip De Haas
> - Tenth Regiment, Colonel Joseph Penrose
> - Eleventh Regiment, Colonel Richard Humpton

- Twelfth Regiment, Colonel William Cooke
- Colonel Timothy Matlock's Philadelphia Rifle battalion.

Detachments from the Pennsylvania Associators:
- Lancaster County Battalions of Colonel Bartram Galbraith, Colonel James Crawford, Colonel Timothy Green, Colonel Thomas Porter. Colonel James Burd and Colonel George Ross.
- Bedford County Battalion of Colonel John Piper.
- Northumberland County Battalions of Colonel James Potter, a company of Colonel Philip Cole's battalion and Captain John Lee's company of Colonel Samuel Hunter's battalions; Bucks County Battalion of Colonel Arthur Erwin.
- Cumberland County Battalion of Colonel Joseph Armstrong; Northampton County Battalions of Colonel George Taylor, Colonel Henry Geiger and Colonel Jacob Stroud.
- New Castle County. Delaware Militia. Major Thomas Duff, commanding; a company of Kent County. Delaware Militia, Captain Thomas Rodney, commanding.
- Four companies of Philadelphia Militia. Captain George Henry, senior officer, commanding.

Mifflin also had the following Marines:
- A detachment from the armed boat Hancock, Captain William Shippen, commanding
- A detachment from Ship Montgomery, Captain William Brown, commanding;
- A detachment under command of Major Samuel Nicholas
- A detachment from the brigantine Andrew Doria, Captain Isaac Craig, commanding

Also, mention is made of a detachment of sailors "used to firing guns," under command of Captain Thomas Read of the Continental Navy.[4]

With the British troop strength in New Jersey at about 12,000, and Washington with far fewer men, Washington was continually on the run to avoid direct confrontations. He could not afford to lose any men. Philadelphia sent about 1,000 troops to him: three battalions of "Associators under Colonel John Cadwalader, Captain Samuel Morris's troop of light horse, and Captain Thomas Forrest's battery of artillery."

Brigadier General Thomas Mifflin was complying with the Continental Congress orders to use all of his persuasive skills to gather up new recruitments in neighboring states. He was successful in his endeavors—perhaps his "silver tongue" was learned from debating skills acquired in college or perhaps it was honed from being a merchant and convincing folk to buy, sell, or trade his goods—whatever the reason, the army now had more men to defend Philadelphia.

Ten. New Jersey Command

After Mifflin returned to army headquarters from his Pennsylvania efforts, he was ordered back again to Philadelphia. Under the threat of an impending British attack, he and General Israel Putnam advised Congress to relocate to Baltimore, Maryland. The only delegates who remained in Philadelphia were Robert Morris, George Walton, and George Clymer. To add to the problem, British sympathizers in the city were an increasing threat. According to Historian Stryker:

> General Thomas Mifflin had been wonderfully successful in obtaining recruits for the army from the neighboring counties, under the instructions to him by Congress ... by all the means in his power to rouse and bring them in to the defense of Philadelphia. On the 27th day of December [Mifflin] sent 500 men from Philadelphia across the Bristol ferry to Burlington [Bristol, Pennsylvania, to Burlington, New Jersey]. The next day 300 more were sent over at the same place, and on December 29 General Mifflin followed in person with 800 soldiers, assuming command of these troops, with headquarters at Bordentown, New Jersey.[5]

On January 1, General Cadwalader received orders to join General Washington's army at Trenton. Cadwalader led his forces along the White Horse road, crossing Doctor's Creek and the Sand Hills. Upon reaching the White Horse Tavern, he was joined by General Mifflin's division. The combined column then proceeded to Trenton.[6]

One often forgets that these soldiers were fighting as the winter set in (walking and camping outside in low temperatures with biting gusts of wind, ice, and snow); this posed significant challenges and a great deal of hardship and discomfort in the personal welfare of both soldiers and animals. The adversity of the weather, traversing roads, making camp and functioning at one's best during war was extremely challenging, yet critical. Sometimes you can get brief glimpses into their daily life. On December 29, 1776, Washington wrote to Congress: "I am just setting out to attempt a second passage over the Delaware with the troops that were with me on the morning of the 26. I am determined to effect it if possible: but know that it will be attended with much fatigue and difficulty on account of the ice, which will neither allow us to cross on foot, nor give us an easy passage with boats."

He proceeds to mention Cadwalader and Mifflin:

> General Cadwalader crossed from Bristol on the 27th and, by his letter of yesterday, was at Bordentown with about eighteen hundred men. In addition to these General Mifflin sent over five hundred from Philadelphia on Friday, three hundred yesterday evening from Burlington and will follow today with seven or eight hundred more. I have taken every precaution in my power for subsisting the troops and shall, without loss of time, and as soon as circumstances will admit of it, pursue the enemy in their retreat—try to beat up more of their

quarters—and in a word adopt in every instance such measures as the exigency of our affairs requires, and our situation will justify.[7]

On December 31, 1776, Mifflin issued these orders to his brigade:

The General returns his most hearty thanks to the brigade for the Alertness shown by them on the Alarm last Evening. Such Conduct does them Honor and gives their Commanding Officer the best expectations of success.

He recommends to all officers of the Brigade to hold their respective Corps in complete order for Marching at a minute's warning for which purpose they must prevent their Men from strolling too far from their quarters. A party of 200 Men goes out this day to harass the Enemy, commanded by Majors [John] Mifflin[8] and Hubley. The commanding officer to call at Head Quarters in this town for orders. Every Man in the brigade must always keep by him dressed Provisions for three Days. This Order must not be neglected as the least Deviation from it may ruin the best concerted Plans.[9]

On January 1, 1777, General Washington informed Congress:

General Mifflin is at Bordentown with about eighteen hundred men and General Cadwalader at Croswix's [Crosswicks, New Jersey] with about the same number. We are now making our arrangements, and concerning a plan of operations, which I shall attempt to execute as soon as possible and which I hope will be attended with some success. As to the number and situation of the enemy, I cannot obtain certain intelligence; but from the accounts most to be relied on, they have collected the principal part of their force from Brunswick and the neighboring posts, at Princeton, where they are throwing up some works. The number there is reported to be from five to six thousand : and it is confidently said they have sent the chief part of their baggage to Brunswick. It is added, that General Howe landed at Amboy a day or two ago with a thousand light troops, and is on his march from thence.[10]

Battle of Princeton

On the morning of January 3, 1777, Continental Army units approached Princeton, New Jersey. The first troops under Brigadier General Hugh Mercer fought British "skirmishers." Soldiers commanded by British Colonel Charles Manwood came at Mercer's brigade with a bayonet charge, which resulted in Mercer being fatally wounded.[11]

The British with bayonets also repelled the Philadelphia Associators led by General John Cadwalader. In a moment of extraordinary bravery, General George Washington personally led a counterattack with Virginia Continental Army troops and Pennsylvania riflemen, rallying his men with the cry, "It is a fine fox chase, my boys!" The British forces, under Manwood, fled.

With most of the British troops gone, a remnant of them occupied

Ten. New Jersey Command

John Trumbull's painting, "The Death of General Mercer at the Battle of Princeton, January 3, 1777." Thomas Mifflin is on horseback on the far left raising his sword (courtesy Yale University Art Gallery).

Nassau Hall on the College of New Jersey campus. At the time, it was the largest stone building in the 13 Colonies.[12] Captain Alexander Hamilton's artillery barrage forced the British soldiers in the building to surrender. The fight ended with about 20 British troops killed and 60 wounded. The Americans lost about 25 killed and 40 wounded. With the British surrender, the Continental Army took about 200 prisoners. After looting the British supply wagons, Washington moved his army north to winter quarters in Morristown, New Jersey.

Although the number of troops engaged and casualty numbers were low, the Battle of Princeton was an inspiration for the colonial soldiers, the Continental Congress, and the residents of the colonies. It also led to the departure of British forces from New Jersey. As army surgeon Alfred Alexander Woodhull noted in his *The Battle of Princeton: A Preliminary Study*, Princeton "was a great battle when its consequences are considered ... especially when one reflects upon the inevitable political result that would have followed a defeat upon that field."[13] Wright and MacGregor write: "Mifflin saw action with the Associators at Princeton. His service in the campaign resulted in his promotion to major general."[14]

Rossman describes how the *Battle of Princeton* affected Washington and Mifflin, as well as the situation in New Jersey at this stage of the war, "Thus was New Jersey, except for two posts, regained from the enemy, and all this in two battles in eight days. It had been accomplished in an audacious and brilliant series of movements in which Mifflin played a great part. Those services did not go unrewarded. And as for Washington, his military reputation was established forever. The cause took on new life."[15]

Back on August 14, 1775, Washington had appointed Mifflin, then a major, as the Army's first Quartermaster General. Except for the four months that Stephen Moylan had served in the role, Mifflin had been quartermaster general ever since.[16]

An idea of the nature of his work in the role of the Continental Army's quartermaster general can be seen by the following exchange of letters between Washington and Mifflin. It was a year and a half after Mifflin took over the position. We can detect Washington's experience with supply matters (undoubtedly partly due to his experiences in the French and Indian War) and we can detect Mifflin looking at everything with the eyes of a businessman and a concern for the practical matter of dollar and cents.

Quartermaster General Duties

Less than a month after the Battle of Princeton, Washington was looking at the campaign ahead, writing to Mifflin:

> The Season is approaching when We shall have Use for Tents; You will therefore pay particular Attention to this Article—All the old ones should be collected & the necessary repairs be made now, that when called for they may be ready—The Tomahawks or light hatchets also deserve your Notice, they should be made light & substantial, so calculated as to be made a part of the Soldier's Accouterments & carried with Convenience—Too much regard cannot be paid to the Wagons; as many should be provided as will serve all the purposes of each Battalion, for their Baggage, Ammunition & Entrenching Tools. I would recommend to you to have Chaises Marine made for the Artillery & Regimental ammunition, light, strong & covered, and not let the Army be encumbered with heavy & unwieldy Wagons when the purposes can be answered with others full as well & probably better—Upon the whole, this is the Time to prepare everything in your department, let me therefore entreat you to spare no pains in equipping Us completely for the ensuing Campaign.[17]

Immediately after reading Washington's letter, Mifflin replied:

> My dear General
>
> The several Points mentioned in your Last Letter have been attended to. I gave to Col. Knox an Order to procure in New England Two thousand Tents. I

have purchased Russia Duck and every other kind of Canvas that I could find in this Town fit for Tents—The Sail Makers are at Work repairing & making Tents. The Ammunition Wagons are on hand—Five are finished—The Tomahawks will be completed—One thousand are brought in. But those Contracts and the Magazines of Forage cannot be prosecuted with the Dispatch required. I have no Cash nor can I procure any from Congress. I sent Mr. Butler to Baltimore for that Purpose—He returned Yesterday with an Order in my Favor on the Loan Office here for 450,000 Dollars—I applied for payment and received in Answer that he (Mr. Smith Commissioner of the Loan) had not One Farthing; but was 12,000 Dollars in Debt. I mention this Circumstance that I may not be responsible for Neglects not my own.

The flat bottom Boats & Artillery Flats go on well—the Workmen are to be paid weekly—my last Dollar has been paid this Morning to Major Ayres to prevent a Delay in his Contract. ... I will do as much as possible without Cash; how long our Credit will hold cannot be ascertained—in many Places it begins to fail already.[18]

On February 13, 1777, Mifflin wrote to Washington from Reading, Pennsylvania, about issues of lack of funds and rising prices

My dear general

I had the Honor to write to you from Philadelphia at which place I was detained near three Weeks by Want of Cash. This being the best Place to purchase Intrenching Tools and Forage I employed Colonel Mark Bird to procure them—He has engaged a very considerable Quantity but is now obliged to stop through Want of Money having expended all his own and a very large Sum which he borrowed. I sent an Express to Philadelphia on Saturday to Mr. Smith; he returned Yesterday without a Farthing and gives me no Encouragement of receiving any in less than many Weeks. In the mean Time the Farmers are taking Advantage of the Season and ask 25 [percent] more for their Grain & Horses than they did two Weeks past.

So many persons are employed to purchase Horses (for the several Troops) in this and the Neighboring Counties, that it is now almost impossible to buy One but at a most extravagant Rate.

Mifflin, who has been on the quartermaster general position for a total of about 14 months, had been considering how the department could be improved. He finished this letter with: "Enclosed I send your Excellency some Thoughts on the new Arrangement of the Quarter Master Generals Department—As other Ideas occur, I will communicate them—I have only to request your Excellency's Orders respecting them as soon as convenient that the Department may have as early as possible its new Coat on."[19]

On February 4, 1777, Mifflin made another request of Washington, one which was not monetary in nature. It involved a prisoner release: "Since I writ the above the enclosed papers were given to me with a Request to forward them to your Excellency, I do not pretend to censure the proceedings of the Gentlemen who imprisoned but I think it bad policy to confine persons who will act the part of Martyrs and who cannot consistently with their own principles take an active part against us. If your Excellency thinks proper to order a Release it will gratify many of your Friends and prevent some who wish to injure our Cause from charging us with Cruelty and an Imitation of the Enemy."[20]

Ten days later, Washington wrote back that he agreed with Mifflin's reasoning, but:

> My Sentiments respecting the treatment proper to be observed to Martyrs coincide with Yours Lenity will operate with greater force in such Instances than Rigor. 'Tis therefore my first Wish to have our whole Conduct distinguished by it. Still it is not my desire, neither indeed is it within my power—to release any Man from Confinement imposed upon him by the Civil power—They best know the Charge & Merits of the Case, consequently should ultimately determine it. For these reasons I dare not comply with your Request.[21]

Five days after this request was denied, Mifflin received the most important promotion of his military career.

Promotion to Major General

On February 19, 1777, Brigadier General Thomas Mifflin was promoted to the rank of major general in the Continental Army. George Washington, serving as the commander in chief, demonstrated a willingness to promote young individuals to the highest military ranks. Washington himself, during the American Revolutionary War, was in his 40s (43 through 49). An illustrative example is the Marquis de Lafayette, who became a major general at the extraordinarily young age of 19, despite lacking any combat experience. Washington's openness to promoting young and inexperienced individuals reflects the dynamic nature of leadership during the Revolutionary War.

Biographer Rawle states of Mifflin: "The sense which Congress entertained of his merits, was evinced by their conferring on him, in the following month of February, the rank of Major General."[22]

Along with Thomas Mifflin, William Alexander (Lord Stirling), Benjamin Lincoln, Arthur St. Clair, and Adam Stephen were also promoted to the rank of major general in the Continental Army by the Continental Congress. Of these five men, Mifflin was the youngest at age 33. Stephen was almost 60, Alexander was 50, Lincoln 44, and St. Clair was approaching his 40th birthday. These promotions are considered to be one of the main reasons a jealous Benedict Arnold turned traitor.[23]

Ten. New Jersey Command

During the American Revolutionary War, 29 men became Continental Army major generals. Thomas Mifflin was the only one who was born in Pennsylvania.

However, in later American history some of the most significant American military commanders came from Pennsylvania: Philadelphia-born Union Army general George B. McClellan (1826–1885) was a prominent Civil War commander who unsuccessfully ran against Lincoln for the U.S. presidency. Another Civil War Union Army general, George Meade (1815–1872), led the forces that won the Battle of Gettysburg. At the onset of the Civil War, he was a brigadier general in the Pennsylvania Reserves. Alexander Haig (1924–2010) was the youngest four-star general in the history of the U.S. Army before he became the Supreme Allied Commander Europe (1974). He was born in Bala Cynwyd, Pennsylvania. World War I hero and later five-star general Henry H. "Hap" Arnold (1886–1950) was known as "the father of the U.S. Air Force." He was born near Philadelphia—at Gladwyne, Pennsylvania.

When the Continental Congress promoted Mifflin, Lincoln, St. Clair, Stephen, and Stirling to major general, all were junior in rank to Benedict Arnold. Washington wrote to Arnold and expressed surprise:

> We have lately had several promotions to the rank of Major General, and I am at a loss whether you have had a preceding appointment, as the newspapers announce, or whether you have been omitted through some mistake. Should the latter be the case I beg you will not take any hasty steps in consequence of it, but allow proper time for recollection, which, I flatter myself, will remedy any error that may have been made. My endeavors to that end shall not be wanting....[24]

About a week later, Arnold wrote the following to Washington at the end of a letter:

> I am greatly obliged to your Excellency for interesting Yourself so much in my behalf in respect to my Appointment, which I have had no Advice of, & know not by what means it was announced.... Congress have doubtless a right of promoting, those, who from their ability, their long, & Arduous Services they esteem most deserving. Their promoting Junior Officers to the Rank of Major Generals, I view as a very Civil way of requesting my resignation, as unqualified for the Office I hold. my Commission was Conferred unsolicited, received with pleasure Only as a means of serving my Country, with equal pleasure I resign it, when I can no longer serve my Country with *honor*.

The reasons for Benedict Arnold's treason has long been debated, but this letter goes a long way in explaining his thought on the matter. It continues:

> It has long been The Person who void Of the nice feelings of honor will tamely Condescend to give up his right, & hold a Commission at the Expense of his reputation, I hold as a disgrace to the Army & unworthy of the Glorious Cause in which we are engaged. When I entered the Service of my Country, my Character was unimpeached, I have sacrificed my Interest, ease, & happiness in her Cause, It is rather a misfortune than fault, that my exertions have Not been Crowned with success, I am Conscious of the rectitude of my Intentions, in Justice therefore to my Own Character & for the satisfaction of my Friends, I must request a Court of Inquiry into my Conduct, & tho I sensibly feel the Ingratitude of my Countrymen, every Personal Injury shall be buried in my zeal for the safety & happiness of my Country, in whose Cause I have repeatedly Fought, & bled, & am ready at all times to risk my life. I shall Cautiously avoid any hasty Step (in Consequence of the Appointments that have taken place) that may tend to Injure my Country.[25]

Two weeks later, Arnold wrote Washington:

> In my last I intimated to your Excellency, the impossibility of my remaining In a disgraceful Situation in the Army, my being Superseded must be Viewed as an Implicit impeachment of my Character I therefore requested a Court of Inquiry Into my Conduct, I believe the Time is near at hand when I can leave, this department without any Damage to the Public Interest when that is the Case I will wait on your Excellency, not doubting my request will be granted, and that I shall be able to Acquit myself of every Charge, Malice, or Envy can bring against me.[26]

The conversation continued as Washington wrote back to Arnold on April 2:

> I was this day favored with yours of the 26th last Month and a few days ago with that of the 11th.
>
> It is needless for me to say much upon a subject, which must undoubtedly give you a good deal of uneasiness. I confess I was surprised when I did not see your Name in the list of Major Generals, and was so fully of opinion that there was some mistake in the matter, that I (as you may recollect) desired you not to take any hasty Step, before the intention of Congress was fully known. The point does not now admit of a doubt, and is of so delicate a nature, that I will not even undertake to advise, your own feelings must be your Guide—As no particular Charge is alleged agt you, I do not see upon what Ground you can demand a Court of Enquiry. Besides, Public Bodies are not amenable for their Actions. They place and displace at pleasure, and all the satisfaction that an individual can obtain when he is overlooked is, if innocent, a consciousness that he has not deserved such treatment for his honest exertions. Your determination, not to quit your present command, while any danger to the public might ensue from your leaving it, deserves my thanks, and justly entitles you to the thanks of your Country.

Apparently, Washington had asked General Nathanael Greene to check on the matter, as the letter to Arnold continues:

Ten. New Jersey Command

Genl Green who has lately been at Philadelphia took occasion to inquire upon what principle the Congress proceeded in their late promotion of General Officers—He was informed that the Members from each State seemed to insist upon having a proportion of General Officers adequate to the number of Men which they furnish, and that as Connecticut [the home state of Benedict Arnold] had already two Majors General it was their full share.[27]

Washington added: "I confess this is a strange mode of reasoning, but it may serve to show you, that the promotion which was due to your seniority was not overlooked for want of Merit in you."[28]

One month later, May 2nd, Congress finally appointed Arnold a major general in the Continental Army. Washington wrote to him six days later.

I am happy to find that a late resolve of Congress of the 2nd instant, has restored you to the continental army. The importance of the Post at Peeks Kill and its appendages has become so great that it is now necessary, to have a Major General appointed to the command of it, you will therefore immediately repair to that Post and take charge of it, till a general arrangement of the army can be effected, and the proper province of every officer assigned.[29]

As the army's quartermaster general, Mifflin was continually hampered by the lack of funds at his disposal. In addition, the devaluation of the currency led many people to refuse payments except in the form of coinage. Both the Continental Congress and the states printed so much paper money that it quickly became worth very little.

Washington, understandably, was very concerned with the operations of the quartermaster general's department. On January 26, 1777, he wrote to Continental Congress President John Hancock:

The hint given by the Convention of New York, of the Necessity and Utility of a Commissary of Forage had struck me before, and had been mentioned by General Mifflin, whose department of Quarter Master General must be eased of part of the load which is at present thrown upon it. He is obliged, in many instances, to act entirely out of his proper line, and instead of being confined to the duty of Quarter Master General, is also Wagon Master and Forage Master General. I have written to two persons that I think qualified to fill the Office of Wagon Master, and I hope one of them will accept. That of Commissary of Forage shall be attended to.[30]

In a letter to Captain Edward Snickers a week earlier, Washington offered Snickers the post of "Wagon Master General to the Army" with "pay of Colonel allowed you. that is, Twenty two pounds ten shillings per Calendar Month." He specified that Snickers should contact "Genl Mifflin, the Quarter Master Genl from whom you will receive your Orders."[31]

George Washington also offered the post of wagon master general to Thomas Rutherford, who, like Snickers, was an old Virginia acquaintance from the French and Indian War. Neither man accepted the post.[32]

In March 1777, Washington wanted Mifflin in camp to perform duties as quartermaster general, but he also needed him in Philadelphia because of a possible British attack there. By June, Philadelphia was anxious about an imminent attack.

On March 13, the commander in chief wrote to Mifflin regarding tents. Probably his comment about Mifflin-rival Greene having a brother who can supply tents didn't sit too well with Mifflin.

> I have not had the pleasure of hearing from you since yours of the 13 February enclosing a Number of Regulations for the Quarter Master Generals department, which, from the multiplicity of Business, I have not been able yet to attend to. What I would principally recommend to you, is the having the Ammunition Wagons and those for carrying Tools got ready as soon as possible. But I think you should turn your attention particularly to providing Tents, because Genl Howe will certainly take the Field as soon as the Weather and Roads will permit, and it will never do for our Army to follow him in a scattered Manner, for want of covering to enable us to keep together.
>
> A Brother of Genl Green's informed me, that he had got a quantity of Duck belonging to the Continent, which he had several times wrote to Congress about, but could not obtain an answer. I desired him to have it made up immediately into Tents, of which Article, we cannot have too many, for our Army suffered extremely last Campaign for want of Shelter from both heat and cold. I shall be glad to hear what forwardness things are in, in your department, and what are your prospects.[33]

Four days later, Mifflin replied with the following account of the status of the army's supplies. It was one month after his promotion to the rank of Major General, and Mifflin was hard at work in his capacity as quartermaster general of the Army. Likely, the most important part of the letter for him was a phrase near the end: "it is my ardent Wish to be in immediate Command of yourself." Mifflin was tired and bored by the quartermaster general position and after almost two years it showed. Undoubtedly, he believed that the rank of major general perfectly positioned him for a more active military role than the clerical position of a quartermaster general ever would.

> The Ammunition Wagons and others go on as fast as possible. I have purchased all the Linen fit for Tents in & near Philadelphia; & have new Ones ready for 12,000 Men only. When any Canvas arrives, it shall be procured & made up. Mr. Hughes has Tents for 3,000 Men. But my chief Supply, which I looked for from Massachusetts, has been cut off by the Assembly of that State; who have engaged all the Sail Cloth that could be procured & have directed a Committee to provide Tents for 12,000 Men: as I am informed—My Agent applied for Sail Cloth for 4,000 Tents but could not obtain One Yard—He has however

been assured by the Council that we may have all the Tents belonging to that State provided we cannot supply ourselves in this Quarter—A Letter from your Excellency to the Government of Massachusetts will make us easy on this Head.

The Tomahawks, intrenching Tools, Horse Shoes & Magazines of Forage will be in Readiness for any Movement of Mr Howes to the North or South of Morris Town.

I have dispatched 36 stout Teems from this Town for Morris Town and will send off 12 more on Saturday next. If Colonel Biddle can find Leisure to begin with some of the Regulations proposed it may save much Trouble & Confusion hereafter; especially if Mr. Howe should think of m[oving] soon.

I [have sent] to Congress for Orders but ha[ve] rece[ived] only some general Hints that it wou[ld] be most agreeable to them to continue me as the Qr Mr Genl.

All I can say on the last Line of your Excellency's Letter is that I will endeavor to do my Duty in whatever Point I may be placed and that it is my ardent Wish to be in immediate Command of yourself.

I expect to have my Accounts in good Order in A Week—When they are completed, I will take a general View of the Department in this State & then most cheerfully wait on your Excellency for Orders. I am with great Attachment Your Obliged Friend & most Ob. Srt.[34]

A couple of days later (March 19), Washington wrote the following to Mifflin. It gives an idea of the type of personnel issues with which Washington had to deal. Although in overall command of the military forces fighting the British Army, Washington still needed to deal with problems very similar to those confronting a modern business executive working on human resources matters:

I have a letter of the 9th from Mr. Snickers, he had not then received your orders for the purchase of Teams, at which he was very uneasy, as the price of Horses was rising daily. I have likewise heard from Mr. Thomas Rutherford, to whom I made the Offer of Wagon Master General, but his ill health renders him unfit to fill so active a department. As I have been unfortunate enough to be disappointed in the only three persons who came within my knowledge, as proper to manage so important a station as Wagon Master General I must leave the matter to you, and hope you will meet with better Success. You well know the necessary qualifications for this Officer, and how much the ease of your own department depends upon him, that I need give you no directions for your Choice.

I have had so many complaints of irregularity & ill Conduct in the deputy Commissaries, which I have in vain endeavored to remedy, that I some time ago directed Colonel Trumbull to come down himself and regulate his own Department. I expect him daily, when I hope he will make strict enquiry into the Conduct of all of them. Capt. Wade may be a man of warm temper, but he has had a sad disaffected set to deal with. Whenever the Settlement of your Accounts will permit you to come to headquarters, I shall be very glad to see you....[35]

CHAPTER ELEVEN

British Occupation of Philadelphia

Philadelphia Spy Network

Another month passes and Washington had quite a different sort of assignment for Mifflin: to establish a spy network in the Philadelphia area. Considering the possibility—or probability—that the British would occupy the city of Philadelphia, Washington, foresaw the value of having trained spies in the city—people who could inform him of British activities. Washington must have remembered well the successful clandestine ride Mifflin had taken with Colonel Rufus Putnam the previous year to reconnoiter the territory north of Manhattan Island. A ride that might well have saved the Continental Army.[1]

Washington had asked the right man. Few people had Mifflin's connections. Not only was Mifflin a native Philadelphian, but his service in government positions made him one of the best known—and best-liked—individuals in Eastern Pennsylvania. The ability to gather intelligence is crucial during wartime, and having someone with Mifflin's background could indeed be valuable for Washington's planning. Following is Washington's April 1777 letter to Mifflin (bold font added).

> From every piece of intelligence which we have lately received, it appears that the Enemy are making hasty preparations to open the Campaign, and Philadelphia seems generally agreed upon as their Object. Whether the expedition will be by land or water is yet a matter of uncertainty, but it is more than probable that it will be by both. **Wherever their Army lies it will be of the greatest advantage to us to have Spies among them,** on whom we may depend for Intelligence. I would therefore have you look out for proper persons for this purpose, who are to remain among them under the Mask of Friendship. I would have some of those in Bucks County, some in Philadelphia and others below Philadelphia about Chester [20 or so miles southwest of Philadelphia], for if any part of their force goes round by Water, they will probably land somewhere

Eleven. British Occupation of Philadelphia

thereabouts. I have directed Genl Putnam to procure similar persons to wait upon them in their way thro' Jersey. I hope we may prevent them from crossing the Delaware, but if that Event should happen, we should be provided. I would therefore have you set about this work immediately and give the persons you pitch upon, proper lessons. **Some in the Quaker line, who have never taken an active part, would be least liable to Suspicion from either party.**

Washington then switched to Mifflin's quartermaster general job:

Every preparation of Defense should be immediately made in Philadelphia from whence the spare Stores should be immediately removed, and the defense of the River below the City particularly attended to. Ten flat Boats to transport Horses, Artillery and Men, should be directly provided, and fixed upon Carriages that they may be transported by land. they should be sent as soon as possible to Bristol or higher up the River, that they may be ordered to meet our Army, wherever it may suit us to cross. When the Enemy begin to advance, the City Militia should be embodied. The Continental Troops that may be there to take post at Bristol and the Ferry opposite Trenton with Ten or twelve pieces of Artillery.

The Continental Frigates, I think, ought to go out of Delaware into Chesapeake Bay, or Boston Harbor, as they are manned.

[Washington, turned to Mifflin—the man who had many contacts, and much influence with Congress and with the Pennsylvania government] "You will please to lay this before Congress, the Continental Board of War, the Pennsylvania Board of War, and any other public Bodies whose Assistance or Advice may be necessary towards carrying the above into Execution."[2]

Mifflin soon went to work on assembling a network of spies. Two Chester County men, Cadwalader Jones and William Dunwoody, were among the first members of Mifflin's spy ring. Another was Ireland-born nurse Lydia Darragh. By the time the British captured Philadelphia five months later, the network was in place.

However, that did not mean Washington expected anything less from Mifflin's quartermaster role. A few weeks later Mifflin sent the Commander in Chief a letter that included mention of the loss of 1700 tents at Danbury, Connecticut, in British General William Tryon's April 21 attack. Tryon had burned houses, storehouses, and whatever supplies that they couldn't take with them. (They were stopped only when surprised by about 500 American troops from New Haven; 66-year-old American General David Wooster was mortally wounded in the fighting.) Mifflin ordered tents from storage at Boston and Portsmouth to Peeks Kills, New York. Mifflin relates that he sent over 1300 Tents with 700 sets of poles to Colonel Biddle and 214 Tents to General Putnam.[3]

Mifflin mentions a Continental navy sloop at Maryland from the island of Martinique with military stores, which included tents. He also brings Washington up-to-date on 24,000 yards of tent cloth that was for sale in Baltimore, but at "a most exorbitant Price which in the opinion of many gentlemen of Congress ought not to be paid."

On May 15, 1777. General Washington wrote the following to Mifflin:

> If you have the number of Tents you mentioned, and there are so many in Martinique, I should suppose, you might decline purchasing the Cloth lately arrived at Baltimore, as it is held at such an exorbitant price; However, as I am not acquainted with the views and expectations of Congress upon this Head, you had better apply to them and obtain their direction for your conduct.
>
> The capture of the La Seine, was rather unlucky; but if restitution has been demanded, in the manner you mention, It may prove a fortunate Event. Our information from abroad, has varied so often from facts, that I wish to hear this confirmed. If the Governor has thus proceeded, I think we may flatter ourselves, that some interesting political events will soon take place. As your continuing at Philadelphia, was founded on the application of Congress, to answer a beneficial purpose; If it has been effected, or is not to be promoted by your remaining there longer, I wish you to repair immediately to Head Quarters. Your Services in Camp are wanted. I am &ca G. Washington.[4]

On May 27, Mifflin responded to Washington from Philadelphia regarding Washington's need for him at army headquarters, the status of the tent difficulty, and a hiring matter. This letter provides a good idea of what the supply-related concerns were of the two men at this time in the war, i.e., halfway between the Battle of Princeton and the British occupation of Philadelphia.

> Mr. Hancock [President of the Continental Congress] has directed me to inform you that upon the Request of several Members of Congress, who judged my Attendance here for some Days necessary, I must remain in Philadelphia unless the Business of the Army cannot be executed to your Satisfaction by the Gentlemen who are now with you as Deputy Quartermaster General.
>
> In the mean Time I have my Hands filled with the Formation of the Department & the Settlement of innumerable intricate Accounts of our Expenses last Campaign.
>
> I have provided almost every Article sufficient for this Campaign except Tents: the Want of which Col. Biddle complains heavily in a Letter dated the 26h Inst. The following is the State of my Tent Account. [Mifflin here gives a detailed account of how tents are distributed.]
>
> It is impossible to gratify the Officers with Marquees at this Time—they must fair as British Officers frequently fair—i.e.—put up with good Tents.
>
> A Major Lutterloh who has been much caressd by Doctor Franklins intimate Friends here waits on your Excellency by Advice of several Members of Congress—He knows the many Blunders which have been committed by hasty Appointments in our Army & will not urge his Interest too far—I believe from his Conduct here that he is a Gentleman of Sense, much Modesty, & Breeding.[5]

In a letter dated the next day, Washington's impatience was obvious:

Eleven. British Occupation of Philadelphia

To Major General Thomas Mifflin
Morris Town May 28th 1777.
Dear Sir

>From your Letter of the 13th, and my answer of the 15th I expected, you would have been in Camp 'ere now; If you are not detained on Business, that is materially interesting and of consequence, I wish you to join me immediately. I this day move to Bound Brook [New Jersey], from whence I came yesterday morning.[6]

A day later, (May 29, 1777), Washington sent the following advice to Mifflin regarding the appointment of the Quarter Master General's deputies and assistants.[7]

> I observe, by the late regulation of the Quarter Master General's department, that the appointment of the Deputies and Assistants is left to you, subject to my approbation. As I must suppose, that you will appoint none, but such as are sufficiently qualified for their respective offices, I hope I shall not be under the disagreeable necessity of putting a negative upon any of your nominations. One matter I would guard you against, and that is, not to suffer the Solicitation of any persons in favor of their Friends, to induce you to make appointments that you would not think fully competent, were you left to the exercise of your own judgment. I know it is often hard to withstand such Solicitations, but the good of the Service and the reputation of your department requires it.

In this letter, Washington had a strong opinion about one of the people who Mifflin was considering for an important position—someone who had powerful connections. Jacob Morris' father was Declaration of Independence signer Lewis Morris, and his uncle was Gouverneur Morris, who in the future would write the Preamble to the United States Constitution. Washington writes:

> Genl Sullivan writes me, that you had appointed the late Major Jacob Morris, Deputy Quarter Master General, to a grand Division of the Army, and desires my confirmation.[8] I suppose the matter is so, but as I have it not from you, I cannot with regularity or propriety give an answer. I would just remark, that Mr. Morris, in my opinion, is by no means qualified for such an Office. He is a very young Man, and cannot have had any experience in the line to which he is promoted. I therefore, fear, that the Solicitation of his Friends and not your own choice has influenced you.

Washington explains the matter further:

> But, if the appointment is made, I must confirm it. Had I known anything of this matter before, I should have made an objection upon another account. Mr. Morris, in a very abrupt manner, and upon the most frivolous pretenses, resigned a Majority in one of the New York Regiments, and I had determined to have kept him from any further promotion, at least till he had fully seen the folly of his behavior, for a majority was as much or rather more than he had a right to expect.[9]

In April, Jacob had written to Washington asking him for a position more fitting for someone of his background, saying he was dissatisfied being a

> major in a Regiment where the Corps of officers are men of very low Births, & no educations, men who I am very conscious are totally ignorant in military affairs who have not sufficient abilities to improve, & who I should be suspicious in time of action might desert me, & thereby leave both my life & Character to be sacrificed, are to me capital objections.[10]

In the May 31, 1777, letter to Mifflin, Washington, addressed the military situation on the Delaware River:

> I have this day transmitted to Congress a full account of our late intelligence of the movements and apparent intentions of the Enemy. As some of their Ships are put out to Sea, we must soon know whether Philadelphia is the object. And as a few days must determine that, I think you had better stay where you are for the present. If any material alterations happen, I will let you know, that you may join the Army, if your presence should be absolutely necessary.[11]

On June 10, Washington wrote to Mifflin:

> I am informed that there are about two hundred Spears, with a joint in the handle, at Philadelphia fit for Horse or light Foot, if so, be pleased to send them instantly up. From every account the Enemy are upon the point of moving, but the Circumstances are so perplexing that it is impossible to say whether part by land and part by Water, or the whole by Water. The deserters generally agree that the orders are for an embarkation of almost the whole and that Skinners and Rogers's Corps and a few Hessians are to be left in Brunswic but that seems impossible.[12] As soon as matters are ascertained you shall have Notice as expeditiously as possible.[13]

Adams Letter to Abigail

On June 14, 1777, the talk in Philadelphia was about an expected attack by British forces. John Adams writes to his wife Abigail Adams:

> ...Mifflin invited the People to assemble in the State House Yard, at the Desire of General Washington, who sent them an Account that the Motions of the Enemy indicated an intention to begin an Expedition, and that every Appearance intimated this City to be their Object.
> Mifflin made an Harangue, in which he applauded the Exertions of the Citizens last December, ascribed the successes of Trenton and Princeton to their Behavior and exhorted them to the same Spirit, Unanimity and Firmness, upon this occasion. Advised them to choose their Officers, under the new Militia Law and meet him in the common on Friday. The Citizens by loud shouts and Huzzas, promised him to turn out, and accordingly, they met him in great Numbers Yesterday.[14]

In his General Orders on July 1, 1777, Washington appointed Thomas Mifflin's cousin Jonathan Mifflin, and Henry Emanuel Lutterloh, Deputy Quartermaster Generals for the Continental Army, specifying that they would have the rank of Colonel, and "are to be respected and obeyed as such."[15]

In addition, Clement Biddle was appointed the Continental Army's Commissary General of Forage. The appointments, it was hoped, would take some of the busy work away from the quartermaster general. In the same orders, the Commander in Chief strongly addressed an issue of army officers abusing the rights of civilians. It's possible that Mifflin was involved in bringing the issue to his attention.

> Notwithstanding the order of June 3rd The General is informed, that many officers are turning their horses into fields of grain and grass, and giving assurances to the proprietors of them, that the damage done shall be paid for by the Quarter-Master General—When he recollects the orders already given, and considers the variety of distresses under which the Inhabitants of New-Jersey are still groaning—The General is astonished to find that neither duty, honor, nor humanity can restrain officers from so cruel and unlawful a practice— He therefore once more, in the most pointed and positive terms forbids it, and orders that no horse be turned into any field whatever, without license first obtained from the Quarter-Master General, or some person acting under his authority. After this second notice, any officers, offending, upon complaint being made, may rest assured that they shall not only be answerable for the damage done, but brought before a Court Martial for disobedience of orders.

British Occupation of Philadelphia

On July 27, 1777, Mifflin writes Washington regarding British troop movements:

> A Gentleman well known in this City is this Minute come to Town from little Egg Harbor. He declares he saw Seventy Sail of Vessels at 4 O'clock Yesterday Afternoon pass by little Egg Harbor [in the center of New Jersey's Atlantic coastline] toward Cape May [on the southern tip of New Jersey about 65 miles south of Little Egg Harbor]. I enclosed to you a Letter from Doctor McGinnis to Colonel Bradford on the same Subject. The Destination of General Howe cannot now be mistaken as Egg Harbor or but a few Hours Sailing from our Capes.[16]

Washington wrote to Mifflin the next day:

> I last night received your favor of yesterday morning. The appearance of the enemy's fleet off little Egg Harbor, if it does not amount to a certain proof that their design is against Philadelphia, is at least a very strong argument of it.
> If the weather had been good this morning, General Green's division would

have reached Coryell's ferry by night, with ease. I am in hopes, as it has now cleared up they will still be able to effect it, though it will be somewhat difficult—General Stephen's with his own and Lincolns division I expect will be at Howell's ferry tomorrow. Lord Stirling is advancing on the rout by Trenton—and General Sullivan is coming on expeditiously in the track we have marched. I have no doubt that all these troops will arrive in full time to unite their opposition against whatever attempts the enemy may make, since, after the fleet arrives in the Capes, it will require some time to get far enough up the Delaware to begin to act, and still more to make the dispositions necessary to be made previous to the commencement of their operations. I had directed General Putnam to hold two of his best remaining brigades in readiness to cross the river, at the shortest notice; I have now given orders for them to cross, and wait for such further directions as events may suggest. As soon as the movements of the enemy make it more evident that Philadelphia is their object, and render it inconvenient to retract I shall order those Brigades to march forward. 'Till then it would be inexpedient to hazard the Highlands [the Hudson Highlands were north of New York City] by drawing off to a distance any of the forces at present behind for their defense. It is far from impossible the enemy may still turn about and make a stroke upon them.

Washington did not write just to keep Mifflin informed of the Army's moves. He had very specific and critical tasks to assign to his former aide-de-camp: reconnoitering the land and getting supplies.

There are several matters on which I wish you to bestow your particular attention and that immediately. reconnoitering well that part of the country in which is likely to be the scene of action all the probable places of landing and all the grounds convenient for incamping that are well situated with respect to those places and for covering and securing the forts—gaining an accurate knowledge of all the roads and by-paths, on both sides of the Delaware (particularly from Wilmington and Chester to Philadelphia) and on the Jersey side where there is a likelihood of the enemy's operating; and procuring good trusty guides well acquainted with all those roads and paths.

I wish you also to obtain drafts, as exact as possible of the country, that I may the more readily have a good insight into its situation and circumstances. From the idea, I at this time have of it I should imagine the main body of our army ought to be incamped on the West-side of Schuylkill for the benefit of good water & good ground and because it has a free and open communication. I would not by any means have the troops enter Philadelphia not only on account of its being pent up between two Rivers but as it would serve to debauch them and introduce disease and would be detrimental to the city and disagreeable to the inhabitants.

The providing a large quantity of hard bread is a thing exceedingly necessary. I would recommend it to you to have all the bakers in the city immediately set to work for that purpose, as in our desultory state we shall have the greatest occasion for it, & shall feel much inconvenience if we do not have it.[17]

CHAPTER TWELVE

Valley Forge

Within the space of less than a month in the early fall 1777, Washington and his army suffered three great blows in eastern Pennsylvania: on September 11, 1777, they were defeated by the British at the Battle of Brandywine Creek, about 30 miles west of Philadelphia; on September 26, 1777, British troops occupied the city of Philadelphia; and on October 4, 1777, the British Army won the Battle of Germantown, a few miles north of Philadelphia.

Just before the British army, totaling 15,000 troops, occupied Philadelphia, the Continental Congress moved westward, meeting for one day at Lancaster, Pennsylvania, on September 27, and then establishing its location at York on September 30. The Congress remained in York for nine months, until June 27, 1778, before returning to Philadelphia by July 2, 1778.

While the British troops occupied the city of Philadelphia, Washington, and his soldiers settled in for a harsh winter at a plateau named Valley Forge, which was only 20 miles west of Philadelphia—about a day's march. In December, 12,000 soldiers and 400 women and children moved to Valley Forge. In addition to George Washington, they included Patriot legends Alexander Hamilton, Nathanael Greene, Henry Knox, and "Mad" Anthony Wayne. Two of the most controversial figures in America history—Benedict Arnold and Aaron Burr—were there as well, as was future U.S. President James Monroe[1] and future chief justice of the United States Supreme Court, John Marshall.[2]

Washington knew that for at least several months the British would not be on the offensive—the roads would be virtually unpassable with the winter weather. It would give Washington an opportunity to have time to train his forces, which were largely composed of state militia units. To help with this were several extraordinary Europe military leaders who arrived from Europe to support the cause: Baron von Steuben of Prussia; Thaddeus Kościuszko and Casimir Pulaski of

Poland; and the Marquis de Lafayette and Baron de Kalb of France. Their help in improving the capabilities and morale of the Patriot forces was invaluable.

Arriving at Valley Forge in December 1777, the first order of business was the construction of log cabins—about 2,000 of them—and the stocking up on supplies. Their biggest problem was to obtain food, clothing, shoes, etc.

In the early days of the camp, the supply of essentials was satisfactory, but by February food shortages began in earnest. By March, the shortage of clothing became critical; almost 3,000 men did not have adequate clothing.

It would not be until June 18, 1778, that General Sir Henry Clinton and 15,000 British soldiers would evacuate Philadelphia. Valley Forge proved to be the worst encampment of the American forces in the war. Never before had the patriot army suffered so much. The extreme shortage of food, clothing and other supplies brought untold suffering and disease.

The British occupation of Philadelphia had both military and political significance, as controlling the colonial capital threatened the sovereignty of the emerging nation. This event surpassed the impact of the earlier British control of Boston, where the British were besieged by colonial forces, rendering them more or less at the mercy of the surrounding Patriot army. An example from later history illustrating the seriousness of occupying an enemy's capital city is the Prussian takeover of Paris in 1871, which led to the subjugation, humiliation, and imposition of significant reparations on France.

Several months before Valley Forge, the Battles of Saratoga pitted the troops of British General John Burgoyne against those of American General Horatio Gates in two confrontations. On September 19 (which was exactly one week before British troops would occupy the colonial capital at Philadelphia, Pennsylvania), Burgoyne attacked with about 7,500 men, while the Americans had about 8,500. Almost 600 of Burgoyne's soldiers were killed or wounded.

Burgoyne, with about 6,800 troops, tried another attack on October 7, 1777. However, the Americans, with their strength increased to over 12,000, counterattacked, forcing Burgoyne to the town of Saratoga. On October 17, the British were surrounded by Gates' soldiers and about 6,000 British and German troops were forced to surrender.

The Battle of Saratoga's importance lies not only in a remarkable military victory but also in its diplomatic consequences. The surrender convinced France to join the American cause against the British, providing crucial support and altering the dynamics of the war.

The day following the second Battle of Saratoga, Thomas Mifflin, in Pennsylvania, requested to be relieved of the position of the Quartermaster General of the Continental Army. In his review of Rossman's biography, Temple University's Harry M. Tinkcom addressed Mifflin's resignations:

> By February, 1777, when he was made a major general, Mifflin's star was at its zenith. Congress had been liberal with its promotions, Washington had confidence in him, and he was very popular in Pennsylvania. But eight months later, on October 8, 1777, he abruptly resigned both his major generalcy and his job as quartermaster general. Here, of course, is one of the big mysteries. Why did he attempt such a complete break at this time? In his letter of resignation Mifflin pleaded ill health.[3]

Mifflin Appointed to the Board of War

Two days after Mifflin's resignation (October 20, 1777), Richard Henry Lee wrote to Washington:

> ...was a good deal surprised to find you had been told that Congress had appointed Gen. Conway a Major General. No such appointment has been made, nor do I believe it will, whilst it is likely to produce the evil consequences you suggest. It is very true, that both within and without doors, there have been Advocates for the measure, and it has been affirmed that it would be very agreeable to the army, whose favorite Mr. Conway was asserted to be. My judgement on this business was not formed until I received your letter. I am very sure Congress would not take any step that might injure the Army, or even have a tendency that way; and I verily believe they wish to lessen your difficulties by every means in their power, from an entire conviction that the purest motives of public good direct your actions.
>
> The business of a Board of War is so extensive, so important, and demanding such constant attention, that Congress see clearly the necessity of constituting a new Board, out of Congress, whose time shall be entirely devoted to that essential department. It is by some warmly proposed that this board shall be filled by the three following gentlemen, Colonel Read, Colonel Pickering the present Adjutant General, and Colonel Harrison your Secretary. And that Gen. Conway be appointed A.G. [Adjutant General] in the room of Colonel Pickering. It is my wish, and I am sure it is so of many others, to know your full and candid sentiments on this subject. For my own part, I cannot be satisfied with giving any opinion on the point until I am favored with your sentiments, which I shall be much obliged to you for Sir as soon as your time will permit. It has been affirmed that Gen. Conway would quit the service if he were not made a M. [Major] General. But I have been told, in confidence, that he would leave it at the end of this Campaign if he *was* appointed, unless his word of honor were taken to continue for any fixed time. And it is a question with me whether the Advocates for Gen. Conway will not miss their aim if he should be appointed

A. General, unless he has the rank of Maj. General also. My reason for thinking so, is, that I have been informed Gen. Conway desires to retire to his family, provided he can carry from this Country home with him, a rank that will raise him in France. It is very certain that the public good demands a speedy erecting, and judicious filling of the new Board of War; and I sincerely wish it may be done in the most proper manner. I do not imagine Congress would appoint Colonel Harrison without first knowing whether you could spare him, nor do I think that so important an office as that of A.G. should be touched without maturest consideration.... Richard Henry Lee.[4]

On November 2, Richard Henry Lee wrote to Mifflin:

> I assure you Sir that having received such original impressions of your firm attachment to the cause of America, I have ever placed you among her first and most valuable friends. Trusting therefore to your patriotism, and my hopes of your returning health, I had ventured to mention your name for one of the three Commissioners of the new board of war—A most important department, on which our righteous warfare eminently depends.

Lee continues:

> Some Gentlemen supposed yr. health would hinder, others observed that the Continental policy forbid the union of two offices in the same person, supposing that you might be prevailed on to retain your commission of M. General could your health permitted action. The spirit of the Continental policy does forbid double Salaries, but the Generalship might be continued with the Board of war Salary. Indeed, the nature of the latter business renders rank and knowledge in War necessary. I love America and venerate its faithful friends, which must render it painful to be deprived, from whatever cause, of the assistance of its surest Supports in this crisis of its fate. I still hope however that returning health will enable you yet to continue your Aid for establishing the glory of North America on the most lasting foundations. I am yours dear Sir with sincere affection.[5]

On November 17, 1777, the old Board of War was terminated by Congress and its duties transferred to a new Board of War and Ordinance. By this time, the Continental Congress had been in existence for over three years, and the Revolutionary War had been raging for about two and a half years. Many in Congress felt that they should have more say in overseeing the military.

On November 7, 1777, Congress accepted Mifflin's quartermaster general resignation and appointed him to the new Board of War along with Timothy Pickering[6] and Robert Harrison.[7]

> The Board of War reported,
> That they have had a conference with General Mifflin on the late establishment made by Congress for conducting the war department, and are unanimously of opinion, that a sufficient number of commissioners have not been appointed for giving due weight to the execution of the regulations which may be recommended by the Board, and adopted by Congress, and particularly for

enabling one of the board of commissioners to visit, from time to time, the different armies, posts, or garrisons, in order to see that the regulations adopted by Congress are carried into execution, and to examine what are the wants of the army, and what defects or abuses prevail, from time to time, in the different departments;

Whereupon, That it would further greatly tend to facilitate the Business of the Department, especially at the commencement of the new Establishment, to secure the Continuation of the Services of the Secretary of the late Board of War, who in their opinion has discharged the Duties of an arduous and complicated Department in its infant Stage, with Honor to himself, and much Disinterestedness, and with Fidelity and advantage to the Public.[8]

Historian Gene Procknow observes:

When Washington successfully defended his position, Mifflin decided to resign the quartermaster position. On one hand he ascribed an unknown illness as the reason for his decision but at the same time also sought an active combat command. Ominously, he resigned as quartermaster in November 1777, just before the trials and tribulations of a supply shortage winter at Valley Forge. Putting himself before the army, he left at an inopportune time—though Congress takes some of the blame as the deliberative body failed to name a successor until the worst of the winter was over.[9]

Articles of Confederation

On November 15, 1777, the Articles of Confederation were adopted by the Second Continental Congress. However, it would take more than three years before it would be ratified by all the states and take effect. It would serve as the first Constitution of the United States until the final constitution was ratified several years later.

The Articles of Confederation were famous for creating a federal government while maintain the authority of the individual states.

Unfortunately, the document had drawbacks: it established only one legislative body, and that entity did not have the power to tax or control commerce between states. Also, the president needed to be a member of the legislature. In addition, all treaties between the new nation and other countries needed to be approved by the individual states.

The major writer of the Articles of Confederation was Delaware's John Dickinson. Known as the "penman of the Revolution," he produced numerous pamphlets, newspaper articles, and speeches in support of the rights of American colonists. He received his legal training in London, England at the Middle Temple and practiced law in Philadelphia during Thomas Mifflin's teenage years. As early as the 1760s, Dickinson's writings were influential in giving voice to American grievances.

In the late 1780's, Dickinson signed and was an enthusiastic supporter of the U.S. Constitution, which replaced the Articles of Confederation.[10]

John Dickinson also served as president of the Delaware constitutional convention in 1791–1792. He was born in Talbot County, Maryland, in 1732 and died in New Castle County, Delaware, in 1808.

On November 24, 1777, the new Board of War stated:

> The Board further beg leave to represent that General Mifflin has expressed a warm Solicitude that Major General Gates should be appointed President of this Board, from a Conviction that his Military Skill would suggest Reformations in the different Departments of the Army essential to good Discipline, Order and (Economy), and that his Character and Popularity in the Army would facilitate the execution of such Reformations when adopted by Congress; a Task in the opinion of this Committee more arduous and important, than the formation of any new Establishment, however wise it may be in Theory![11]

Siege of Fort Mifflin

Stone-and-wood Fort Mifflin,[12] and other defensive installations, along the Delaware River were built to protect the new nation's capital of Philadelphia. In September 1777, the British attacked the city by land and took control. However, their ships couldn't supply them because Fort Mifflin stood in the way. It had to be taken if the British were to bring ships in with food, clothing, gunpowder, etc. These supplies were especially important as they would enable the British forces to pursue the Continental Army before it could go into the safety of its winter encampment.

Major General Horatio Gates. After his troops defeated the British forces at the Battles of Saratoga in 1777, some people in Congress and in the army felt that he should be commander-in-chief of the Continental Army. That effort became known as the Conway Cabal (courtesy Yale University Art Gallery).

Fort Mifflin was built on the Delaware River to protect the nation's capital of Philadelphia. Initially called the Mud Island Fort, it was named after General Thomas Mifflin by 1777. In that year, about 2,000 British soldiers attacked the 400-man Fort Mifflin garrison. It took an estimated 10,000 cannon balls for them to overcome the American troops (photograph by author).

Located less than 10 miles from the center of Philadelphia, Fort Mifflin sat on an island in the Delaware River that was so muddy it was named Mud Island. The fort's original name was appropriately enough Mud Island Fort. At least by 1777, it was unofficially renamed after Thomas Mifflin who in February of that year became a major general in the Continental Army.[13]

On November 10, 1777, about two months after they had secured control of Philadelphia, 2,000 British troops attacked Fort Mifflin, which was manned by only 400 men. The British, with a fleet and 228 cannon, overcame the garrison on November 15 after an intense bombardment, inflicting 240 casualties. An estimated 10,000 cannon balls were shot in what has been called the heaviest artillery bombardment of the war.

The last defenders of Fort Mifflin ran out of ammunition, but were able to escape by rowing across the Delaware river to Fort Mercer on the New Jersey shore.[14]

It had taken weeks for the British to overcome the small Fort Mifflin garrison, and that was enough time for Washington to move his troops to the relative safety of a winter encampment at Valley Forge.

Post-war, Fort Mifflin was reconstructed and went on to serve as a prison in the Civil War and a munitions storage facility in both World War I and World War II. In the 21st century, it is known as the American fort in the longest continuous service.

After Fort Mifflin was taken by the British, General Howe was able to get whatever supplies were needed by ship. He also was emboldened to immediately pursue Washington. On December 4, he went after the Patriot army with 10,000 to 15,000 troops. His plan to destroy the Continental Army was foiled by the actions of a 49-year-old midwife.

One of the most successful Philadelphia spies was Ireland-born nurse, Lydia Darragh.[15] In December 1777, British General William Howe's top officers took over a large room in her house for a secret meeting. They didn't suspect the Darraghs of having any connections with the patriot military forces because they were Quakers. They, of course, never read Washington's words of eight months earlier: "Some in the Quaker line, who have never taken an active part, would be least liable to Suspicion from either party."

Eavesdropping from an adjacent closet, Lydia Darragh heard the details of a planned British surprise attack on Washington's forces, which was to occur two days later at Whitemarsh, Pennsylvania. Obtaining a pass to leave the city the following day, to visit a mill for flour, Darragh encountered Colonel Thomas Craig as she approached the Continental Army encampment. As Craig was commander of the 3rd Pennsylvania Infantry Regiment, it wasn't difficult for him to immediately get word of the surprise attack to General Washington.[16]

Because of Darragh's information, the Continental Army was now fully prepared when the British attempted to surprise them with over 10,000 troops. Instead of causing the destruction of Washington's main force, they were forced to retreat to Philadelphia. Lydia Darragh is sometimes considered the first female spy in the history of the United States—and certainly one of the most successful.

Washington Letter to State Leaders

In December 1777, the Continental Army troops began their suffering of the winter at Valley Forge, Pennsylvania. British-occupied Philadelphia was just 20 miles away.

On December 29, 1777, Washington sent to state leaders the following message from his headquarters at Valley Forge. This particular copy was sent to New York governor, George Clinton. While there is some variation among the letters, more than 90 percent of the text is the same. The first issue addressed by the Continental Army Commander was the need for additional troops:

> I take the liberty of transmitting you the enclosed Return, which contains a State of such of the New York Regiments, as are in the Army immediately under my command. By this you will discover how deficient—how exceedingly short they are of the compliment of Men, which of right according to the establishment they ought to have. This information I have thought it my duty to lay before you, that it may have that attention which its importance demands; and in full hope, the most early and vigorous measures will be adopted not only to make the regiments more respectable but complete. The expediency and necessity of this procedure are too obvious to need arguments. Should we have a respectable force to commence an early Campaign with, before the Enemy are reinforced, I trust we shall have an opportunity of striking a favorable and an happy stroke; But if we should be obliged to defer it, It will not be easy to describe with any degree of precision what disagreeable consequences may result from It.

The second—and more pressing issue—Washington raises is the matter of adequate clothing for the troops at the Valley Forge encampment.

> ...No pains—no efforts on the part of the States can be too great for this purpose. It is not easy to give you a just and accurate Idea of the sufferings of the Army at large—of the loss of Men on this account. Were they to be minutely detailed, your feelings would be wounded, and the relation would probably be not received without a degree of doubt and discredit. We had in Camp on the 23d Inst. by a Field return then taken, not less than 2898 Men unfit for duty by reason of their being bare foot and otherwise naked. Besides this number sufficiently distressing of itself, there are many others detained in Hospitals and crowded in Farmers Houses for the same causes....[17]

Chapter Thirteen

Conway Cabal

Conway Cabal, October 1777

Biographer Rawle mentions Mifflin's dissatisfaction with the state of affairs in the early fall of 1777:

> In what may be termed the *political* conduct of Gen. Mifflin in *the army*, we cannot wholly exculpate him from the charge of being frequently *discontented* and *out of humour* with the course of proceedings: at times, if we are to believe Wilkinson, (in his Memoirs,) quite despondent of ultimate success. He was naturally *free* and *unguarded* in his conversation; and it is very probable that *some* of his remarks reached the ears of the commander in chief.[1]

Rawle states that Mifflin (at the time Nathanael Greene's star was rising) was not a favorite at [Washington's] headquarters, and hence we may account for his never having had a separate command...." However, Rawle, mostly incorrectly, believed that "...although suspected of being a party to the unworthy plot concerted at York to remove Gen. Washington from the command of the army, [Mifflin] was altogether innocent of it. The writer of this article has accidentally become possessed of a correspondence between him and the late Colonel Delany, which appears to vindicate him entirely from the charge."[2]

Rawle continues:

> In a letter dated February 1, 1778, the general [Mifflin] observes,
> As a man of sense and honor, you must judge what my feelings must be, when I am told that my old acquaintance Colonel Delany had charged me with a design of ruining General Washington, and of setting up Gen. Gates in opposition to him. As a friend to my country, I have spoken my sentiments on public matters with decency and firmness. *I love and esteem Gen. Washington, and know him too well, even to wish for a change. I love my country, and for her sake deprecate the idea of such a change.* But I have seen, and among my friends have said, that Gen. Washington's judgment in military points was frequently counteracted by what I believed a dangerous influence. I have quoted Long Island and Mount Washington as instances of that influence, and have lamented that

the general did not consider the"³ *great value* of his own *private judgment*, a judgment universally admitted and admired.

In answer, Col. Delany threw the blame on an officer from the southward, from whom he had heard the charge when dining at a friend's house, and did not attempt to support it himself.⁴

In the opinion that Gen. Washington sometimes allowed his own excellent judgment to be overruled by the suggestions of others, Mifflin did not stand alone. Wilkinson observes, that General Wayne "wished our worthy general would follow his own good judgment, without listening too much to some counsel."

Who were meant as giving this counsel, is not explained. I have heard from military men, that the loss of the battle of Germantown was imputable to the suggestions of *General Knox*, that an advancing army ought not to leave a garrison in its rear. *C.J. Marshall* has explained and vindicated the remaining with so many troops on *Long Island*, and the unfortunate attempt to defend *Fort Washington* now appears to have been the act of *General Greene*.⁵

The *Encyclopædia Britannica* defines the word *cabal* as "a private organization or party engaged in secret intrigues; also, the intrigues themselves." The Conway Cabal was an effort in late 1777 by several prominent Continental Army officers and members of the Continental Congress to replace George Washington as the Commander in Chief of the American military forces in the American Revolutionary War against Great Britain. Their choice of a replacement was Major General Horatio Gates.

From the viewpoint of the 21st century—with the benefit of hindsight—this seems absurd, but at the time it attracted the interest of some of the most powerful and respected people in America.

Historian Gene Procknow explains the situation well: "With the loss of Philadelphia by Washington juxtaposed with Horatio Gates' phenomenal victory at Saratoga, a chorus of voices sprang up that Gates should replace Washington as Commander in Chief. Unfortunately for Mifflin, he joined the insurgents in what historians have termed the Conway Cabal and advocated the replacement of Washington with Gates."⁶

At the time, General Washington had suffered recent military defeats at the battles of Brandywine and Germantown, while General Gates' reputation was at an all-time high. In October 1777, Gates' forces had defeated and captured British General John Burgoyne's army at Saratoga, New York. Considered by many historians to be the main turning point of the American Revolutionary War, it was the event—more than any other—that convinced the French government to enter the war on the side of the American colonists.

The actions of the anti–Washington group of men have gone down in history with the name, the "Conway Cabal." The man it was named for, and who most historians have believed to be its ringleader, was Continental Army Brigadier General Thomas Conway, who, under the command of Washington, had recently led men in action at the battles of Brandywine and Germantown.

An Irish-born veteran of the French military, Thomas Conway had moved to North America to support the American colonists and their efforts to achieve independence from Great Britain. On May 13, 1777, after his participation at Brandywine and Germantown, the Continental Congress commissioned Conway a brigadier general. However, Conway wanted more than that—he wanted Washington to recommend him for the position of Major General—even though he had been a brigadier for only a matter of a few months. It has been said that his objective was to acquire the higher rank so he could return to Europe and immediately receive a similar rank in the French Army.[7]

Apparently, Commander in Chief Washington was reluctant to agree to the request, fearing that other, more senior, officers would resent being passed over for a similar promotion. At the time, there were 24 brigadier generals with more seniority than Conway in the Continental Army.[8]

Seething from Washington's lack of support, Conway encouraged General Horatio Gates to strive to replace Washington. In October 1777, Conway wrote a letter to Gates, arguing that "Heaven has been determined to save your Country, or a weak General and bad Councilors would have ruined it." Conway also sent letters to members of the Continental Congress in which he disparaged Washington.

A member of General Stirling's staff heard Gates' aide-de-camp James Wilkinson (who was under the influence of alcohol) speak of Conway's letter. He told General Stirling what he had heard. General Stirling, in turn, told Washington. After Washington read copies of the letters, he confronted Gates and Conway. Gates apologized. When Washington told Conway that he was aware of the contents of his letter, the latter claimed that he never wrote the words "weak general." On November 5, 1777, Thomas Conway wrote a letter to Washington in which he said:

> My opinion of you sir without flattery or envy is as follows: you are a Brave man, an honest Man, a patriot, and a Man of great sense. your modesty is such, that although your advice in council is commonly sound and proper, you have often been influenced by men who Were not equal to you in point of experience, Knowledge or judgment.
>
> these are my sentiments; i have expressed them in private conversation with some General officers, and in particular to General Mifflin at reading before Doctor Craig. I think they Will be found such in my Letter to General Gates.

Thirteen. Conway Cabal

Other major American leaders who have been considered part of the Cabal include Dr. Benjamin Rush. Immediately after the victory of Gates' forces at Saratoga, Rush wrote the following anti–Washington letter to arguably Massachusetts' most influential delegate to the Continental Congress—John Adams.

> To John Adams from Benjamin Rush, 21 October 1777
> From Benjamin Rush
> Reading Octbr: 21. 1777
>
> I have heard several Officers who have served under General Gates compare his Army to a well regulated family. The same Gentlemen have compared Genl. Washington's imitation of an Army to an unformed mob. Look at the Characters of both! The one on the pinnacle of military glory—exulting in the Success of Schemes planned with wisdom, and executed with vigor and bravery—and above all see a country saved by their exertions. See the Other outgeneraled and twice beaten—obliged to witness the march of a body of men only half their number thro' 140 miles of a thick settled country—forced to give up a city the capital of a state and After all outwitted by the same Army in a retreat. If our Congress can witness these things with composure, and suffer them to pass without an enquiry I shall think we have not Shook off monarchical prejudices, and that like the Israelites of old we worship the work of our hands.[9]

Historian Mark Edward Lender's *Cabal! The Plot Against General Washington, The Conway Cabal Reconsidered* provides the most comprehensive account of the Conway Cabal. He mentions Mifflin's "antipathy toward Washington" and Greene replacing Mifflin in "Washington's confidence." Dr. Lender goes on to state: "but Mifflin's antagonism also was borne of an honest concern for the patriot cause and a fear that Washington was not the man to set things right."[10]

In 1777, Congress established a new Board of War consisting of three members, each chosen for their expertise in military matters rather than being members of Congress. On November 7, 1777, Congress elected Thomas Mifflin, Colonel Timothy Pickering of Massachusetts, and Lieutenant Colonel Robert Harrison of Maryland as the initial members. Later, on November 24, 1777, at Mifflin's recommendation, two additional members were added: Major General Horatio Gates and Richard Peters of Pennsylvania, with Joseph Trumbull of Connecticut replacing Robert Harrison. General Horatio Gates served as the chairman of the Board. While the choice of members may not have always been optimal, the inclusion of individuals with solid military knowledge and experience was considered a significant improvement.

Less than a year later, on October 29, 1778, Congress further modified the Board of War. This time, it specified that two of the five members must be delegates to the Continental Congress, while the remaining three should not be delegates. Additionally, Congress mandated that a quorum required three members.

Friction between Generals Gates and Washington rose to a new level after Gates' victory at the Battle of Saratoga in October 1777. He directly informed the Continental Congress of the victory, bypassing his immediate superior, Washington. In addition, Washington had lent troops to Gates for the New York campaign, and Gates was slow to return them. Worst of all, Washington received word in late 1777 that Gates was involved in a conspiracy among Continental Army officers to have Washington replaced—with Gates himself taking over.

Richard Henry Lee wrote to Washington late in November 1777:

> As it appeared by the letters of Gen. Mifflin that he objected only to serve in the Quartermasters department, that his health was returning, and that he was willing to continue his aid to the public cause, Congress appointed him one of the Commissioners of the new Board, because he is competent to the right discharge of its duties, because that would best suit his valetudinary state, and as shewing a just sense of his uniform, vigorous, and well founded patriotism.[11]
>
> General Mifflin has proposed a plan for the Quartermaster department that appears judicious, and well fitted to answer the purpose of good service and œconomy at the same time. He would divide this department into its military and civil branches, the former to be filled by a person well qualified to discharge its duties, and the latter, again to be divided into Commissaries of Teams, of Forage, of Tents &c. &c. to be governed in their purchases by estimates from the Quarter Master general who is to touch no money but a moderate tho sufficient salary.[12]

In the fall of 1778, Congress modified the board composition to two legislators and three individuals from outside the legislative body.[13]

In 1781, with the war essentially over, Congress established a War Office, composed of members who were not legislators. It appointed General Benjamin Lincoln as its head and gave his position the title Secretary at War. These appointments were made under the Congress of the Confederation. Lincoln from Massachusetts held his position from 1781 to 1783, and was succeeded by General Henry Knox, also from Massachusetts, who served as Secretary at War from 1785 to 1789.

When the war ended, many functions of the Board of War were assumed by the new War Department. Under the new U.S. Constitution of 1789, the position's title was changed to Secretary of War. Knox continued his duties into the presidential cabinet of George Washington until 1794. The title Secretary of War endured through the War of 1812, the American Civil War, and two world wars. In 1947, President Harry S. Truman renamed the cabinet position the Department of Defense, and its head became the Secretary of Defense.

Rawle discusses Mifflin's roles in 1777:

In the course of this year, his health became so much impaired that he was under the necessity of requesting leave to resign, but his application was unsuccessful. He was not even relieved from the fatigues of the quarter-master general's department. On the contrary, his labours were increased, by being appointed a member of a new board of war. It would seem, however, that this body did not immediately go into operation, for a report was soon afterwards made to Congress, by one of their committees, that *he* had been consulted with, and his *advice* taken as to supplying the army with flour, and other matters which related to the quarter-master general's department.[14]

Rawle addresses Valley Forge:

The ensuing winter is known to have been one of *dense* and heavy *gloom* in our public affairs. The REMNANTS of an army, protected from the severity of the weather by huts hastily erected at *Valley Forge*, were suffering almost *every privation*, while the enemy *rioted in enjoyment* at Philadelphia. Much complaint was made of bad management *somewhere*, and General Mifflin came in for a share of the blame. On the 2d of March a new appointment of quarter-master general was made, and he was directed to render to Congress and to General Greene, his *successor*, a statement of the preparations for the next campaign, and deliver the articles on hand to General Greene.[15]

Rawle states at this time Mifflin was in a serious disagreement with Congress, He believed he should not be "responsible for the conduct of *others*, over whom he had no *efficient control.*" Congress, on the other hand, insisted that, in general, "great servants of the public" are so responsible. Rawle continues:

The great want of order and subordination in many departments of the army, which was partly owing to the erroneous systems adopted at different times by Congress itself, and partly to the novelty of the predicaments in which we were placed, threw on the head of a department no *small difficulties*; and Mifflin, who, so far as related to his own receipts and disbursements of public money, was above suspicion, very reasonably conceived that he ought not to be responsible for the conduct of *others*, over whom he had no *efficient control*. A resolution to a different effect was passed, however, by Congress, on the 19th of May, declaring as a general rule, that the "great servants of the public" are *accountable* to it, and that it must depend on *particular circumstances*, of which Congress will judge, whether, in any case, the payment of money to deputies or assistants shall discharge the principal. No progress was made in the inquiry at *this time*, and on the 21st of May, Mifflin, who with others foresaw the speedy evacuation of Philadelphia, and was anxious to participate in those military measures, which the event would probably give rise to, obtained leave to join the main army.[16]

On December 30, 1777, as the Conway Cabal was winding down, 20-year-old Major General Lafayette sent a letter to Washington in which he stated: "You Shall See Very plainly that if You were lost for

America, there is no Body who Could keep the army and the Revolution for Six months. there are Oppen dissentions in Congress, parties who Hate one another as much as the Common enemy." Lafayette continued:

> Stupid men who without knowing a Single word about war undertake to judge You, to make Ridiculous Comparisons; they are infatuated with Gates without thinking of the different Circumstances, and Believe that attacking is the only thing Necessary to Conquer. those ideas are entertained in their Minds by Some jealous men and perhaps Secret friends to the British Government who want to push You in a moment of ill Humor to Some Rash enterprise Upon the lines or Against a much stronger army. I should not take the liberty of mentioning these particularities to You if I did not Receive a letter about this matter from a Young Good natured Gentleman at York whom Conway Has Ruined By His Cunning Bad advice But Who entertains the Greatest Respect for You.[17]

Apparently, Lafayette did his own research into Conway. After all, Lafayette had his own highly-placed contacts in the French government. Lafayette wrote:

> And the reason of such behavior for me is that he wishes to be well spoken of at the French court, and his protector the marquis de castries is an intimate acquaintance of mine—but since the letter of Lord Stirling I inquired in his character, I found that he was an ambitious and dangerous man—he has done all [in h]is power by a cunning maneuvers to take off my confidence and affection for you—his desire was to engage me to leave this country—now I see all the general officers of the army revolted against Congress, such disputes if known by the enemy, can be attended with horrid consequences—I am very sorry when ever I perceive trouble raised among the defender of the same cause, but my concern is much greater when I find officers coming from France, officers of some character in my country to whom any fault of that Kind may be imputed—the reason of my fondness for Conway, was [h]is being by all means a very brave and very good officer—however that part of maneuvers &c. which seems so extraordinary to Congress is not so very difficult for any man of common sense who applies himself to it—I must pay to gal portail [sic] and some French officers who came to speak to me the justice to say that I found them as I could wish upon this occasion—for it has made a great noise among many in the army—I wish indeed those matters could be soon pacified—I wish your excellency could let them Know how necessary you are to them and engage them in the same time to Keep peace and a simulate love among themselves till the moment where those little disputes shall not be attended with such inconveniences—it would be a too great pity that slavery, dishonor, ruin, and unhappiness of a whole world should issue from trifling differences betwixt some few men.
>
> ...I am now fixed to your fate and I shall follow it and sustain it as well by my sword as by all means in my power—I beg you will keep the letter secret—you will pardon my importunity in favor of the sentiment which dictate it—youth and friendship make perhaps myself too warm, but I feel the greatest concern of all what happens since some time. with the most tenderest and

profound respect I have the honor to be dear general Your most obedient humble Servant

The Marquis de Lafayette[18]

General Washington sent a very interesting letter to his friend and Virginia congressional delegate Richard Henry Lee at the beginning of the Conway Cabal affair. On October 16, 1777, he wrote: "...if there is any truth in the report which has been handed to me, viz.—that congress has appointed Brigadier Conway to be Major General in this Army, it will be as unfortunate a measure, as ever was adopted—I may add (& I think with truth) that it will give a fatal blow to the existence of this army—upon so interesting a subject I must speak plain—the duty I owe my country—the ardent desire I have to promote its true interests—and justice to Individuals require this of me." Washington states [bold print added]:

> **General Conway's merit then, as an officer, and his importance in this Army, exists more in his own imagination than in reality**; for it is a maxim with him to leave no service of his own untold nor to want anything which is to be obtained by importunity; but, as I do not want to detract from any merit he possesses, and only wish to have the matter taken up, on its true ground (after allowing him everything that his warmest friends can contend for) I would only ask why the youngest Brigadier in the service (for I believe he is so) should be put over the heads of the oldest, & thereby take Rank, and command Gentlemen who yesterday only, were his Seniors—Gent[n] who I will be bold to say (in behalf of some of them at least) of sound judgment & unquestionable Bravery.

Washington goes on to advise Lee that good officers passed over for promotion because of Conway will have "good pretexts for retiring." He adds: "I have been a Slave to the service: I have undergone more than most men are aware of, to harmonize so many discordant parts but it will be impossible for me to be of any further service if such insuperable difficulties are thrown in my way—You may believe me my dear Sir, that I have no earthly view, but the public good in what I have said—I have no prejudice against Genl Conway...."[19]

Two weeks later, Washington wrote the following to Richard Henry Lee:

> The report of Genl Conway's promotion was so prevalent, and came from such authority—among others from Baron Kalb, who told me, that by some Members of Congress he was informed that it either had, or would take place—that I had not a single doubt remaining upon my Mind of the Fact. What I said in my last, was with no design to injure General Conway—nor with a view to serve any individual—I then said, and still think, it would have an exceeding bad tendency; not, as I before observed, that I had formed my opinion from anything I had heard, because to this moment I have not exchanged directly;

or indirectly, a single word with any Brigadier in the Service on the subject, but from the nature of the case; well knowing that all Officers are apt to entertain as high an opinion of their own merits as they deserve, and few of them are actuated by such pure and disinterested motives as to submit to what they conceive a slight, in which light the promotion of a younger Officer over them undoubtedly would be considered. These, & these only, were my motives for the letter I wrote you. how far he is qualified to discharge the duties of Adjutant Genl in case the present Gentn is appointed to, & accepts any other Office, you can judge almost as well of as I—He must, no doubt, be well acquainted with the detail duty of an Army from the length of his Services; but then, he is a bad scribe, which however may in some measure be remedied by good Assistants (which he or any other Adjutant Genl must have)—what weight their may be, in his being a Foreigner, you can judge as well of as I can.

There is a Gentn, if Colo. Pickering should go out of the Office, who I am told is well qualified to supply his place, he was formerly Deputy Adjt Genl to the Northern Army, and of the name of Flemming—he has been an Officer in the British Service, well acquainted with detail duty, and a good disciplinarian— He was in very bad health at the time Genl Gates left that Office; which was, I believe, the principal reason why he was not thought of as a successor—that he was not, caused his resignation. The part he has acted since, & his political Sentiments, can be known perhaps with precision from the Representatives of New York, where he formerly resided, and those of Jersey, where he is at present a resident; and in whose Treasury, I understand, he has imbarkd his all. a good security if true.

The three Gentn you have in contemplation for constituting a Board of War (not from your own body) are, in my judgment, equal to any you could make choice of. They want, what is not to be found among a people unused to war, a competent knowledge of the business; but they have a large share of understanding—great application—and as much experience in the business as any I know having had as good opportunities of seeing, and feeling our wants as any among us. at the same time men of unquestionable attachment, and Integrity. The advantages of having able Members solely confined to this department are too obvious & important; & the benefits to my self, & the army at large, too diffusive & extensive, to suffer local conveniences to interpose; for which reason if Messrs Harrison & Pickering should Incline to accept the appointment, it will meet with my ready concurrence.

I congratulate you most sincerely on the important events to the Northward; but cannot help complaining, most bitterly, of Genl Gates's neglect in not giving me the earliest authentic advice of it; as an Affair of that magnitude might, and indeed did, give an important turn to our Operations in this Quarter—at least in our designs—but which, for want of confirmation, we began to doubt the propriety of—from the time I wrote Congress on the 18th (Inclosing the first acct I had of the Surrender, which was not altogether authentic) till the 26th I heard not a little more of it (and actually began to doubt the truth of it)—nor have I to this moment recd the least advice of this Important transaction from General Gates. I wish Sir, the Situation of your Troops in this Quarter, & our Force, could give you well-grounded hopes of a similar event; but as this will shortly become the Subject of a Letter to Congress, I shall not inlarge upon it at present, in this.

Although the Surrender of General Burgoyne is a great, and glorious event highly honourable to our Arms, and to those who were immediately opposed to him. and although I am perfectly well satisfied that the critical situation in which Genl Gates was likely to be thrown (by the approach of General Clinton up the No. River) would not allow him to insist upon a more perfect Surrender; I am nevertheless convinced, that this event will not equal our expectations; and that, without great precaution, & very delicate management, we shall have all these Men—if not the Officers—opposed to us in the spring. without the necessary precautions (as I have just observed) I think this will happen; and unless great delicacy is used in the precautions, a plea will be given them, & they will justify, a breach of the Covenant on their part—do they not declare (many of them) that no faith is to be held with Rebels? did not the English do the very thing I am now suspecting them of, after the Convention of Closter Seven, upon changing their Commander? will they hold better faith with us than they did with the French? I am persuaded myself, that they will not—and yet, I do not see how it is to be prevented, without a direct violation of the articles ourselves, or by attempting to guard against the evil, give them a plea of justification on theirs.

It is reported among us, that Genl Mifflin has resigned his Offices in this army—the truth you must know—It is also said, that Baron Kalb is desirous of going into that Department, being the one he has been regularly trained in for a great numbers of years in the French Service. Whether, admitting this to be the case, as it is a department not only of great trust but through whose hands much of the Public Money is to pass Congress would choose to Entrust the Baron is left to themselves to determine; certain it is a knowing Man will be much wanted, & as certain it is I know of none such among ourselves.[20]

Conway sent the following December 29, 1777, letter to Washington six days after he was appointed inspector general by Congress:

Coll Fitzgerald mentioned to me yesterday that your excellency Wished to Know the method I intended to proceed upon in the new office to Which I was appointed. the first step, is to take your orders concerning the instruction of the troops the returns of Which Models, are to be sent to the Different Regiments concerning the Clothing, arms, rations, Regimental pay Books, &c. &c. are not yet printed, nay I Believe the form of these returns is not yet Determined by the Board of War, and some time may elapse before they are sent Down, and of consequence before I can commence the reviews. in order to Make use of every Moment I propose to your Excellency to Begin Without Delay the instruction of the Troops.

The Method I thought the Most efficacious is to assemble one or two officers and noncommissioned officers from each Regiment in *pott's grove* or some other convenient place your excellency may Direct; there to instruct them in all Maneuvers necessary for a Battalion, a Brigade, a Division, this I think I can with some assiduity effect in a Month's time. when the officers and noncommissioned officers are thoroughly instructed, they are to repair to their respective Regiments in order to spread the instruction. I have seen this followed Both in the imperial and French army, and more than two hundred thousand men trained up in the space of three Months. No army wants instruction more than this army, where no two Regiments Maneuver alike, and where there are hardly two officers in each Regiment able to command the Maneuvers. it is impossible for a general to promise himself any solid success with Such troops.

Let the men be ever so Brave, and the generals plan ever so judicious and well formed. it is also impossible that the commander in chief should personally attend this instruction, as his whole time must be taken up in Watching the enemy, in opposing the enemy's Designs, and in carrying his own into execution. having been employed constantly in training up troops, and having been concerned in working on the Late instruction given to the French army I accepted of the office of inspector general with the view of being instrumental to the Welfare of the cause, and to the glory of the commander in chief in Making his troops fit to execute his orders. the rank of Major General which was given me is absolutely requisite for this office in order to be vested with proper authority to superintend the instruction, and the internal administration. there is no inspector in the European army under a Major general. however sir if my appointment is productive of any inconvenience or any Ways Disagreeable to your excellency, as I neither applied nor solicited for this place, I am very ready to return to France where I have pressing Business; and this I will do with the More satisfaction that I expect even there to be useful to the cause. I am With Respect Sir your obedt humble servant. Ts Conway[21]

In January 1778, Major General Nathanael Green and nine brigadier generals (Jedediah Huntington, Henry Knox, William Maxwell, Lachlan McIntosh, John Paterson, Enoch Poor, Charles Scott, James Varnum, and George Weedon) protested the promotion of Conway.

Behind the scenes Conway did his best to further the notion that Horatio Gates would be a better Commander in Chief than Washington, in what became known as "the Conway Cabal."

Toward the end of the war, Conway retuned to France where he served in the French Army in Flanders and India. During the French Revolution, he fled France to escape the revolutionaries.

On January 4, 1778, Washington wrote the following letter to General Gates in which he discusses what he knows about what would be later known to history as the Conway Cabal:

> ...I am to inform you then, that Colonel Wilkenson, in his way to Congress in the Month of October last, fell in with Lord Stirling at Reading; and, not in confidence that I ever understood, informed his Aid de Camp Major McWilliams that Genl Conway had written thus to you "Heaven has been determined to save your Country; or a weak General and bad Counsellors would have ruined it"—Lord Stirling, from motives of friendship, transmitted the acct with this remark—"The enclosed was communicated by Colonel Wilkenson to major McWilliams, such wicked duplicity of conduct I shall always think it my duty to detect."

In consequence of this information, and without having anything more in view than merely to shew that Gentn that I was not unapprised of his intriguing disposition, I wrote him a Letter in these words. "Sir—A Letter which I received last night contained the following paragraph." "In a Letter from Genl Conway to Genl Gates he says 'Heaven has been determined to save your Country; or a weak Genl and bad Counsellors would have ruined it—I am Sir & ca."

Neither this Letter, nor the information which occasioned it, was ever, directly, or indirectly, communicated by me to a single Officer in this army (out of my own family) excepting the Marquis de la Fayette, who having been spoken to on the subject by Genl Conway, applied for, and saw, under injunctions of secrecy, the Letter which contained Wilkinson's information—so desirous was I, of concealing every matter that could, in its consequences, give the smallest Interruption to the tranquility of this army, or, afford a gleam of hope to the enemy by dissensions therein.

Thus Sir, with an openness and candor which I hope will ever characterize and mark my conduct, have I complied with your request. the only concern I feel upon the occasion (finding how matters stand) is, that in doing this, I have necessarily been obliged to name a Gentn whom I am persuaded (although I never exchanged a word with him upon the subject) thought he was rather doing an act of Justice, than committing an act of infidelity; and sure I am, that,

Washington expresses his surprise that Conway and Gates corresponded with each other:

till Lord Stirling's Letter came to my hands, I never knew that Genl Conway (who I viewed in the light of a stranger to you) was a correspondent of yours, much less did I suspect that I was the subject of your confidential Letters—pardo[n] me then for adding, that so far from conceiving, that the safety of the States can be affected, or in the small[est] degree injured, by a discovery of this kind; or, that I should be called upon in such solemn terms to point out the author, that I considered the information as coming from yourself; and given with a friendly view to forewarn, and consequently forearm me, against a secret enemy; or, in other words, a dangerous incendiary; in which character, sooner or later, this Country will know Genl Conway.[22]

On February 2, 1778, Washington military aide Tench Tilghman wrote to Continental Congress leader Robert Morris:

Our enemies have already heard of and exult at this appearance of division and faction among ourselves and the officers of the army who have been all of them at one time or another under his command are exasperated to the highest degree at a thought of displacing him I have never seen any stroke of ill fortune affect the General in the manner that this dirty underhand dealing has done It hurts him the more because he cannot take notice of it without publishing to the world that the spirit of faction begins to work It therefore behooves his friends to support among us him against the malicious attacks of those who can have no reason to wish his removal but a desire to fill his place.[23]

Washington's Reputation

Given Washington's well-deserved reputation as the "indispensable man" of the American Revolution, it is difficult to understand how Mifflin, Gates, Rush and other prominent military and civilian leaders doubted his abilities in 1777 and 1778. It's helpful to recognize this was a low point in Washington's military career for reasons that were mostly beyond his control. Ultimately, criticism of Washington went nowhere at the time, soon fizzled out, and ended up doing absolutely no harm to Washington's place in history.

In subsequent centuries, other great anti-colonial military and government leaders have been measured against Washington. Dr. Sun Yat Sen has been called the "George Washington of China," Kenya President Jomo Kenyatta the "George Washington of Africa," Gen. Charles de Gaulle the "George Washington of France," Benito Juarez the "George Washington of Mexico," and José de San Martín the "George Washington of Southern South America."

However, perhaps the most famous comparison of them all was Venezuelan leader Simón Bolívar, who has frequently been called the George Washington of Venezuela, and of Bolivia, and of Colombia, and of Panama, and of Ecuador and of Peru. Or simply the "George Washington of South America," since he led each of those countries to independence from the Spanish Empire.

During the 19th century, pictures of George Washington were prominently displayed in the walls of almost every government office and schoolroom in the United States. Even in the 21st century, Washington is very popular. A 2021 CBS News Poll of Americans found: 39 percent of them chose George Washington as their "favorite Founding Father," Benjamin Franklin came in second at 21 percent, and Thomas Jefferson was third with 15 percent. None of the remaining best-known founders (Hamilton, Madison, Adams, Paine, and Jay) polled more than 5 percent.[24]

As mentioned, in February 1778, four months after the American patriots won the major victory over the British at Saratoga, New York, France entered the American Revolutionary War on the American side. Nothing was to prove more critical to the ultimate American victory than the French partnership.

In a March 1778 letter to Patrick Henry, Washington, discusses military issues: the supply situation as the troubles of Valley Forge, the arrival of a French ship, and most importantly of all, the Conway Cabal. Washington minces no words when he tells Henry about an anonymous letter by a Cabal activist that Henry had forwarded to him: "The

Anonymous Letter, with which you were pleased to favor me, was written by Doctor [Benjamin] Rush, so far as I can judge from a similitude of hands [handwriting]. This Man has been elaborate & studied in his professions of regard for me; and long since the Letter to you."[25]

Then Washington discusses

> the intrigues of a faction, which I know was formed against me ... it appeared in general, that General Gates was to be exalted, on the ruin of my reputation and influence. This I am authorized to say from undeniable facts, in my own possession, from publications, the evident scope of which, could not be mistaken, and from private detractions industriously circulated. Genl Mifflin it is commonly supposed, bore the second part in the Cabal; and General Conway, I know, was a very active, and malignant partizan but I have good reasons to believe that their machinations have recoiled most sensibly upon themselves.[26]

The following letter is from George Washington to General Thomas Mifflin on April 24, 1778: "In conformity to a Resolve of Congress, of which the enclosed is a Copy, I am to inform you that a Council of War, at which I request your attendance, will be held at this place to deliberate and determine upon the measure recommended by Congress. As the meeting of the Council, will depend upon the arrival of Genl Gates, to whom I have written, you will be pleased to enquire of him when he will be here, and regulate yourself accordingly."[27]

On that same day, George Washington wrote to Major General Horatio Gates: "It being indispensably necessary that some general plan of operation should be settled for the present Campaign; and perceiving that Congress have been pleased to appoint you to command on the North River—I am to request, if you should not find it too inconvenient, that you will make a digression from your route thither, and favor me with a call at this Camp, that we may enter upon a discussion of the point, and form some general System. The propriety of this measure, particularly at this advanced period, will be so obvious to you, that it is unnecessary to add upon the subject."[28]

Two months later, on June 18, 1778, General Sir Henry Clinton (April 16, 1730–December 23, 1795) and 15,000 British soldiers evacuated Philadelphia. General Clinton had taken over as the British Commander in Chief in America. He was to have charge of all His Majesty's troops until the end of hostilities in 1782. Originally, he had been sent over to Boston in May 1775, and the following month he had played a major role in securing the British victory at the Battle of Bunker Hill.

The Cadwalader Duel

In an interesting after effect of the Conway Cabal, on July 4, 1778—which was a month after the British left Philadelphia, Thomas Conway and Continental Brigadier General John Cadwalader[29] engaged in a duel. Like Thomas Mifflin, Cadwalader was a successful Philadelphia merchant before the war, attended "Philadelphia Academy" and was an early supporter of colonial independence. Cadwalader commanded Pennsylvania Militia at the Battle of Princeton, and also fought at the Battles of Brandywine, Germantown, and Monmouth.[30]

The duel between Thomas Conway and John Cadwalader was a result of Conway's slander and libel of George Washington. Cadwalader, defending General Washington's honor, challenged Conway to the duel. Cadwalader was not injured; Conway was shot in the mouth and believed he would soon die.

The fact that Cadwalader challenged Conway to the duel in defense of Washington's honor was rather ironic since Washington—along with Thomas Jefferson, Benjamin Franklin, and many other leaders of the time, opposed dueling. Writing to English physician Thomas Percival in 1784, Franklin said: "It is astonishing that the murderous practice of Dueling, which you so justly condemn, should continue so long in vogue. ... How can such miserable Sinners as we are, entertain so much pride as to conceit that every Offence against our imagined Honor merits Death! ... Yet every one of them makes himself Judge in his own Cause, condemns the Offender without a Jury, and undertakes himself to be the Executioner."

Thinking it likely that he would die from his injury, 19 days after the duel (July 23, 1778), Conway wrote the following letter to Washington:

> I find myself just able to hold the pen During a few Minutes, and take this opportunity of expressing my sincere grief for having Done, Written, or said anything Disagreeable to your excellency. my career will soon be over, therefore justice and truth prompt me to Declare my Last sentiments. you are in my eyes the great and the good Man. May you Long enjoy the Love, Veneration and Esteem of these states whose Liberties you have asserted by your Virtues. I am With the greatest respect sir your Excellency's Most obedt humble Servant Ths Conway.[31]

Thomas Mifflin Resigns as Major General

On August 17, 1778, Thomas Mifflin resigned his commission as a major general. He wasn't the only key Continental Army officer to resign in the middle of the war because Washington couldn't find a better person to fill his position. Alexander Hamilton's resignation is even better known. Both Mifflin and Hamilton resigned because they were continually denied any of their requests to move into other positions. Today, it might be called job burnout, due to fatigue, overwork, or prolonged stress.

In 1775, Alexander Hamilton joined the militia and the following year was promoted to captain of a New York Infantry company. He saw action at the Battle of White Plains and later at the Battles of Trenton and Princeton. Impressed with Hamilton's service, Washington chose him to be an aide-de-camp on his headquarters staff. He also promoted Hamilton to lieutenant colonel. Hamilton was only twenty. As the war progressed, Hamilton's desire to command a regiment of his own grew, even as Washington denied each of his requests to be reassigned. Finally, seeing the war could soon come to a conclusion, Hamilton resigned from his role as an aide-de-camp in 1781. Subsequently, he did get opportunities to command one of the Marquis de Lafayette's battalions, and, led a successful night attack at the Battle of Yorktown.[32]

When Mifflin resigned as major general, he realized that his future in the army was totally dependent on one man: General George Washington. However, Washington had put up with Mifflin for one reason—he thought he had no one else who could fulfill the duties of the quartermaster general anywhere near as well. Despite what he knew of Mifflin's role in the Conway Cabal, he was willing to overlook the past if it meant that he had the best people in key positions. (Later, Washington, would find that there was another general officer who could be as competent as Mifflin in the position—Nathanael Greene.)

The end result of the Conway Cabal for Thomas Mifflin wasn't that he would be banished to a European country like Thomas Conway, or that his actions would reveal significant defects as a military leader as was the case with Horatio Gates. No, it was that Mifflin lost much of the trust and support of George Washington. In 1777, the 33-year-old Mifflin believed he was putting his country first when he saw costly mistakes Washington was making, and he believed that Gates was a far better military leader than he would turn out to be. Mifflin overlooked the fact that by voicing criticism of Washington (even behind the scenes), he was jeopardizing the most important thing for his military career—Washington as a friend and mentor.

Ultimately, the alienation of Washington did not play a part in Mifflin's non-military career, but it did permanently prevent his advancement in the American military. No longer would Washington consider Mifflin for a command role as he did at the Battles of Long Island,

Trenton, and Princeton. The one thing Mifflin wanted most from his participation in the Revolutionary War was a chance to prove himself to be a great military commander. Never would he get that chance after the winter of 1777–1778. Mifflin would need to look elsewhere if he wished an influential role in the creation and development of the new country. That he did find—in politics. He was always a very competent politician, but after the war, he would prove himself to be one of the master political leaders of his time.

As for Washington, he had a war to win and ultimately incredibly important service to perform as the first president of the United States. He was too big a man to let resentment toward Mifflin interfere with that. In the future dealings—and there some significant ones—between the president of the country and the governor of arguably the most important state, Washington was cool, but always respectful and fair toward his former subordinate. Mifflin, for his part, was equally respectful and cooperative in his relations with Washington.

They would not let past differences interfere with what would be best for their respective states and their country.

Fort Wilson Riot

In August 1779, hostility arose among the working class of Philadelphia against well-to-do citizens, particularly merchants. The former demanded price controls in the face of rampant inflation. Many of the wealthiest citizens objected to price controls. The protesters posted inflammatory notices throughout the city, and a group of likeminded militiamen captured four wealthy men, parading them through the streets. When former Continental Army Major General Thomas Mifflin attempted to intervene, a militiaman struck him with a musket. As historian Thomas Fleming described it, "The blow shocked more than a few spectators; in 1776, Mifflin had been a hugely popular leader of the militia."[33]

Approximately two months later, tensions escalated into violence during what became known as the Fort Wilson Riot. In Philadelphia, at Walnut Street west of South Third Street is an historical marker with the title "Fort Wilson." However, it didn't mark the spot of a fort or a fortification of any kind. It was the site of a house where American patriot leaders fended off an attack by radical elements of the patriot cause. The marker states in full:

> On this site, in 1779, resided James Wilson a signer of the Declaration of Independence, and a leading lawyer in Philadelphia. Having represented certain

Tories accused of treason, Wilson incurred the wrath of patriotic elements after the British Army left Philadelphia [The British left on June 18, 1778], these feelings culminated in a riot in which the mob fired on Wilson's home and killed several persons.[34]

In early fall, 1779, word spread that a meeting of the activists was planned for October 4, 1779, at Philadelphia's Byrne's Tavern with the possible aim of rounding up Wilson, Robert Morris (who like Wilson had been a signer of the Declaration of Independence),[35] and other wealthy and influential leaders. Thomas Mifflin and about two dozen other community leaders gathered at the large Wilson home to offer them protection.

An unruly mob composed mostly of militiamen passed by the Wilson house, chanting and threatening. When the main body was almost past, one officer in the house, a one-armed veteran named Campbell, opened a third-story window and began to address them. Some say Campbell shot his pistol into the street.[36]

Eyewitness Allen M'Lane stated, "I saw Captain Campbell, of Colonel Hazen's regiment of the Continental Army, at one of the upper windows, at Wilson's house; heard him distinctly call out to those in arms to pass on."[37]

The activists turned around, came back to the window, and began firing on the house. Thomas Mifflin, at this point, stepped out onto a balcony to address the mob. A window sash next to him was hit by bullets, barely missing him. Mifflin returned fire as did others from inside the house.[38] Philip Hagner, another eyewitness, stated:

> While Mifflin was endeavouring to make himself heard, a man near me fired at him, and though the ball did not hit its aim, it struck the sash near Mifflin's body, and broke it. The General immediately discharged both his pistols into the street. Upon my asking the man if he knew who he had fired at, he replied, "he supposed some damned Tory." and when I informed him that it was General Mifflin, he expressed his surprise and regret.[39]

Allen M'Lane continues:

> We concluded we would run into Wilson's garden, but there we found ourselves exposed to the fire of both the mob in the neighbors' yards, as well as those of Wilson's friends in the house. In a few minutes we were discovered by General Mifflin, who recognized us as officers of the Continental army, and ordered one of the doors of the back building to be opened; at this moment several persons in the house became much alarmed, and jumped out of the second story windows. The back door of the house was immediately opened, and we entered. General Mifflin and Thompson met us on the lower floor, and requested us to follow them upstairs....
>
> When I reached the third story, I looked out of one of the windows in Third

Street, looked up Third Street, could see no person in the street nearer than Dock Street, where the mob had dragged a field-piece. I looked down Third Street, and saw a number of desperate-looking men in their shirt sleeves, coming out of Pear Street, moving towards Wilson's house, armed with bars of iron, and large hammers, and in a minute reached the house, and began to force the doors and windows; they presently made a breach in Third Street, but on entering the house, they received a fire from the staircases and cellar windows, which dropped several of them; the others broke and dispersed, leaving their wounded in the house. Some of Wilson's friends ran down stairs, shut the doors, and barricaded them with tables and chairs, &c.[40]

Then, President Joseph Reed[41] appeared with Continental Army and Philadelphia horsemen and all fighting ended. Arrests were made and the attacking parties carried away.[42] The exact number of casualties is unknown, but reports suggest that "six or seven people were killed, and between seventeen and nineteen were 'dangerously wounded.'"[43] According to the 1847 biography of Joseph Reed, several individuals were killed.[44]

The Fort Wilson Riot reflected the economic and social tensions in Philadelphia during that period. In the 1770s, the city was home to large numbers of fervent patriots, loyal supporters of the king, and Quakers who were pacifists.

The day following the Fort Wilson incident, former president of the Continental Congress Henry Laurens wrote to John Adams: "We are at this moment on the brink of a precipice and what I have long dreaded and often intimated to my friends, seems to be breaking forth a convulsion among the People. Yesterday produced a bloody scene in the streets of this City, the particulars you will probably learn from other friends—and from circumstances which have come to my knowledge this Morning there are grounds for apprehending much more confusion."[45]

In his next letter to Laurens, Adams referred to the riot: "The Convulsions at Philadelphia, are very affecting and alarming but not entirely unexpected to me. The state of Parties and the Nature of their Government, have a long time given me disagreeable Apprehensions. But I hope they will find some Remedy."[46]

Some of the insurgents were jailed; others were freed on bail. In the end, the Assembly granted a blanket pardon and no similar violence occurred again.

Chapter Fourteen

Mifflin's Properties

Mifflin biographer Rossman states that although Mifflin and Washington needed to work closely after the Revolution, their relationship after the Cabal incident cooled, but never broke. Rossman elaborates: "Sometimes, as during the Conway Cabal and the Whiskey Insurrection, relations between them were severely strained. These differences with Washington, although honorable and sincere, have been sufficient to damn Mifflin for posterity. Yet during their lifetimes, the two men remained on good terms despite their differences."[1]

An example of the apparently cordial relationship between Washington and Mifflin in the years following the Conway Cabal appears in a George Washington's diary entry for Sunday, July 22, 1787: "Left town by 5 oclock A.M.—breakfasted at Genl Mifflin's—Rode up with him and others to Spring Mills. and returned to Genl Mifflin's to Dinner after which proceeded to the City."[2]

Similarly, in a diary entry for the same day, French immigrant and vineyard owner Peter Legaux wrote: "This day Gen. Washington, Gen. Mifflin and four others of the Convention did us the honor of paying us a visit in order to see our vineyard and bee houses. In this they found great delight, asked a number of questions, and testified their highest approbation with my manner of managing bees, which gave me a great deal of pleasure."[3]

Despite the cordiality, it's noted that Washington sometimes retained a certain coolness toward Mifflin. Shortly after Washington's death, Charles Biddle, who had been vice-president of the Supreme Executive Council of Pennsylvania when Thomas Mifflin was speaker of the Pennsylvania Provincial Assembly (1785–1787), wrote of Washington[4]:

> When he was elected President of the United States, he lived during the whole of the time that he was in Philadelphia nearly opposite to me. At that time I saw him almost daily. I frequently attended his levees to introduce some friend or acquaintance, and called sometimes with Governor Mifflin. The General

always behaved politely to the Governor, but it appeared to me that he had not forgotten the Governor's opposition to him during the Revolutionary war.[5]

Falls of Schuylkill Estate

At the latter part of his life, Thomas Mifflin had three places of residence: 248 High Street in Philadelphia, a house on Ridge Road at the Falls of Schuylkill, and his farm in Berks County.[6]

In 1779, while still a major general in the Continental Army, Mifflin chose the Falls of Schuylkill, several miles north of Philadelphia, as the location of his rural estate. The 22-acre property, purchased for an annual rental of 60 pounds "payable throughout the lifetime of the grantor." was described in the deed as a "Messuage or Tenement and two Tracts ... of Land."[7] One of these pieces was along the bank of the Schuylkill River, while the other one, on the other side of Ridge Road was the location of Mifflin's house, which was owned by him until 1799. When the property was up for sale in 1833, it was described as "a splendid country seat" with "views of the most picturesque scenery in the Union."[8]

Circa 1850 lithograph of Thomas Mifflin's rural estate at Fountain Green, in Fairmont Park, which was located several miles north of Philadelphia. It was one of his main homes until 1799 (Library of Congress).

Fourteen. Mifflin's Properties

In 1845, a letter in the *New York Mirror* stated:

> I have passed a night at "Fountain Park," the beautiful country seat of a mutual friend of ours. My object in writing now is simply to catalogue the beauties of this enchanting spot, which, taking into view its location, natural advantages, and artificial improvements, is, perhaps, without a rival in the country. The mansion was built, and the grounds originally laid out by Gov. Mifflin, the first chief magistrate of the then new state of Pennsylvania, and apparently without regard to expense or labor.

The letter writer noted that Fountain Park was located on the north side of the "Wissahiccon or Ridge turnpike road at the Falls of the Schuylkill" and about four miles from Philadelphia. He stated that everyone approaching it from the city noticed "its beautiful green sloping lawn, studded with iron and marble jets and fountains in constant play—its stocked deer park, marble statues, flower garden, gardener's cottage, etc." He continued: the mansion

> is built of brown hewn stone, square in front, two and a half stories high, with semi-circular wings, and a portico along the entire front extending to the roof, supported by four massive fluted columns with a raised balcony on the top. The house is surrounded and delightfully shaded by towering sycamores, drooping willows, graceful pines, and fragrant magnolias. A carriage way encircles the mansion, branching off in various directions, embowered with vines, and cooled and refreshed by dripping fountains. The view from the road is greatly improved by the octagonal stone buildings which form the wings or outposts of the central building, and are used as ice-house, bath-house, and hot house, while the background of the picture is filled up with capacious and substantial barns, stables, coach houses, smoke-house, work-shop, etc. Although placed on a healthful eminence some forty feet above the level of the Schuylkil, it is surrounded by an amphitheater of loftier hills, protecting it from the wintry winds, and in summer looking like a green curtain hung against the sky.[9]

The writer goes on to describe the grounds which

> extend to some twenty acres, are remarkably diversified with orchard, meadow, upland woodland, flower and vegetable gardens, etc., and on the northern extremity a never failing rivulet is formed into a couple of lakes, from one of which the summer stock of spring water ice is gathered, while the other by means of pipes is conveyed to the mansion, stables, bath and green houses, garden, lawns, etc. where it is disembogued in half a score hydrants and numerous fountains, whose ceaseless plashing imparts a soothing and delightful air to the place.[10]

There were some features that definitely were not there in Mifflin's time, notably the Norristown and Philadelphia railroad, which in 1845 passed every "hour or two" through the estate's land a half-mile to the rear of the mansion. Years after Mifflin's death, Fountain Green was the site of a brewery and beer garden. Ultimately, the mansion was demolished.

Although Mifflin had left his business enterprises to serve with the army and in government positions, he was still quite wealthy in land holdings. An inventory of about 1779 showed that Mifflin owned a substantial amount of property: his Philadelphia house (at the corner of Front and Chestnut streets); 1,230 acres of land in Cumberland County, Pennsylvania (about 129 miles west of Philadelphia); his farm in Berks County with 620 acres (about 65 miles northwest of Philadelphia); two lots in New Jersey; a country seat five miles from Philadelphia; and houses owned by his wife, Sarah.[11]

Chapter Fifteen

The Continental Congress

Elected to the Continental Congress, 1780

The year 1780 marked the end of Mifflin's military service with the Continental Army. It had been five years since Washington had given him his big break—naming him as his first aide-de-camp. 1780 was also the year that Mifflin was again elected to the Continental Congress. He also was chosen to represent Berks County in the Pennsylvania General Assembly. Even his popularity with the electorate could not overcome the fact that he and John Dickinson (Mifflin's fellow delegate in the First Continental Congress in 1774), had split the non–Federalist vote.

Even if Mifflin had stayed with the army, it is unlikely he would have played much of a role. In 1780, Revolutionary War military activity switched from the northern and middle Atlantic colonies to the southern ones: Virginia, North Carolina, South Carolina, and Georgia. The "man of the hour"—who was in charge of the forces of the South for Washington—was Mifflin's nemesis Nathanael Greene, and the "men of the hour" were leaders like southerner Daniel Morgan, who distinguished himself at both the battles of Saratoga and of Cowpens.

In one of the most important British victories of the war, the British forces captured Charleston, South Carolina, on May 12, 1780. The Patriot army of over 2,500 men surrendered. It was not a promising start for General Greene, but things would soon improve. Later in the month, after a British victory at the Battle of Waxhaws, 26-year-old British cavalry Lieutenant Colonel Banastre Tarleton's troops reportedly massacred American Patriot soldiers who had surrendered. This led to the colonial battle cry of "Tarleton's quarter." The word *quarter* meant a promise not to kill a surrendering enemy. Few British army officers were as despised by American troops as Tarleton. Another one of course, who was equally despised by American patriots, was former Continental Army General Benedict Arnold—who, after turning traitor, actively fought against the very men who a few years before had been his comrades in arms.

As much, or more, than anywhere else in the thirteen colonies, South Carolina residents were divided between those loyal to the King—the Loyalists—and those supporting the independence movement—the Patriots. The former were mostly living in or near the cities, while the latter's support was centered on people in the western part of the state—known as the backcountry.

The nation was clearly divided along political lines. The clear evidence of this was on October 7, 1780, which marked the first significant American win following Britain's May 1780 invasion of Charleston, South Carolina—the battle of Kings Mountain. Taking place south of the border between North and South Carolina, it saw Patriot militia from North Carolina, South Carolina, Virginia, and the future state of Tennessee pitted against loyalist militia. British soldiers were not involved. The Patriots with about 900 troops suffered almost 30 soldiers killed and about 60 wounded. The Loyalists had about 1100 soldiers of which about 250 were killed, 160 were wounded, and almost 700 were captured.

Three months after Kings Mountain, the Patriot forces achieved another major victory by Continental Army troops and backwoods militia, which were commanded by Saratoga hero General Daniel Morgan.

The result of this January 17, 1781, battle of Cowpens, was that Morgan and his men soundly defeated British troops led by Tarleton. The British suffered 110 soldiers killed, while only 12 of Morgan's men died. The number of wounded was similarly uneven: British 200 or more and the Americans 60. In addition, the 500 captured British troops put a serious dent into the ability of the Crown's forces to control the southern part of the United States.

Confederation Congress

After the Articles of Confederation went into effect, the Confederation Congress had its first session on March 2, 1781. It elected Samuel Huntington of Connecticut as its president. He served for four months. He was followed by Delaware's Thomas McKean,[1] who was in the position for a little over three months, and Maryland's John Hanson, who served for a year. Elias Boudinot of New Jersey was next for another year and then came Thomas Mifflin who was president of the Confederation Congress from November 3, 1783, to November 30, 1784, which was one of the most eventful terms of them all. It included the resignation of

Fifteen. The Continental Congress

General Washington as Commander in Chief of the Continental Army, as well as the signing of the peace treaty that ended the American Revolutionary War.

Three of these Confederation Congress presidents went on to serve as governors of states: Huntington served as Connecticut governor for ten years, Mifflin and Kean were governors of Pennsylvania—each for nine years. After Thomas Mifflin, five other men became president of Congress: Richard Henry Lee, John Hancock, Nathaniel Gorham, Arthur St. Clair, and Cyrus Griffin. In 1789, the U.S. Constitution was ratified and the new executive branch of the national government was headed by another "president"—President of the United States George Washington.

The fall of 1781 saw the most decisive battle of the war—the Battle of Yorktown. French and American forces combined outnumbered (almost 20,000 to 9,000 British) and outfought the British who sustained great losses during the three-week siege. They also contained a huge British force on Virginia's Yorktown peninsula after a French fleet prevented the British from leaving by sea, the latter were left with only one alternative—surrender.[2]

On October 19, 1781, British General Lord Cornwallis, along with 8,000 British soldiers and seamen surrendered at Yorktown. By their action, the war, for all intents and purposes—was over. The British could no long afford to fight with the colonists; they were running out of resources, had mounting debt, and were also at war with France and Spain. By November 1781, London heard of Cornwallis's surrender, and on March 5, 1782, the British Parliament passed a bill to make peace with America. The Americans won their independence by defeating the most powerful military force in the world.

In 1782, Continental Congress delegate Theodorick Bland proposed the creation of "a list of books to be imported for the use of the United States in Congress Assembled." In other words, a reference library for the Continental Congress. Bland represented Virginia in the Continental Congress and, at the end of his life became a member of the newly-created United States House of Representatives.

James Madison was appointed as chairman of a committee to research and recommend the composition of the list. The two other committee members left Congress after a short time and were replaced by Thomas Mifflin and North Carolina delegate Hugh Williamson.[3]

As can be guessed from the backgrounds of Mifflin, Madison, and Williamson, the resultant list of over 500 titles (in 1,600 volumes) included a great number of books on political theory, government, law, treaties, geography, and history. Some of the historical categories were:

Greek, Roman, Italian, German, Dutch, French, British, Scottish, Irish, Spanish, Portuguese, Prussian, Russian, Danish, Swedish, Polish, Swiss, Chinese and Turkish. Some of the best-known books on political theory on the list were: Plato's *Republic*, Aristotle's *A Treatise on Government*, Thomas More's *Utopia*, John Locke's *Two Treatises on Government*, and Machiavelli's *The Prince*. The research committee presented this book list to Congress on January 23, 1783.

Although Congress did not act in 1783 on the compilation of books, 17 years later it appointed another committee to create a similar list and did purchase books for use by members of Congress. That collection was the foundation of the Library of Congress.

Elected President of the Continental Congress

From 1782 through 1784, Thomas Mifflin was a member of the Continental Congress, now known as the "Confederation Congress." Anti-Mifflin propaganda did not have a significant long-term impact on his career. About six years after the "Cabal" controversy, Mifflin ascended to the highest public office in the United States at that time when he became president of the Continental Congress. One day later, November 3, 1783, General Washington ordered the disbanding of the Continental Army.

The Articles of Confederation, often considered the country's first constitution, established a unicameral Congress, i.e., a government with only one legislative house or chamber. Delegates were appointed by state legislatures, similar to the first and second Continental Congresses. The president of Congress under the Articles of Confederation was required to be a member of Congress.

Throughout the Continental Congress's existence (1774 to 1788), 12 individuals served as its president. Virginia had three representatives, while Massachusetts, Pennsylvania, and South Carolina each had two. Connecticut, Delaware, Maryland, New Jersey, and New York each had one. Term lengths varied, with Henry Middleton of South Carolina serving for only four days, and John Hancock of Massachusetts holding the position for nearly two-and-a-half years.

Thomas Mifflin, elected as the fifth president of the Continental Congress, served from November 3, 1783, until his term concluded on November 30, 1784. During his tenure, he presided over significant matters of the time, including the approval of the first trade mission to China, the appointment of Thomas Jefferson as minister to France, and the enactment of the Ordinance of 1784, which divided the Northwest Territory into self-governing districts.

The United States Department of State website describes the first American trade mission to China as follows:

> A ship called the *Empress of China* became the first vessel to sail from the United States to China, arriving in Guangzhou (Canton) in August [1784]. The vessel's supercargo, Samuel Shaw, had been appointed as an unofficial consul by the U.S. Congress, but he did not make contact with Chinese officials or gain diplomatic recognition for the United States. Since the 1760s, all trade with Western nations had been conducted at Guangzhou through a set group of Chinese merchants with official licenses to trade. Some residents of the American colonies had engaged in the China trade before this time, but this journey marked the new nation's entrance into the lucrative China trade in tea, porcelain, and silk.[4]

Samuel Shaw went on to serve as the first consul to China from 1786 to 1794. Shaw earlier played another part in the history of the United States—he had reported misconduct by the commander in chief of the Continental Navy, Esek Hopkins. One of the charges was that Hopkins, against orders of the Continental Congress, had tortured British prisoners of war. He then retaliated with a criminal libel suit against Shaw and another whistleblower, Richard Marven. Congress paid the legal expenses of the two sailors. This led to Congress's passage of the first whistleblower law in 1778. Today, July 30 is celebrated as National Whistleblower Day in the United States to recognize the passage of this law and " the crucial role whistleblowers play today in defending our nation from waste, fraud and abuse."

The 1778 Continental Congress resolved "That it is the duty of all persons in the service of the United States, as well as all other the inhabitants thereof, to give the earliest information to Congress or other proper authority of any misconduct, frauds or misdemeanors committed by any officers or persons in the service of these states, which may come to their knowledge."

Congress ordered that "the secretary of Congress furnish the petitioners with attested copies of the records of Congress, so far as they relate to the appointment of Esek Hopkins, Esq., to any command in the continental navy, and his dismission from the same, and also to the proceedings of Congress upon the complaint of the petitioners against."[5]

The Ordinance of 1784

On April 23, 1784, the Ordinance of 1784 was approved by the Confederation Congress, which was convened in Annapolis, Maryland. This ordinance established "a framework for the establishment of territorial governments" in the area obtained from Great Britain situated west of Pennsylvania, south of the Great Lakes, north of the Ohio River, and east of the Mississippi River.[6] Composed by Thomas Jefferson of Virginia, with assistance from Jeremiah Townley Chase of Maryland, and David Howell of Rhode Island, the Ordinance paved the way for the division of the western territory, known as the Northwest Territory, into individual states that would be equal to the original thirteen states. Significantly, the Ordinance of 1784 initially prohibited slavery in the territory. However, after debate, this provision was dropped in order to secure its final approval. The Ordinance of 1784 was later superseded by the Ordinance of 1787, which did prohibit slavery in the territory.

On December 23, 1783, in the Maryland State House in Annapolis, George Washington resigned his commission as the commander in chief of the Continental Army. Thomas Mifflin's responsibility in his capacity as president of the Continental Congress, was to accept Washington's resignation. Horace Elisha Scudder describes the scene in his 1889 Washington biography:

"General George Washington Resigning His Commission" on December 23, 1783, to the Congress of the Confederation. Accepting it is president of the Congress, Thomas Mifflin, who is on the left side. Completed in 1826, this 12 ft × 18 ft painting by John Trumbull is in the United States Capitol Building's rotunda in Washington, D.C.

Fifteen. The Continental Congress

On December 23 1783, Congress was assembled at Annapolis. The gallery was filled with ladies. The governor, council, and legislature of Maryland, several officers, and the consul-general of France were on the floor. The members of Congress were seated and wore their hats to signify that they represented the government. The spectators stood with bare heads. General Washington entered and was conducted by the secretary of Congress to a seat. When all was quiet, General Mifflin who was then president of Congress, turned to Washington and said "The United States, in Congress assembled, is prepared to receive the communications of the commander in chief." Washington rose and read a short address, in which he resigned his commission.[7]

George Washington responded:

Mr. President, the great events on which my resignation depended having at length taken place; I have now the honor of offering my sincere Congratulations to Congress and of presenting myself before them to surrender into their hands the trust committed to me, and to claim the indulgence of retiring from the Service of my Country.

Happy in the confirmation of our Independence and Sovereignty, and pleased with the opportunity afforded the United States of becoming a respectable Nation, I resign with satisfaction the Appointment I accepted with diffidence. A diffidence in my abilities to accomplish so arduous a task, which however was superseded by a confidence in the rectitude of our Cause, the support of the Supreme Power of the Union, and the patronage of Heaven.

The Successful termination of the War has verified the most sanguine expectations, and my gratitude for the interposition of Providence, and the assistance I have received from my Country-men, increases with every review of the momentous Contest.

While I repeat my obligations to the Army in general, I should do injustice to my own feelings not to acknowledge in this place the peculiar Services and distinguished merits of the Gentlemen who have been attached to my person during the War. It was impossible the choice of confidential Officers to compose my family should have been more fortunate. Permit me Sir, to recommend in particular those, who have continued in Service to the present moment, as worthy of the favorable notice and patronage of Congress.

I consider it an indispensable duty to close this last solemn act of my Official life, by commending the Interests of our dearest Country to the protection of Almighty God, and those who have the superintendence of them, to his holy keeping.

Having now finished the work assigned me, I retire from the great theater of Action; and bidding an Affectionate farewell to this August body under whose orders I have so long acted, I here offer my Commission, and take my leave of all the employments of public life.[8]

Washington handed the paper of his speech to President Mifflin, who replied:

The United States in Congress assembled receive with emotions too affecting for utterance this solemn resignation of the authorities, under which you have led their troops with success through a perilous and a doubtful war.

Called upon by your country to defend its invaded rights you accepted the sacred charge before it had found alliances and whilst it was without funds or a government to support you.

You have conducted the great military contest with wisdom and fortitude, invariably regarding the rights of the civil power through all disasters and changes. You have by the love and confidence of your fellow citizens enabled them to display their martial genius and transmit their fame to posterity. You have persevered till these United States aided by a magnanimous king & nation have been enabled, under a just Providence, to close the war in freedom, safety and independence, on which happy event we sincerely join you in congratulations.

Having defended the standard of liberty in this new world, having taught a lesson useful to those who inflict and to those who feel oppression you retire from the great theatre of action with the blessings of your fellow citizens: But the glory of your virtues will not terminate with your military command: it will continue to animate remotest ages.

We feel with you our obligations to the army in general and will particularly charge ourselves with the interests of those confidential Officers who have attended your person to this affecting moment.

We join you in commanding the interests of our dearest Country to the protection of Almighty God, beseeching Him to dispose the hearts and minds of its citizens to improve the opportunity afforded them of becoming a happy and respectable nation; And for you we address to Him our earnest prayers that a life so beloved may be fostered with all his care—that your days may be happy as they have been illustrious and that He will finally give you that reward, which this World cannot give.[9]

Connecticut artist John Trumbull's 12-foot-high by 18-foot-wide painting of the event was finished in 1824.[10] Titled *General George Washington Resigning His Commission*, it resides today in the Rotunda of the U.S. Capitol building in Washington, D.C. After completing the painting, Trumbull (1756–1843) toured with it to Providence, Hartford, Albany, Philadelphia, and elsewhere.

Washington's relinquishment of power served as a powerful example in history, demonstrating the importance of a military leader yielding authority to a democratically elected civilian government. Washington's act was not only a model of a peaceful transfer of power but also set a precedent for limiting presidential terms. Until the 1940s, all U.S. Presidents followed Washington's lead, restricting their time in office to two four-year terms. This changed in 1940 when President Franklin Roosevelt sought and won a third term. In 1947, Congress passed an amendment to the U.S. Constitution, ratified in 1951, limiting the president to two terms. Rawle speaks of Washington's resignation of his commission:

In this capacity, [Mifflin] had the distinguished honor of receiving at Annapolis, from one of the first of warriors, and best of statesmen, the resignation of that commission which had borne him to glory, and his country to independence. The *answer* of the president to the dignified, yet respectful address of the commander in chief, *closely resembled* the manly and simple eloquence of the latter. They are both recorded in the journals of Congress, but those journals could *not record* the *feelings* which the occasion inspired. The audience was public, and the impressions made as well by the act itself, as by the manner in which it was conducted, long remained on the minds of all who were present.[11]

In 1783, the war was over, and despite the memories of the Conway Cabal, Thomas Mifflin was again elected as a Pennsylvania delegate to the Continental Congress. It was the year of the Treaty of Paris, which was to end the American Revolutionary War. This Treaty of Paris is not to be confused with other treaties of the same name: the Treaty of Paris of 1763, which concluded the French and Indian War,[12] and the Treaty of Paris of 1899, which ended the Spanish-American War and officially recognized the independence of Cuba while ceding Guam and Puerto Rico to the United States.[13]

To get the needed number of delegate signatures for the Treaty of Paris with Britain, Mifflin sent Josiah Harmar to the delegates representing New Jersey, Connecticut, and South Carolina, who had not shown up at the Continental Congress signing. That task was completed on January 14, 1784, and on that day Congress voted to ratify the Treaty of Paris. President of Congress Thomas Mifflin presided over the ratification, which would officially end the American Revolutionary War. Next, it was needed to send it back to Paris by March 3, 1784.

The original, ratified Treaty of Paris document was signed by only two people: President Mifflin, and the Secretary of the Congress Charles Thomson. Interestingly, Thomson (1729–1824) was also one of only two men to sign the Declaration of Independence document on July 4, 1776. For the Declaration, Thompson in his capacity as the secretary of congress, was joined by John Hancock who was serving as the president of Congress.

Notably, when the ratified versions of the Treaty of Paris were exchanged on May 12, 1784, Thomas Mifflin, as president of the only national governing body at the time, became the first person in history to be recognized by the British government as the "President of the United States."

On January 14, 1784, from Annapolis, Maryland, Thomas Mifflin wrote to the American Peace Commissioners, informing them that Colonel Josiah Harmar had been chosen by Congress to carry the ratified treaty to Europe.[14] Mifflin wrote:

This day, nine States being represented in Congress, Vizt: Massachusetts, Rhode Island, Connecticut, Pennsylvania, Delaware, Maryland, Virginia, North Carolina, and South Carolina, together with one Member from New-Hampshire, and one Member from New-Jersey, The Treaty of Peace was ratified by the unanimous Vote of the Members; This being done, Congress by an unanimous Vote, ordered a Proclamation to be issued, enjoying the strict and faithful Observance thereof, and published an earnest Recommendation to the several States in the very Words of the 5th. Article—They have likewise resolved, that the Ratification of the Definitive Treaty of Peace between the United States & Great Britain, be transmitted, with all possible Dispatch, under the Care of a faithful Person, to our Ministers in France, who have negotiated the Treaty; to be exchanged; and have appointed Colonel Josiah Harmar to that Service.[15]

Biographer Rawle states:

General Mifflin, after discharging the duties of president of Congress, with much dignity and effect, was left out of the new delegation from Pennsylvania, and for a short time remained in private life. But his native state, accustomed to see his name enrolled in the list of her public servants, did not long leave him in retirement.

In 1785 he was chosen a member of the state legislature, and when that body convened, they elected him their speaker. In 1788 he was placed by popular suffrage in the seat which had been occupied by Franklin, and became first a member, and afterwards president of the supreme executive council.[16]

The relationship between Mifflin and Washington was certainly at least cordial a half-a-dozen years after the Conway Cabal fizzled out. On May 31, 1784, Mifflin wrote to his old Commander in Chief from Annapolis, Maryland:

On Friday I expect to have the Pleasure of seeing Mount Vernon in Company with Mrs. Mifflin and Mr. Lloyds family—But there is a possibility that we shall not proceed farther than Alexandria on that day as the setting of Congress on Thursday may be so late as to prevent my leaving Annapolis before Friday Morning. at every event I have determined not to see Philadelphia before I have the Satisfaction of paying a Visit at Mount Vernon. I am with the greatest sincerity and Attachment Dear Sir Your Obedient humble Servant. Thomas Mifflin.[17]

Thomas Mifflin's political career in Pennsylvania saw him elected as the 35th speaker of the Pennsylvania General Assembly on October 27, 1785. He was re-elected on October 26, 1786. However, due to illness, Mifflin resigned as speaker on December 21, 1786. Gerardus Wynkoop II served as speaker in his absence.[18] On December 26, 1787, Mifflin resumed his role as speaker after recovering from his illness. During this period, Thomas Mifflin was unanimously elected for a third term as speaker of the Pennsylvania General Assembly on October 24, 1787.[19]

It's worth noting that only four individuals, including Thomas Mifflin, have served terms as both speaker of the Pennsylvania General Assembly and governor of Pennsylvania, with the others being Simon Snyder (1808–1817), Joseph Ritner (1835–1839), and William F. Packer (1858–1861).

During his tenure as speaker of the Pennsylvania House, Thomas Mifflin actively participated in two constitutional conventions, one for the federal constitution and the other for a state constitution. He represented the Commonwealth of Pennsylvania at the United States Constitutional Convention in 1787 and served as the president of the Pennsylvania Constitutional Convention, which met from 1789 through 1790.

Throughout his life, Mifflin faced accusations from political adversaries regarding his alleged alcohol consumption. Rossman in his biography of Mifflin evaluates the stories: "That an old warrior like him was a heavy drinker was probably true, as it certainly was true of many revolutionary heroes and prominent figures in those early years of the republic. But then the attitude toward drinking alcoholic beverages was different from our own."[20]

Rossman believed that "far more disabling to Governor Mifflin than drink was his chronic sickness." He notes that "Although its exact nature is still unclear, the letters, diaries, newspapers, account books, and executive minutes from revolutionary times to the day of his death, are strewn with continuous references to his illness."[21] Rossman noted two occasions when illness most affected Mifflin's duties to the detriment of his reputation: his resignation from the Quartermaster's Department during the Conway Cabal and during inauguration ceremonies after his third gubernatorial win.[22] The first of these contributed to the disaster at Valley Forge; the second of these led to his death at a relatively early age.

In his review of Rossman's biography, historian John H. Powell states: "Thomas Mifflin is usually remembered today in Pennsylvania for two regrettable things: his part in the Conway Cabal and his enthusiastic way with wine after dinner. Dr. Rossman, in this first biography of Mifflin ever prepared, sensibly explains.... Mifflin's drinking was, and has always been, grossly exaggerated."[23]

The source of Mifflin's illnesses at key times in his career has been discussed for more than 200 years. During his life, his political enemies often chalked it up to overindulgence in alcohol. While there is no evidence Mifflin ever abstained from alcohol, the question of his dependence on it remains unanswered. Other contemporaries contended he had a serious health issue—or issues—throughout his life. After all, he only lived to age 56—but that was longer than both parents, with his mother passing at 37 and his father at 44 years old.

Mifflin's health challenges were not unique among Revolutionary War generals. His rival, Nathanael Greene, missed one of the most critical battles of the war—the Battle of Long Island. Greene had organized the American defensive positions, but he was bed-ridden with a high fever during the August 27, 1776, battle.[24] British General Cornwallis claimed illness during the surrender at Yorktown in 1781. Additionally, Union Army General John Sedgwick missed the First Battle of Bull Run in 1861 due to cholera.

In the 1700s, many illnesses and deaths could be attributed to poor hygiene, sanitation, diseases, and the lack of medical knowledge. A year earlier than Mifflin's death, George Washington's doctors tried to balance the fluids in his body, and he was bled four times—with the last extraction taking 32 ounces of blood. He died at age 67.

Chapter Sixteen

The Constitutional Convention

Constitutional Convention of 1787

In preparation for the Constitutional Convention of 1787, each state legislature selected delegates to create a new constitution for the United States. Pennsylvania was represented by Thomas Mifflin, Benjamin Franklin, Gouverneur Morris, Robert Morris, George Clymer, Thomas Fitzsimons, Jared Ingersoll, and James Wilson. The Convention's first scheduled meeting was on May 14, 1787, at the State House in Philadelphia, which was the same building where the Declaration of Independence was signed. However, a quorum was not achieved until May 25. The average age of a delegate to the Constitutional Convention was approximately 44 years old. Mifflin was 43.

Of the 55 delegates who attended the Constitutional Convention, 40 had served as delegates to the Continental Congress. Mifflin was one of seven signers of the Constitution who had also signed the Continental Association in 1774. The others were: George Washington, Roger Sherman, George Reed, John Dickinson, John Rutledge, and William Livingston.

A total of six Constitution signers had signed the Declaration of Independence (1776), and five had signed the Articles of Confederation (1777–1781).[1] Interestingly, at the Constitutional Convention the delegates referred to themselves and other delegates as *deputies*.

Many of the most famous Americans of the time represented their states at the Constitutional Convention: George Washington, Benjamin Franklin, James Madison, and Alexander Hamilton. Thomas Jefferson and John Adams were notable exceptions—Jefferson was in Paris serving as the American minister to France, and Adams was in London as the United States minister to Great Britain.

Of the 55 delegates, only Thomas Mifflin and 38 others signed the resulting Constitution on September 17, 1787. More than one-half of the signers were lawyers (20 or 21).[2]

Non-lawyer merchant signers included Mifflin and fellow Pennsylvanians Clymer, Fitzsimons, and Morris, as well as Gilman and Langdon from New Hampshire, Broom from Delaware, and Gorham from Massachusetts.

Regarding religious affiliation, 26 of the 55 attendees and 19 of the 39 signers were what would be known as Episcopalians.[3] After the Episcopalians, the next most common religious affiliation of the U.S. Constitutional Convention delegates were Presbyterians (about 11), and Congregationalists (about 7). Only John Dickinson of Delaware and George Clymer of Pennsylvania shared Mifflin's Quaker background. (Both Dickinson and Clymer later joined the Episcopal Church, while Mifflin in later life identified as a Lutheran.)

Twenty-three of the Constitution's signers were veterans of the Revolutionary War.[4] Surprisingly, of the 89 men who served as either a brigadier general or a major general in the Continental Army during the Revolutionary War, only two were among the 39 delegates who signed the U.S. Constitution—George Washington and Thomas Mifflin. Rawle discusses Thomas Mifflin's role at the Constitutional Convention of 1787:

> Prior to this, however, in 1787, when it became obvious to all that the confederation of the states was inadequate to their safety and happiness, and a convention for the purpose of framing a constitution was agreed on, he was chosen a member.... Of the share which he took in the formation of that unequalled constitution, which has so much conduced to the fame and happiness of our country, we have no satisfactory knowledge. Their proceedings were secret, and we can only glean from the imperfect journal of Mr. Gates part of their debates. His name appears as one of the illustrious band who signed the constitution, of whom *but one now* remains![5]

When Rawle's short biography of Mifflin was published in 1826, only one signer of the U.S. Constitution was still living—James Madison, who signed for the state of Virginia along with George Washington and Judge John Blair.[6] Madison passed away in 1836 at age 85. After the Constitutional Convention, he worked to get the Constitution ratified by all of the states, served in the House of Representatives (1789–1797), and was United States secretary of state (1801–1809). (Between 1809 and 1817 Madison served two terms as the fifth president of the United States.)

Sixteen. The Constitutional Convention

Mifflin Reads Constitution to Pennsylvania Assembly

On Tuesday, September 18, 1787, at 11:00 a.m. the new United States Constitution was presented to the Pennsylvania Assembly by three of the Constitutional Convention's best-known delegates: Benjamin Franklin, Thomas Fitzsimons, and Thomas Mifflin. Mifflin took on the task of reading the entire document to the lawmakers and citizens gathered for this event. The *Pennsylvania Gazette* reported that the "large crowd of citizens, who stood in the gallery of the Assembly room, and who testified the highest pleasure in seeing that great work at last perfected, which promises, when adopted, to give security, stability, and dignity to the government of the United States."[7]

In November, Jefferson and Adams exchanged opinions on the new national constitution from their posts in Paris and London respectively. Jefferson's letter of November 13, 1787, expresses his reservations:

> "How do you like our new constitution? I confess there are things in it which stagger all my dispositions to subscribe to what such an assembly has proposed. the house of federal representatives will not be adequate to the management of affairs either foreign or federal. their President seems a bad edition of a Polish king. he may be reelected from 4. years to 4. years for life. reason & experience prove to us that a chief magistrate, so continuable, is an officer for life. when one or two generations shall have proved that this is an office for life, it becomes on every succession worthy of intrigue, of bribery, of force, & even of foreign interference. it will be of great consequence to France & England to have America governed by a Galloman or Angloman. once in office, & possessing the military force of the union, without either the aid or check of a council, he would not be easily dethroned, even if the people could be induced to withdraw their votes from him. I wish that at the end of the 4. years they had made him forever ineligible a second time. indeed I think all the good of this new constitution might have been couched in three or four new articles to be added to the good, old, & venerable fabric, which should have been preserved even as a religious relic.—"[8]

In a letter dated December 6, 1787, Adams responds that he would have "given more Power to the President and less to the Senate." Interestingly, in less than ten years, Adams will occupy that very position—President of the United States. Adams states that he differs from Jefferson regarding the new Constitution and continues:

> You are afraid of the one—I, of the few. We agree perfectly that the many Should have a full fair and perfect Representation.—You are Apprehensive of monarchy: I, of Aristocracy.—I would therefore have given more Power to the President and less to the Senate. The Nomination and Appointment to all offices I would have given to the President, assisted only by a Privy Council of

his own ... but not a Vote or Voice would I have given to the Senate or any Senator, unless he were of the Privy Council. Faction and Distraction are the sure and certain Consequence of giving to a Senate a Vote in the distribution of Offices.

You are apprehensive the President when once chosen, will be chosen again and again as long as he lives. So much the better as it appears to me.—You are apprehensive of foreign Interference Intrigue, Influence.—So am I.—But, as often as Elections happen, the danger of foreign Influence recurs. the less frequently they happen the less danger.—and if the Same Man may be chosen again, it is probable he will be, and the danger of foreign Influence will be less. Foreigners, Seeing little Prospect will have less Courage for Enterprise.

Elections, my dear sir, Elections to Offices which are great objects of ambition, I look at with terror.—Experiments of this kind have been so often tried, and so universally found productive of Horrors, that there is great Reason to dread them.[9]

U.S. Constitution, 1787

Amazingly, the final version of the U.S. Constitution, consisting of about 4,500 words, was ready for signatures in less than a hundred

The Assembly Room of Philadelphia's Independence Hall. The Declaration of Independence (1776) was signed by delegates of the Second Continental Congress in this room. Eleven years later, the U.S. Constitution was signed in this room at the Constitutional Convention (Library of Congress).

Sixteen. The Constitutional Convention

working days.[10] The approval of only nine out of the 13 states was needed for the Constitution to pass, and this occurred on June 21, 1788, when the ninth state, New Hampshire, ratified the Constitution. It then became the supreme governing document of the country.

In many countries—including Great Britain—virtually any laws can be changed by the nation's legislative body—in the case of Britain, Parliament—at any time. However, provisions found in the U.S. Constitution can only be changed by a long and involved amendment process.

Notably, George Washington was sworn in as the nation's first president on April 30, 1789, several months before North Carolina and Rhode Island ratified the Constitution. North Carolina ratified it on November 21, 1789, and Rhode Island ratified it on May 29, 1790, the same day that Thomas Mifflin's former commanding officer, General Israel Putnam, passed away.

Thirty-three of the signers of the Constitution either were or had been members of the Continental Congress. Thomas Mifflin and Nathaniel Gorham had served as Continental Congress presidents. Of all the members of the Constitutional Convention, perhaps only George Washington, Robert Morris, Daniel Carroll, and Daniel of St. Thomas Jenifer were wealthier than Thomas Mifflin.

Signature of Thomas Mifflin appears here on the last page of the U.S. Constitution. Mifflin and 38 other men signed it in 1787. George Washington's name can be seen in the upper portion of this image, and Benjamin Franklin's signature appears directly above Mifflin's.

With the passage of the U.S. Constitution, the new nation began to take shape.[11] As the Constitution took effect, important issues arose that required immediate attention. The new federal government was burdened with debt incurred during the Revolutionary War. Proposals to create a national bank arose. Former general Alexander Hamilton was chosen by his commander in chief to be the first secretary of the treasury. Washington also selected another trusted general, Henry Knox, to be in charge of the military affairs of the federal government as the first secretary of war.

Mifflin Farm

During the time just before and just after the Constitution Convention, Mifflin played an active role in state affairs as a member of the General Assembly for Philadelphia County (1785 to 1788).

It was during this period that he had a farm named Angelica near Redding, Pennsylvania. He would own it for about 20 years. It was located only about 13 miles west of pioneer Daniel Boone's birthplace.[12] The Boone family sold its home in 1750, which was about 24 years before Thomas Mifflin bought the Angelica property.[13]

On April 9, 1788, writer John Penn,[14] the former chief proprietor of the province of Pennsylvania, visited Thomas Mifflin at Angelica. Penn later wrote in his *John Penn's Journal of a Visit to Reading, Harrisburg, Carlisle, and Lancaster, in 1788*:

> The General and Mrs. Mifflin received us in a neat farmhouse, and being very early themselves, provided a second breakfast for us, though it was then only half past seven. He took us around some of his improvements, and I rode with him to various points of view which commanded the town of Reading and circumjacent hills and valleys. He farms about twelve hundred acres and has a Scotch farmer, who conducts the business. One hundred [acres] of meadow-land he waters. One neighbor of the General's is one of the marrying Dunkers. They live in their own houses like other countrymen, but wear their beards long.
>
> [Penn went on to relate:] General Mifflin, with agreeable frankness and affability, pressed us both to stay for an early dinner, to which we sat down about one o'clock. After dinner I mounted my horse and came into Carlisle Road about three miles off, at Sinking Spring.[15]

Thomas Mifflin's influence and legacy extended beyond his political roles, with many towns, streets, schools, etc., named after him. Mifflin County in Pennsylvania was formed on September 19, 1789, from parts of Cumberland and Northumberland Counties; this county bears

Thomas Mifflin's name as a recognition of his significant contributions during the Revolutionary War and his leadership at the state and national levels.

In the 19th century, 411–square-mile Mifflin County's position near the geographical center of Pennsylvania, combined with the railroad and the Pennsylvania Canal, made it a major transportation hub.[16] As of 2022, the county had a population of approximately 46,000.[17]

The practice of naming counties after prominent individuals, particularly those who played pivotal roles in the Revolutionary War and the founding of the nation, was very popular in the late–18th century and throughout the 19th century as new states were added to the Union. A number of years after Thomas Mifflin was governor; the second and third governors of the state, Thomas McKean and Simon Snyder, respectively, would also have Pennsylvania counties named after them. Thomas Mifflin wasn't alone among Revolutionary War generals with a Pennsylvania county named for him. Other Revolutionary War generals would each have a namesake county like: John Armstrong, Richard Butler, Nathanael Greene, Marquis de Lafayette (Fayette County), Hugh Mercer, James Potter, John Sullivan, Joseph Warren, George Washington, and Anthony Wayne.

Few people in the United States have had as many towns, streets, schools, and buildings named after them as Thomas Mifflin. This is a reminder of the place he held in the hearts of the people who elected him to serve and represent them on the municipal, state, and federal levels.

In 1981, the Pennsylvania Historical and Museum Commission installed a historical marker in Lewistown, Mifflin County, Pennsylvania. It reads: "Mifflin County Formed September 19, 1789 from Cumberland and Northumberland counties, and named for Thomas Mifflin, Governor, 1790–99. County seat, Lewistown, was laid out 1790; incorporated 1795. Important in Pennsylvania's canal development and early iron industry."[18]

Chapter Seventeen

President of the Supreme Executive Council of Pennsylvania

The Supreme Executive Council of Pennsylvania was created by the Pennsylvania Constitution of 1776. Thomas Mifflin served as its seventh and final president from October 1788 to October 1790. He replaced Benjamin Franklin, who had served in that position from 1785 to 1788.

Pennsylvania Constitutional Convention Called, 1789

As the deficiencies of the existing Pennsylvania state constitution of 1776 became apparent in light of the new U.S. Constitution, a Pennsylvania Constitutional Convention was convened in 1789 with the purpose of replacing the outdated document. Pennsylvania, over the years of its inclusion in the United States, has had five state constitutions, enacted in 1776, 1790, 1838, 1874, and 1968.

There was much heated debate within Pennsylvania as the prospect of an amended Pennsylvania State Constitution was considered. Its citizens just broke free of a monarchy that curtailed individual freedoms and imposed unfair taxation. How could Pennsylvania avoid this—and yet govern effectively? State leaders looked at the construction of the federal government's constitution with its three separate branches of government, and their discussions involved topics like: electors, the governor's executive powers, length of time to serve, and property and personal taxation.

Chief Justice Thomas McKean identified what in his opinion were the main defects of the 1776 constitution: "The balance of the one, the few and the many is not well poised in the State; the Legislature is too powerful for the executive and judicial branches. We have now but one branch; we must have another branch, a negative in the executive, stability in our laws and permanency in the magistracy before we shall be reputable, safe and happy."

Ten years older than Thomas Mifflin, Thomas McKean was born in New London Township, Pennsylvania. It was only a few miles from the spot where Pennsylvania, Maryland, and Delaware meet. After studying law with a cousin, McKean received some of the best legal education in the world at Middle Temple in London, England. A long-time member of the Delaware colonial assembly, in 1774 he became a Delaware delegate to the first Continental Congress and served most of the time until 1783. During those years, he signed both the Declaration of Independence (he was the last to sign it—on January 18, 1777), and the Articles of Confederation. For a short time in 1781 he served as president of the Continental Congress. During the Revolutionary War he was a Pennsylvania militia colonel.

Always a busy man, at one time McKean served as president of Delaware while he was also chief justice of Pennsylvania (he held the latter position for 22 years). McKean served as both a delegate to the state convention that ratified the United States Constitution in 1787, and a delegate to the Pennsylvania Convention of 1789–90. In 1799, former Federalist McKean ran for governor of Pennsylvania as a Democrat-Republican. Defeating a Federalist candidate, he succeeded Mifflin as governor. (Mifflin was prohibited by the state constitution from running a fourth time.) McKean was reelected as governor twice, and died at age 83 in 1817.

Rawle discusses Mifflin's part in the Pennsylvania State Constitutional Convention:

> The imperfections of our state constitution, which had long been complained of, seemed to be rendered more visible on comparing it with the constitution of the United States, and a convention was speedily called for the purpose of amending it. [Thomas Mifflin] was president of this convention.
>
> "In the formation of political constitutions, [Mifflin] was not expected to take a lead. His natural disposition and confirmed habits were of an *ardent* and *active* kind: he was *unaccustomed* to and perhaps unqualified for slow deliberation and patient investigation. To the great leading principles of individual and political rights, he was no stranger; but his knowledge on those subjects was rather *intuitive* than *acquired*.

Rawle continues with a review of the issues considered by the state convention delegates:

> In the great *division* of the powers of government-its partition into *three parts-all* concurred, but there were some diversity of opinion, and some

warmth of debate, in respect to several important articles, and the charges of *aristocracy* and *anarchy* were reciprocally, but decently made. The manner of electing the governor—for all agreed that the executive power ought no longer to remain in the hands of a council—was *one* subject of warm and frequent debate. A close conformity to the constitution of the United States in this respect, by making use of the medium of *electors*, was much pressed. Experience has shown how entirely nominal this mode of election has become in respect to the president of the United States; and such would *undoubtedly* have been the result, if we had adopted it in the *state*. Another serious subject of contest—*universal suffrage*—was advocated as part of the inherent rights of man, while some of the members, highly respected for talents and influence, fruitlessly endeavored to establish a compound ratio founded on property and personal taxation....

As president of the convention, Mifflin was not required to vote, but in committees of the whole he could both debate and vote, yet his *voice* was seldom heard. His *suffrages* were always on the popular side.[1]

Pennsylvania Constitution Adopted, 1790

William Rawle provides insights into Mifflin's terms as governor of Pennsylvania during the late 1700s, drawing from his own experience as the U.S. district attorney for Pennsylvania during that period. It is important to remember that Rawle knew and worked with Thomas Mifflin before he wrote Mifflin's biography. Rawle knew many people of that period as he worked inside Pennsylvania's government. He had access to them, the opportunity to interview them, and perhaps most important of all, he had firsthand knowledge of Mifflin's character, accomplishments, leadership abilities, etc. Rawle discusses Mifflin's terms as governor, saying:

> As soon as the [state] constitution went into operation, the election of a governor became an interesting subject. Wilson, whose views in the convention were entirely theoretical and abstract, *deserted* his new associates, and concurred with a small number of citizens in recommending General *St. Clair* for this high office. St. Clair then possessed a good military reputation. He was a man of no extraordinary attainments, but his private character was fair, and he was much approved of by the federal party; yet *many* of the federalists *regretted* the nomination, and foresaw that, by opposing the election of Mifflin, he would be driven into the *opposite* political ranks. The mode of election finally adopted by the convention was admitted to render the success of St. Clair *exceedingly doubtful*.

Rawle also points out one of Thomas Mifflin's finest attributes—one that allowed him to have success in his civilian career: "His *happiest* exhibitions were those of an *executive* character. He was *ready* to conceive, and *prompt* to execute whatever the duties of such an office required."[2] Rawle states:

> The nine years which limited [Mifflin's] continuance *in office*, were not altogether years of quiet, regular detail. In 1793, the public mind was disturbed by the indiscretions of the minister from France [Edmond-Charles Genêt]; and during that and two or three succeeding years, the administration of the United States received from the Governor of Pennsylvania a ready and efficient compliance with *all its* requisitions. In this he evinced the merit of subjecting, to his sense of duty, those predilections in favor of France, which he entertained in common with numbers of his fellow citizens.[3]

Rawle then reminds the reader that his own position as the U.S. district attorney for Pennsylvania during the last decade of the 1700s gave him a front row seat from which to observe Thomas Mifflin and rate his effectiveness as governor of Pennsylvania:

> The present writer then filled a station which gave him the best opportunities of observing the official proceedings of Governor Mifflin, and he bears a willing testimony to his *prompt* and *effective* compliance with the requisitions of the President on every occasion. He did not, like the executive council in 1783, on the occasion already adverted to, *deliberate* and *discuss* when it was his duty *to act*. It was a strong practical proof, that the *executive power* in a republic is most safely confided to a single hand.[4]

The year 1790 also marked the passing of Pennsylvania's most famous person. On April 17, 1790, Benjamin Franklin died in Philadelphia at age 84. The Rev. William Smith, the first provost of the College of Philadelphia, wrote about the night of Franklin's death:

> On the evening of his death a company of gentlemen were seated at the dinner table of Governor Mifflin, at the Falls of Schuylkill. It consisted of Thomas McKean, Henry Hill (a private gentleman of rank in old Philadelphia), the Hon. Thomas Willing, David Rittenhouse and Dr. Smith. During the dinner 'a great thunderstorm arose' and the group received word that Franklin had passed away.[5]

The Reverend Smith, "under the impulse of the moment, wrote the following lines without leaving the table":

> Cease! cease, ye clouds, your elemental strife,
> Why rage ye thus, as if to threaten life?
> Seek, seek no more to shake our souls with dread,
> What busy mortal told you "Franklin's dead?"
> What, though he yields at Jove's imperious nod,
> With Rittenhouse he left his magic rod.[6]

Mr. Willing, not to be outdone by Dr. Smith, immediately wrote the following:

> What means that flash, the thunder's awful roar-
> The blazing sky-unseen, unheard before?
> Sage Smith replies, "Our Franklin is no more."
> The clouds, long subject to his magic chain,
> Exulting now, their liberty regain.[7]

Four days later, Franklin was buried in Christ Church graveyard at the corner of Arch and Fifth Streets. It was estimated that 20,000 people lined the route of the funeral procession. It was quite a number for a city that only had 6,700 homes. Dr. Smith described the scene:

> The mourners were preceded by all the clergy of the city, including the readers of the Hebrew congregation. The corpse was carried by citizens. The pall was borne by Governor Thomas Mifflin, Chief Justice McKean, Thomas Willing, president of the Bank of North America, Samuel Powell, the mayor of the city, William Bingham and David Rittenhouse. Bells were tolled and minute guns were fired during the time that the procession was passing. In the line of the procession were the Supreme Executive Council, the General Assembly of the State, the Judges of the Supreme Court, members of the bar, the corporation of the city, the printers of the city, with their journeymen and apprentices, the Philosophical Society, the College of Physicians, the Faculty and students of the College of Philadelphia, and various other societies, besides a numerous and respectable body of citizens.[8]

Political Parties and the New Republic

The first years of the new republic were times the political party structures were in a state of formation. Washington was elected by a unanimous vote of the electors. No other U.S. president would enjoy that amount of popularity.

The dominant political parties of the 1790s were the Federalists—composed of strong supporters of Washington and his polices—and the Democratic-Republicans, which was formed according the ideas and polices of Thomas Jefferson and his allies.

The differences between the two factions could be profound: what powers did the federal government have? What powers belonged to the individual states? What if the federal and states disagreed upon an action? What about the third branch of government—the Supreme Court? When could they override actions of the national or state governments? The U.S. Constitution answered many of these questions,

Seventeen. President of the Supreme Executive Council

but certainly not all. The framers of that document were intelligent and far-sighted leaders, but they could not predict the future with unerring accuracy. The only certainty was that new issues and concerns *would* arise in the future.

To make the situation more complex, the new United States of America did not exist in a vacuum. There were other nations just as legitimate—or more so—that posed additional issues of international trade and commerce, and even conflicts and wars. What role would the U.S. states play in international affairs, if any? The U.S. no longer had the foreign policies of the British government to fall back upon. In a few words: The 13 former British colonies were on their own.

Like many in the political and party systems of the time, Thomas Mifflin drifted from being called a federalist, to a supporter of the Democratic-Republicans. For many political actors, that was not a big problem, but Mifflin was the chief executive officer of one of the major states for over a decade. His actions carried weight and set precedents.

For his three Pennsylvania gubernatorial elections, Thomas Mifflin was considered a Democratic-Republican. However, he ran without an official political party endorsement. But with his popularity with the voters, he didn't need it. Between 1790 and 2024, there were 48 individuals who held the office of Pennsylvania governor; only Mifflin ran without a political party endorsement.

As governor, he was not only setting precedents, but also his actions had an immediate effect on the lives and welfare of many thousands of Pennsylvania citizens.

Chapter Eighteen

Governor of Pennsylvania

Pennsylvania Governor Election of 1790

In 1790, the voters of Pennsylvania selected the person who would be the first to serve in the office of governor, which was newly-created by the state constitution of 1789. "On December 21, 1790, Thomas Mifflin was the last President of Pennsylvania as well as the first governor of the Commonwealth of Pennsylvania."[1] It would mark a milestone in the move to transition Pennsylvania from a political entity governed by a colonial charter to a state of a new nation—a state that was governed by a state constitution that was created by leaders elected by the people.

Unlike when he had served as president of Pennsylvania, Governor Mifflin now had the power to make all civil appointments. As Rossman notes, under the new Pennsylvania constitution, the governor "appointed the secretary of the commonwealth, the attorney general, the adjunct general, the auditor general, the surveyor general, the secretary of the Land Office, the entire judicial establishment of the state, the auctioneers, the heads of state institutions, and innumerable petty officers like gaugers, inspectors, and measurers."[2] After McKean became the second governor of Pennsylvania, he wrote to John Dickinson: "A Governor of Pennsylvania has more duty to perform than the President of the United States or any Governor in the Union."

In the Pennsylvania gubernatorial election of 1790, two former Continental Army generals ran against each other: Democratic-Republican Thomas Mifflin and Federalist Arthur St. Clair. In addition to the fact that both had been successful generals in the Revolutionary War, both had also been presidents of the Continental Congress. At the time of the gubernatorial election, it had been six years since Thomas Mifflin had presided over the Congress, while it was only three years since Arthur St. Clair had been its president.

The results of Pennsylvania's first gubernatorial election couldn't have been more lopsided—with Supreme Executive Council of Pennsylvania President Thomas Mifflin accruing over 90 percent of the vote. He carried all 23 counties, and received a statewide total of 27,974 votes, while his opponent—Major General Arthur St. Clair, captured only 2,864 votes.[3]

In 1790, the state of Pennsylvania had a total of about 434,000 people which was about 11 percent of the United States' total population of 3,965,000. One of the most lopsided tallies occurred in Thomas Mifflin's namesake Mifflin County where he received 1,404 votes to St. Clair's 17 votes.[4]

Mifflin was governor of one of the most populous states at a time when the relationship between the new Federal government and the state governments was in the process of being developed. His experience as a long-time member of both the Confederation Congress and state and local governments was invaluable in this new role.

Inauguration, 1790

On December 17, 1790, the members of the Pennsylvania House of Representatives met in the Senate chamber. Thomas Mifflin was acknowledged as the winner of the election. Four days later, in the Senate Chamber, the Chief Justice of the Commonwealth Thomas McKean, administered the oath of office to Mifflin as prescribed by the Pennsylvania constitution, as well as the oath required by the U.S. Constitution. Following the ceremony, the new governor along with the legislators formed a procession to the court house on High Street.

The procession to the court house was one of the most impressive Philadelphia had ever seen:

Order of Procession

Constables with their Staffs.
Sub Sheriffs with their Wands.
High Sheriff and Coroner with their Wands.
Judges of the Supreme Court and Judge of the
High Court of Errors and Appeals.
Attorney General and Prothonotary of the Supreme Court.
Wardens of the Port of Philadelphia.
Treasurer, Comptroller and Register General.
Secretary of the Land Office.
Receiver General and Surveyor General.
Justices of the Peace.
Prothonotary of the Court of Common Pleas and
Clerk of the Court of Quarter Sessions.

Clerk of the Mayor's Court and the Corporation.
Mayor, Recorder and Alderman.
Common Council, two and two
Master of the Rolls and Register of Wills.
Register of German Passengers, and Collector of Excise
in the City and County of Philadelphia.
Assistant Secretary of Council.
Secretary of Council.
Members of Council two and two.
The Governor-elect.
Sergeant-at-Arms of the Senate.
Clerk of the Senate.
Speaker of the Senate.
Members of the Senate, two and two.
Doorkeeper of the Senate.
Sergeant at Arms of the House of Representatives.
Assistant Clerk of ditto.
Clerk of ditto.
Members of ditto, two and two.
Doorkeeper of ditto.
Provo and Faculty of the University and College, two and two.
Officers of the Militia Citizens.[5]

When the procession ended, the certificate of the election was read by the Clerk of the Senate, and the official proclamation was thrice made by the clerk of the court, declaring Thomas Mifflin Governor of the Commonwealth of Pennsylvania and Commander in Chief of its Army and Navy. Then, the procession returned to the Senate chamber. The Governor was placed in the Speaker's chair with the Speaker of the Senate and the Speaker of the House of Representatives on either side of him. Members of both houses were also seated. Governor Thomas Mifflin then gave his inaugural address.

Mifflin most likely spent a great deal of time reflecting about what he needed to accomplish and how they were to "get the job done" before composing his inaugural address to the legislature. George Washington felt the two-party system of politics would damage American society. Mifflin must have thought the same; he did not affiliate himself with either political party when he ran for governor. He was savvy enough to know that moving forward, there would be heated debates between the parties: Federalists, whose leaders were Alexander Hamilton and John Adams, and Anti-Federalists with Thomas Jefferson and James Madison. Hamilton recognized the success of the British government model with a strong national government, while Jefferson thought we just threw off the yoke of a monarchy and so promoted individual liberties and state rights. By the 1790s, the two parties also clashed over the economy and foreign policy.

Inaugural Address of Governor Mifflin

Mifflin addressed both state houses, reminding the elected officials that their energy and interests shouldn't be political but for the residents. As George Washington said, "If we mean to support the liberty and independence which has cost us so much blood and treasure to establish, we must drive far away the daemon of party spirit and local reproach." Mifflin stated in his inaugural address that the senate, the house, and the governor needed to work together and to look toward the future as they took care of today's business within the confines of Pennsylvania's new constitution. All needed to keep their citizens in the forefront of their minds as they as they began the challenging tasks ahead. Governor Mifflin said:

> *Gentlemen of the Senate and House of Representatives:* There cannot be a subject of fair congratulation, and that which the establishment which the new constitution presents at this time to every patriotic citizen of Pennsylvania. The wisdom, the candor and the liberality of the late convention have not only produced a system that promises political energy and happiness to the State, but have been the means of diffusing the blessings of confidence and concord among the people. A just sense of the common interest has happily prevailed and for the advancement and security of that interest, we are now convened to organize and administer a government which has been sanctioned by the warmest approbation and is supported by the best wishes of our constituents.
>
> The task assigned to us is not, however, less difficult than it is important; for whatever we analyze the nature and extent of our relative connection with the Union, or contemplate the increased population of the Commonwealth, the extensive cultivation of her soil, the flourishing state of her commerce and the enterprising spirit of her inhabitants, we shall be equally impressed with the magnitude and variety of her objects that command the care and consideration of the Government. But reflecting on the other hand, that to cherish the springs of national felicity and opulence by encouraging industry, disseminating knowledge and raising our social contact upon the permanent foundation of liberty and virtue must be pleasing to that being by whom the order and harmony of the universe were established. We shall find a great and constant consolation amidst all the difficulties of prospecting our public duties, and are justified in the grateful hope that our zeal and our labors for the prosperity of our country will not be vain and ineffectual.
>
> I am sensible gentlemen, that the reputation and success of government depends ... upon the conduct of its officers and the good understanding that can subsist among them. Permit me, therefore, to take this first opportunity

to bespeak a mutual confidence between the legislative and executive departments.

Mifflin then addresses his hope for a positive working relationship between the legislature and his executive branch of government:

> As public servants our duty, our interests and our objects are the same, and so perfectly do I rely on your wisdom and integrity that in every act, which can promote the common weal which is necessary to accomplish the patriotic views of the Legislature, you may be assured on my part of the most cheerful assistance and co-operation, while on your part I am persuaded that I shall experience a cordial support in the constitutional exercises of my official powers, since next to the ambition of promoting the happiness of our fellow citizens and of advancing the honor and reputation of the Commonwealth, I shall cherish the desire of conciliating and preserving your esteem.
>
> As soon, gentlemen, as the necessary arrangements shall be made, I will lay before you such business as will, in my opinion, require your attention in the present session.

Historian William Henry Egle notes that "This, the first inauguration day, was closed with every demonstration of joy and respect, such as the ringing of bells, firing artillery, etc., etc. On the days following various bodies of tradesmen and society organizations waited upon the Governor and tendered their congratulations, and upon the first day of January, following, city councils, with the mayor and recorder, waited upon his Excellency and formally congratulated him on his accession to his high office."[6]

As Governor Mifflin prepared for what would become nine years leading the major state of Pennsylvania as its governor, he had some new and unique problems to confront. It would be the first time in Pennsylvania history that the state would have a chief executive officer whose duties were prescribed in the new state constitution. It would also be necessary to work hand and glove with the first federal presidential administration, which was also given powers and restraints under the new national constitution—the Washington Administration.

New and often unique situations would arrive. Article One, Section 19 of the new Federal Constitution, which every state was bound to follow, stated:

> No State shall enter into any Treaty, Alliance, or Confederation; grant Letters of Marque and Reprisal; coin Money; emit Bills of Credit; make any Thing but gold and silver Coin a Tender in Payment of Debts; pass any Bill of Attainder, ex post facto Law, or Law impairing the Obligation of Contracts, or grant any Title of Nobility.
>
> No State shall, without the Consent of the Congress, lay any Imposts or Duties on Imports or Exports, except what may be absolutely necessary for

Eighteen. Governor of Pennsylvania

executing it's inspection Laws: and the net Produce of all Duties and Imposts, laid by any State on Imports or Exports, shall be for the Use of the Treasury of the United States; and all such Laws shall be subject to the Revision and Controul of the Congress.

No State shall, without the Consent of Congress, lay any Duty of Tonnage, keep Troops, or Ships of War in time of Peace, enter into any Agreement or Compact with another State, or with a foreign Power, or engage in War, unless actually invaded, or in such imminent Danger as will not admit of delay.

But the Federal government did not have total power. Mifflin, and the other state governors and the state legislators, had many other powers—powers too numerous to enumerate in detail in this founding document. The tenth amendment to the Constitution stated: "The powers not delegated to the United States by the Constitution, nor prohibited by it to the States, are reserved to the States respectively, or to the people."

A showdown between individual states and the federal government in the first decade under the new U.S. Constitution was inevitable. Many disputes over this could be—and were—referred to the U.S. Supreme Court. A major problem was that the Court was also a product of the new Constitution—and thus entering uncharted territory.

Into this situation, stepped two men: one man who more than anyone else was receiving credit for the winning of the Revolutionary War and the benefits of freedom that resulted from it. Second, was a man who had at one time wanted to replace the first man as head of the army. If these two men were petty and vain, they would be at loggerheads over the issues, and the whole nation would suffer. But Washington and Mifflin were honorable men—albeit with differences of opinion—who would continue to put the interests of the new nation ahead of past disagreements. They were men who—just as both had done throughout the Revolution—put the love of liberty and dedication to the new country in first place.

Mifflin's three terms as governor of Pennsylvania in the 1790s were not times of total tranquility. Looking back in 1813 was a man who was vice president of the United States, and then president of the United States, during those years. John Adams spoke of the turmoil of that time in Pennsylvania in a letter to Thomas Jefferson. (We will read about the Genêt affair, the insurrections, and the Yellow Fever epidemic shortly.)

> I believe You never felt the Terrorism of Gallatins Insurrection in Pennsylvania [known as the Whiskey Rebellion]: You certainly never realized the Terrorism of Fries's, most outrageous Riot and Rescue as I call it, Treason, Rebellion as the World and great Judges and two Juries pronounced it. You certainly never

felt the Terrorism, excited by Genêt, in 1793. when ten thousand People in the Streets of Philadelphia, day after day, threatened to drag Washington out of his House, and effect a Revolution in the Government, or compel it to declare War in favor of the French Revolution, and against England. The coolest and the firmest minds, even among the Quakers in Philadelphia, have given their opinions to me, that nothing but the Yellow Fever, which removed Dr. Hutchinson and Jonathan Dickenson Sargent from this World, could have Saved the United States from a total Revolution of Government.

Adams continues with mention of Governor Mifflin:

I have no doubt you were fast asleep in philosophical Tranquility, when ten thousand People, and perhaps many more, were parading the Streets of Philadelphia, on the Evening of my Fast Day.[7] When even Governor Mifflin himself, thought it his Duty to order a Patrol of Horse and Foot to preserve the peace, when Market Street was as full as Men could Stand by one another, and even before my Door; when Some of my Domesticks [domestics] in Phrenzy, determined to Sacrifice their Lives in my defense; when all were ready to make a desperate Salley among the multitude, and others were with difficulty and danger dragged back by the others; when I myself judged it prudent and necessary to order Chests of Arms from the War Office to be brought through bye Lanes and back Doors: determined to defend my House at the Expense of my Life, and the Lives of the few, very few Domesticks and Friends within it. What think you of Terrorism, Mr. Jefferson? Shall I investigate the Causes, the Motives, the Incentives to these Terrorisms?[8]

Mifflin's First-Term Agenda

When Mifflin became governor, one of his major objectives was to improve Pennsylvania's infrastructure of roads and canals. Businesses and individuals of the Philadelphia area had long been urging the creation of a major road to the agricultural lands of Central and Western Pennsylvania.

In 1790, Governor Mifflin told the state legislature: "The commercial policy of insuring the transportation of our produce from the interior counties to the capital is, dependent upon the ease and facility of the communications that are established throughout the State; and when we consider Pennsylvania not only as the route that actually connects the extreme members of the Union, but also as a natural avenue from the shores of the Atlantic to the vast regions of the western territory, imagination can hardly paint the magnitude of the scene which demands our industry, nor hope [to] exaggerate the richness of the reward which solicits our enjoyment."[9]

On December 10, 1791, Pennsylvania Governor Mifflin addressed the state's senate and house of representatives: "The improvement of our roads and inland navigation will, I am persuaded, continue to be a favorite object with the Legislature.... While I offer these remarks, I am aware, Gentleman, that the want of a good and permanent road is, at present, the principal defect in the communication between the middle counties and the metropolis."[10]

With the cooperation on the Pennsylvania legislature, Governor Mifflin was able to begin a major road across much of the state. Begun in 1792, the Philadelphia and Lancaster turnpike was completed in 1794. Built by a private company, the stone and gravel road was 62 miles long and cost more than $450,000. This was a time that a quart of cider cost less than four cents, and an attorney would draw up a lease for half-a-dollar.[11]

Much of the road's construction (and maintenance) costs were recouped with the installation of tolls. Not only was the road used extensively to transport goods eastward, but as western lands became available, eastern settlers from many states used the road with their west-bound stagecoaches and covered wagons.

About four decades after the Philadelphia and Lancaster turnpike was built, railroads and canals supplanted it as the primary means by which freight and people were moved across a long distance. The pendulum swung back in the highway's favor with the invention of the automobile in the late 19th century. Today, the Philadelphia and Lancaster turnpike is part of the 3,000-mile-long U.S. Route 30, which travels from Atlantic City, New Jersey, to Astoria, Oregon.

Besides improving transportation systems, two other important issues to Governor Mifflin were judicial system reform and improving prison facilities. As Rawle states in his biographical piece, Thomas Mifflin was a proponent "in relieving the distressed always active and humane ... [and] in the business of others scrupulously just." This included the incarcerated. Among Mifflin's duties as governor of the Commonwealth, were "remitting forfeitures and fines, granting reprieves and pardons." For example, accompanied by judges, he visited the debtors' and criminals' sections of the Philadelphia prison. He found the debtors conditions so poor that he requested that the legislature initiate corrections, which they did.[12]

Emily and Joseph Hopkinson

Thomas Mifflin's wife Sarah died several months before he was first elected governor of Pennsylvania. That left his daughter Emily to take on the duties usually reserved for a colony's (or state's) first lady. In

Mifflin's will of November 29, 1797, he gave his daughter Emily his collection of drawings and paintings. As Rossman says, he was most concerned with providing "for her children since he had so generously provided for [Emily] at the time of her marriage."[13]

Emily Mifflin's husband, Joseph Hopkinson, a Philadelphia judge, gained fame as the writer of the words for "Hail Columbia," a song that became an unofficial national anthem of the United States. The music for the song was composed by German immigrant Philip Phile (c.1734-c.1793) and played at George Washington's inauguration in 1789. Joseph Hopkinson wrote the lyrics in 1798.

"Hail Columbia's" first stanza reads:

Emily Mifflin, a daughter of Thomas Mifflin, was born in Philadelphia, Pennsylvania, in 1774. Thomas Mifflin biographer Kenneth Rossman described Emily as "one of the most brilliant of the younger set, and an artist of some ability." She presided over Governor Mifflin's household after the death of his wife, Sarah Mifflin (public domain, via Wikimedia Commons).

> Hail Columbia, happy land!
> Hail, ye heroes, heav'n-born band,
> Who fought and bled in freedom's cause,
> Who fought and bled in freedom's cause,
> And when the storm of war was gone
> Enjoy'd the peace your valor won.
> Let independence be our boast,
> Ever mindful what it cost;
> Ever grateful for the prize,
> Let its altar reach the skies.

Its chorus is:

> Firm, united let us be,
> Rallying round our liberty,
> As a band of brothers joined,
> Peace and safety we shall find.

A few weeks after the song became popular, Hopkinson wrote to former President Washington: "As to the Song it was a hasty thought and a hasty composition, and can pretend to very little *intrinsic* merit—Yet I believe its public reception has at least equaled anything of the kind. The theatres here and at New York have resounded with it night after night, and the men and boys in the Streets sing as they go. I mention these things as pleasing and convincing testimonies of the great change that has taken place in the *American* mind, when American tunes and American sentiments have driven off those execrable French murder shouts—which not long since tortured our ears in all places of public amusement, and in every lane and alley in the United States."[14]

Washington responded: "...I will unite with you in a fervent wish, and hope, that greater unanimity than heretofore, will prevail; for enough, I think we have seen, to remove the mist entirely; and that, the young men of the present day, will not suffer the liberty for which their forefathers fought—bled—died—and obtained—be lost by them: either by supineness, or divisions among themselves, disgraceful to the Country."[15]

Joseph and Emily Mifflin Hopkinson were pleased that throughout the 1800s, many people considered "Hail Columbia" the national anthem of the United States of America. It's said that President Lincoln mentioned he had to stand up and take off his hat when "Hail Columbia" was sung.

In 1931, U.S. President Herbert Hoover proclaimed "The Star-Spangled Banner" the nation's official national anthem. "Hail Columbia" became the official song of the vice president of the United States, and it is played after each vice president takes the oath of office at their inauguration.[16] It is also used as the entrance song for the vice president of the United States in the same way that "Hail to the Chief" is played for the president.

Pennsylvania Governor Election of 1793

In the Pennsylvania gubernatorial election of 1793, incumbent Thomas Mifflin, considered a Democrat-Republican, faced off against former Lutheran minister Frederick Muhlenberg.[17] Less than three years earlier, Muhlenberg was ending his term in office as the first speaker of the U.S. House of Representatives in the history of the United

States. (He was speaker from April 1, 1789, to March 4, 1791). Less than a year after losing the Pennsylvania governor election to Mifflin, Muhlenberg was back in the U.S. House of Representatives as speaker again. This second time he served from December 2, 1793, to March 4, 1795.[18]

Thomas Mifflin's attention to the needs of the people, his ability to listen and put duty first, his eloquent speaking skills to persuade others, his ethics and ability to work with all produced accomplishments that must have resonated with Pennsylvania's citizens as they put him back in office. He received almost exactly two-thirds the vote with Muhlenberg pulling in the remaining one-third. Although Mifflin had been disowned by the Quakers almost two decades earlier when he joined a Pennsylvania militia unit, he still had a lot of Quaker support. They came out in good numbers whenever he sought political positions in the Philadelphia or Pennsylvania governments. Muhlenberg, of course, had a great deal of German-American support, but that was somewhat lower in the 1793 election, as Mifflin was also affiliated with the Lutheran Church.[19]

Genêt Affair

In 1793, after King Louis XVI was executed, French revolutionaries declared France a republic. Other European monarchies—notably Britain and Spain—began fearing for their own safety and wars began between their countries and France.

The other monarchies had every reason to fear. The American Revolution was fought to free the 13 North American colonies from British rule, leaving the mother country's soil untouched by violence. The French revolutionaries went much further—they sought to overthrow the French monarchy, and radically reshape their society and culture. The American Revolution led to a nation that strove to uphold the rights of individuals, while the French Revolution led to one of the bloodiest revolutions in history. Under the French revolutionaries' Reign of Terror, by 1794 about 17,000 people had been executed by the government and thousands more had died in prison.

France, seeking allies, sent Edmond-Charles Genêt to the United States as the French minister. Without permission from the U.S. federal government, he attempted to recruit American citizens to attack British Canada and Spanish Florida. He also tried to arrange for American privateers to raid British and Spanish ships.

President George Washington, recognizing the risks of war with Britain and lacking a comparable navy, opted for neutrality. In addition, Britain posed a threat with its control of Canada and its Native

American allies on America's western frontier. Washington demanded that Genêt stop his efforts, and the latter refused.

At this time, a British ship—the *Little Sarah*—was captured and brought to Philadelphia. U.S. Secretary of State Thomas Jefferson told Genêt that U.S. law prohibited him from arming the ship when it was in an American port. Genêt did it anyway, enlisting a crew of 120 men and moving 14 guns to the *Little Sarah*. Secretary of the Treasury Alexander Hamilton alerted Governor Mifflin to Genêt's action. Mifflin sent in the Pennsylvania militia with orders to detain the ship. He only allowed the militia to leave after Jefferson personally met with Genêt and assured Mifflin that the ship would not violate U.S. law. President Washington told Genêt the ship must remain in Philadelphia. Genêt ignored him and ordered the ship to leave.

In 1794, at Washington's request, Genêt was recalled by his government. The end result was that at the very beginning of the United States' existence as a nation, the principle of neutrality in foreign affairs was established. In addition, the authority of the federal government in such matters would thereafter supersede that of state governments.

Understanding that Genêt's life was in danger due to the radicals now in power in France, the Washington administration compassionately granted him asylum in the United States. Genêt married New York Governor George Clinton's daughter; moved to a farm about six miles south of Albany, New York;[20] and died in 1834.

Rossman, in his Mifflin biography, adds: "Governor Mifflin's conduct during the Genêt affair, despite his predilections in favor of France, was meritorious. He knew his duty, and he readily and efficiently co-operated with the [Washington] administration in compliance with all its requests. He was determined to preserve the peace and neutrality of the port of Philadelphia, even going beyond Jefferson's cautious manner of dealing with [the ship]."[21]

Like many incidents in the years immediately following the adoption of the U.S. Constitution, the Genêt affair help develop and settle the relationship of the federal government and the individual states. Mifflin's cooperation with the Washington administration—which included powerful political foes of Mifflin—set a precedent that affected not only Pennsylvania, but also the nation as a whole.

Kidnapping of John Davis

In 1791, three slave-catchers from Virginia—Francis McGuire, Baldwin Parsons, and Absalom Wells—were accused in Pennsylvania of kidnapping John Davis, a free African American. They took Davis to Virginia, where they sold him into slavery. Governor Thomas Mifflin argued that Davis was a free man and requested his return to Pennsylvania and the extradition of the kidnappers. However, Virginia's Governor Beverly Randolph refused, stating that the U.S. Constitution and Virginia law did not cover the dispute.

A Pennsylvania anti-slavery organization, the "Washington Society for the Relief of Free Negroes and Others Illegally Held in Bondage," went to Virginia and brought Davis back to Pennsylvania.

On November 29, 1791, the Virginia House of Delegates referred the demands of Pennsylvania Governor Mifflin, for the extradition of fugitives from justice, to a committee. "In December, it delivered a report and proposed resolutions, which were passed by both houses of the General Assembly passed on 20 Dec, charging that Pennsylvanians had encouraged slaves to flee from Virginia" (JHDV, Oct. 1791, pp. 91, 97, 137–38, 144–45).[22]

Governor Mifflin requested President George Washington's help since under the new U.S. Constitution it was a matter that concerned a dispute between two states, and in that case the federal government had jurisdiction.

As Richard Hildreth writes in his "Despotism in America," Virginia's Governor Randolph responded to Mifflin:

> This opinion having been transmitted to Mifflin, with Governor Randolph's regrets that no means had yet been provided for carrying into effect so important an article of the Federal constitution, it was forthwith laid before President Washington, with copies of all the other documents, enclosed in a letter from Mifflin, in which he pointed out Innis's apparent ignorance of act of Pennsylvania under which the indictments had been found (and which indeed had only been enacted March 29, 1788), by which the forcibly carrying any person out of the state to be sold as a slave was subjected to a fine of a hundred pounds, and imprisonment to hard labor for not less than six nor more than twelve months.[23]

Washington asked Congress for legislation that would cover "interstate extradition" and "fugitive slave activity." As a result, on February 12, 1793, Congress passed the Fugitive Slave Act of 1793. The law required the opposite of what Mifflin wanted. It made it legal for enslaved people seeking freedom to be captured in the North and returned to their masters. It also made it illegal for northerners to help those people. In a sad postscript, members of the Washington Society were not able to force John Davis's return to Pennsylvania. It is believed he died an enslaved man.

Fifty-seven years after the Fugitive Slave Act, the U.S. Congress passed the Fugitive Slave Act of 1850 that required the return of slaves who fled their owners. It would take another 15 years and a Civil War before this act would be nullified by the Thirteenth Amendment to the Constitution of the United States, which formally abolished slavery in 1865.[24]

A relative of Thomas Mifflin's who shared his disgust of slavery was his second cousin Warner Mifflin, who was one of the most famous abolitionists of the late 18th century. A year and a half younger than Thomas, Warner was also raised a Quaker, but unlike Thomas, he grew up in a slaveholding family in Virginia. After freeing the enslaved people on his farm, Warner moved to Delaware and became internationally famous for helping enslaved people gain their freedom. His efforts including leading groups in non-violently demanding the legislatures of several states, as well as the Continental Congress, outlaw slavery and the slave trade. He also, along with other Quakers, met with American General George Washington and British General William Howe during the Revolutionary War to try to initiate a peace agreement.[25]

Historian Michael R. McDowell writes: "Mifflin gave most of his adult life in both time and other resources to the anti-slavery cause, and the assistance of both enslaved and free African Americans, calling this service no more than his duty."[26]

After Warner Mifflin's death, Richard Allen, the founder of the African Methodist Episcopal Church and formerly an enslaved man, wrote, "We cannot but regret the loss of that great and good man Warner Mifflin, ... whose labors and anxiety were great for the freedom of our race; who for many years devoted his time to that service, and who has been instrumental in the hands of God, in liberating hundreds, if not thousands of the African race.... We hope that every slave he has been instrumental in freeing, is a star in his garment, and that he will shine unto the perfect day."[27]

Yellow Fever, 1793

During the 1700s and 1800s, the United States suffered from yellow fever epidemics that were brought north by ship from the Caribbean Sea. Philadelphia and other eastern seaboard port cities were hit the hardest, but sometimes ships carried it up the Mississippi River. A recent study estimates that a total of between 100,000 and 150,000 Americans died in the epidemics.[28]

Caused by a virus transmitted by a mosquito, relatively small yellow fever outbreaks began in the late 1600s. Many believe that it came to the 13 British colonies on trading ships' water barrels. The feared disease caused the yellowing of eyes and skin, and the vomiting of blackened blood.

The first major yellow fever epidemic in the Atlantic seaboard states began in August 1793 in Philadelphia, Pennsylvania. Not only was the city one of the great trading and cultural centers of the new country, but it was the headquarters of both the national government, then led by President George Washington, and the Pennsylvania state government, then headed by Governor Thomas Mifflin, who was in his first term of office. At the time, there were only about 400 doctors with medical degrees in the American colonies, but fortunately Philadelphia had more than its share.

In Philadelphia approximately 5,000 people—almost ten percent of the population—died. It would be 125 years before another epidemic of similar magnitude attacked Philadelphia—the Spanish flu of 1918, which killed over 12,000 people in the city.

The combination of a record hot, humid summer, a city surrounded by swampland, and hundreds of refugees from the island of St. Domingue in the Caribbean proved deadly. Thousands more left the city. Many federal and state officials moved to Germantown. The disease was at its worst in early October, and it began to subside later in the month as the temperatures cooled. It was especially hard on recent immigrants from countries that traditionally did not have yellow fever, i.e., people without immunities. In the following century, most epidemics of yellow fever occurred in the ports of the Southern states. The last major occurrence in the U.S. was in 1905 in New Orleans, Louisiana.[29]

As one of the major health crises in North American history, the 1793 Philadelphia epidemic was a serious test of Governor Mifflin's ability to handle a major and unexpected disaster at a time that scientific knowledge of the disease and its treatment was at its earliest stages. From his office in Germantown, he worked on arrangements to convert an estate north of the city into a temporary hospital.

The main physician treating the victims of Philadelphia's epidemic was the best-known medical doctor of the new country, Benjamin Rush. Rush believed strongly in bleeding and purging patients to cure diseases. It's been said that he used this "cure" for almost all diseases—even mental illness. Rush would often bleed a patient of six to eight pints of blood over a period of several days, believing that the human body replenishes its blood supply in one or two days. Later research found it usually takes weeks.

In September 1793, Dr. Rush publicized his cure for yellow fever—bleeding and purging the patients. Without adequate record keeping,

Eighteen. Governor of Pennsylvania

it's not known if more of his patients died from his therapies than died from yellow fever itself. By November, the yellow fever epidemic had almost stopped. President Washington moved back into the city, and businesses reopened. In December, the Pennsylvania legislature opened for its winter session.

On November 14, 1793, in his role as governor of the state, Thomas Mifflin issued a Thanksgiving Day proclamation. It demonstrates not only Mifflin's leadership responsibilities, but also his personal religious faith.

By THOMAS MIFFLIN,
Governor of the Commonwealth of Pennsylvania.
A PROCLAMATION,
Appointing a day of General Humiliation,
Thanksgiving and Prayer.

WHEREAS it hath pleased ALMIGHTY GOD to put an end to the grievous calamity, that recently afflicted the city of Philadelphia, and it is the duty of all, who are truly sensible of the Divine Justice and Mercy, to employ the earliest moments of returning health in devout expressions of penitence submission, and gratitude: THEREFORE I have deemed it proper to issue this Proclamation, hereby appointing THURSDAY, the Twelfth day of December next, to be holden, throughout the Commonwealth, as a DAY OF GENERAL HUMILIATION, THANKSGIVING AND PRAYER AND I earnestly exhort and entreat my Fellow-Citizens to abstain, on that day, from all their worldly avocations [hobbies], and to unite in confessing with contrite hearts, our manifold sins and transgressions;—in acknowledging, with thankful adoration, the mercy and goodness of the Supreme Ruler and Preserver of the universe,—more especially manifested in our late deliverance;—and in praying, with solemn zeal, that the same mighty power would be graciously pleased to instill into our minds just principles of our duty to Him, and to our fellow creatures;—to regulate and guide all our actions by his Holy Spirit;—to avert from all mankind the evils of War, Pestilence, and Famine;—and to bless and protect us in the enjoyment of Civil and Religious Liberty. AND all Officers of the Commonwealth, as well as all Pastors and Teachers are, also, particularly requested to make known the Proclamation, and, by their and advice, to recommend a punctual observance thereof within their respective jurisdictions and congregations;—so that the voice of the people, strengthened by it unanimity, and sanctified by sincerity, ascending to the throne of grace, may there find favour and acceptance.

GIVEN under my Hand and the great Seal of the State, at Philadelphia, this Fourteenth day of November, in the Year of our LORD, One Thousand Seven Hundred and Ninety-Three, and of the Independence of America the Eighteenth.

THOMAS MIFFLIN.

By the Governor,
A.J. DALLAS, *Secretary of the Commonwealth*[30]

At the time of the 1793 yellow fever epidemic, Philadelphia's population of more than 50,000 was about 94 percent white and 6 percent black.[31] Many people of the city, as well as medical professionals, mistakenly believed that black people were resistant to yellow fever. Even Dr. Benjamin Rush believed it, writing to one of the city's most respected African American ministers: the "malignant and contagious fever, which infects white people of all ranks, but passes by persons of your color."[32]

That pastor, Richard Allen (mentioned earlier as the founder of the African Methodist Episcopal Church), and another black minister, Absalom Jones, organized the free black community to help nurse the sick, transport the sick to locations outside the city, and bury the dead. One white victim of the disease, Isaac Heston, wrote that he didn't know what the people would do, if not for the blacks, as "they are the principal nurses."[33]

After the epidemic was over, the reverends Jones and Allen wrote a pamphlet that described the role of the Philadelphia's African American community in caring for the victims. This is known as the first copyrighted pamphlet by African Americans in American history.[34]

Municipal Issues

The time of Thomas Mifflin's service as Pennsylvania governor occurred during the first years of the new republic, when the roles of the chief executive officers of the states were evolving. These were days immediately following the adoption of the U.S. Constitution and many state constitutions—including Pennsylvania's. Many questions needed to be addressed in detail. What was the relationship between the governor of a state and the federal government? What about between two or more states? Or between the governor and local government? What about an executive branch of government and the judiciary?

A notable case of the latter occurred in 1793 when a riot broke out in Myerstown, Pennsylvania, which was about 80 miles northwest of Philadelphia. Founded by German immigrants, Myerstown was originally called Herclerode, then Tulpehocken Town, and lastly given the name, Meier-Town—or Myerstown.

In December 1793, a drunken confrontation between German immigrant townspeople and Scotch-Irish canal workers threatened to escalate out of control. German farmer Martin Glass complained to fellow townsmen that he had earlier been insulted by one of the canal workers. After they were drunk, Glass and his group headed over to another tavern where the canal workers were drinking and started a fight. The next day, a mob of Irish canal workers with clubs and other makeshift weapons entered Myerstown, looking for Glass, his friends, and anyone else who got in their way.

Later, 101 citizens of Myerstown petitioned Governor Mifflin that they were "insulted, abused, and threatened both as to Person and Property" by "lawless men belonging to the Schuylkill and Susquehanna Canal armed with clubs, etc." The petition asserted that "One of the Overseers at the Canal had ordered Clubs to be made for the Hands, and Men were employed (with promise of Pay) for that purpose." One hundred men had entered Myerstown "armed with unmerciful Weapons (abusing the Inhabitants as they went) Clubs, etc., headed by an Overseer with Pistols to the great Terror and Disturbance of the good people under pretense of seeking for Persons (supposed) to be guilty of some Offence; they made Prisoners of some innocent Boys, some of whom they beat."

Governor Mifflin responded to them: "It is my duty and it will always give me great satisfaction to see that the laws are faithfully executed and that every injury offered to the property or persons, of my Fellow Citizens, is satisfactorily redressed, by the regular authority. With this view, therefore, I have requested the Judge of Dauphin County, immediately to investigate the subject of your complaint, and to proceed therein according to law and justice."

Governor Thomas Mifflin wisely added that it was not in the power of the "Executive Magistrate" to made a final decision, but it is left to the judiciary. He assured them that the duty of the judges was to protect them from "outrage" and encouraged them to "promote the harmony and peace of the Community."

Mifflin sent copies of the complaint and his response to the president and managers of the canal company. President Robert Morris (who is famous as the "financier of the American Revolution," and later a United States senator representing Pennsylvania in the first Congress under the Constitution of 1787), replied to Mifflin with the promise to have the superintendent of the Canal project investigate the overseers and workmen, and discharge any that are to blame for the violence.

Several weeks later, the judges of the Court of Common Pleas responded: "His Excellency the Governor considering the Subject proper for a Judicial investigation, has requested the Judges of Dauphin County, to take the same into immediate consideration." The Judges fined nine of the canal men and ten of the townspeople. The Court declared "it takes two parties to make a quarrel," but decided that Martin Glass and the citizens of Myerstown were more responsible for the conflict than the canal men.[35]

Presque Isle

Following the Revolutionary War, there were various disputes among the states over their respective borders. One of the most significant concerned the Erie Triangle, which was a piece of land in Northwestern Pennsylvania with frontage on Lake Erie. When New York and Pennsylvania negotiated their borders, the Triangle was left, and it became federal land. It had formerly been the site of forts occupied by the French, the British, and the United States.

In 1788, the Confederation Congress offered the Erie Triangle for sale to the state of Pennsylvania. With the authorization of his state legislature, Governor Mifflin in 1792 purchased its approximately 200,000 acres for $151,000. Although relatively small, the Triangle fit well within the goals of the Commonwealth government to establish a Pennsylvania infrastructure that included roads and canals that could efficiently transport agricultural and other goods between the Philadelphia area and the west regions. A Pennsylvania port on the Great Lakes would be a wonderful addition to this system. As a merchant by trade, Mifflin understood well the benefits of access to the Great Lakes.

Once having ownership of the Erie Triangle, the Pennsylvania legislature voted to begin a settlement at the part of the Triangle called Presque Isle, which is a peninsula of land that reaches out into Lake Erie. This was to the delight of most western Pennsylvanians, who often perceived the state legislature as favoring residents of the eastern part of the state.

Fearing a general Indian war in the region, as well as the complication of a hostile actions by nearby British troops, the Washington administration asked Mifflin to put the Presque Isle development on hold. He did, although he protested that he was obligated by acts of the Pennsylvania legislature to either proceed with the Presque Isle establishment within a time frame proscribed by it, or else reconvene the legislature and request them to amend their legislation. In September 1794, Mifflin spoke to the Pennsylvania legislature, and declared his power to settle the Presque Isle situation was limited, but "if you shall be of opinion, that the interest of the Union, requires in any degree, a sacrifice of the local interest of the state, your power is competent to decide the question."

On September 23, the legislature authorized Mifflin to suspend the Presque Isle project. However, within weeks, negotiations with the Six Nations of the Iroquois Confederacy were held and a treaty concluded. A major Indian war was avoided.[36] In April of 1795, the Pennsylvania legislature passed an act to allow the establishment of a town at the Presque Isle area of the Triangle. It would be called Erie. Erie, as well as the rest of the Triangle was surveyed in 1795. Today, Erie is the fifth largest city in Pennsylvania, and Presque Isle, with almost a dozen beaches, has the only seashore in the Commonwealth of Pennsylvania.[37]

The Whiskey Rebellion

In the years following the Revolutionary War, three notable rebellions occurred in the United States: Shays' Rebellion in Western Massachusetts (August 1786–February 1787), the Whiskey Rebellion in Western Pennsylvania (1791–1794), and Fries' Rebellion in Pennsylvania (1799–1800). Thomas Mifflin, as the chief executive officer of the Commonwealth of Pennsylvania, played a crucial role in the government's response to the Whiskey and Fries Rebellions.

Shays' Rebellion was an insurrection by people who were hit by high taxes and foreclosures of their homes and farms. The rebels closed several courts so they could not proceed with the foreclosures. The most significant action was the September 1786 attack on the federal government's arsenal at Springfield, Massachusetts, by leader Daniel Shays and approximately 1,200 men who were mostly farmers and veterans of the Revolution. Defeated, they retreated and were overtaken by militia troops. As a result of the rebellion, the state legislature took action to reduce the tax burden of citizens who were suffering from the severe economic conditions in Massachusetts.

By the 1790s, debts incurred by the United States government due to the American Revolutionary War hampered the functioning of the federal government. President Washington's Secretary of the Treasury, Alexander Hamilton, pushed for an excise tax on whiskey and other distilled liquors. A bill authorizing it was passed by Congress in 1791. This triggered what has become known as the Whiskey Rebellion. Farmers in western Pennsylvania resented the tax, which they believed unfairly singled them out. In 1794, the protestors turned violent. On July 16, about 400 rioters harassed tax collectors. On August 7, 1794, Governor Thomas Mifflin issued the following proclamation:

> In the NAME and by the AUTHORITY of the Commonwealth of PENNSYLVANIA, By THOMAS MIFFLIN, GOVERNOR of the said Commonwealth, A PROCLAMATION.
> Whereas it appears in and by a Proclamation of the President of the United States, bearing even date herewith, that certain acts have been perpetrated in the western parts of the commonwealth of Pennsylvania, which he is advised amount to treason, being overt acts of levying war against the United States;

that James Wilson, an Associate Justice, on the fourth instant, by writing under his hand, did, from evidence which had been laid before him, notify to the President, that in the Countries of Washington and Allegheny in Pennsylvania, laws of the United States are opposed, and the execution thereof obstructed, by combinations too powerful to be suppressed by the ordinary course of judicial proceedings, or by the powers vested in the Marshal of the district; and that in the judgment of the President it is necessary, under the circumstances of the case, to take measures for calling forth the Militia, in order to suppress the combinations aforesaid, and to cause the laws to be duly executed: AND WHEREAS it appears to me expedient, that, on this extraordinary occasion, the General Assembly should be convened...

Mifflin perceived that the state needed the manpower to step in if there was a rebellion against federal or state laws. He concluded his proclamation by calling for the Pennsylvania General Assembly to convene at the State House in Philadelphia on September 1 "for the purpose of ... devising the necessary means to maintain the peace and dignity of the commonwealth, and of providing more effectually, than the existing laws provide, for organizing, arming and equipping the Militia, in order to insure a prompt and faithful compliance with the orders of government, and of such requisitions, as the President shall, make in pursuance of his constitutional and legal powers."[38]

When Mifflin directly called up the Pennsylvania militia to quell the rebellion, he helped that action become established as a state right.

In August, President Washington sent a peace commission to western Pennsylvania. After it was unsuccessful, he raised a force of militia from Virginia, New Jersey, Pennsylvania, and Maryland to deal with the insurrectionists. Governor Thomas Mifflin was commander in chief of the Pennsylvania militia. By the time the troops arrived in Western Pennsylvania, the main opposition was nowhere to be found. By November, about 150 of the rebels were arrested. The rebellion was effectively ended at that point. The following July, Washington pardoned two of the leaders who had been found guilty of treason.

Mifflin biographer Rawle's writes about the insurrection of 1794: "The absurd insurrection of 1794, could only be suppressed by the display of great military power; and at the head of that portion of the militia of Pennsylvania which went on the service, Gen. Mifflin cheerfully put himself under the orders of Gen. Lee,[39] governor of Virginia, who in the regular army during the war had been his inferior in rank. In this he showed his reverence for the Constitution of the United States; which, rendering the President commander in chief of the whole, authorized him to assign particular services to such officers as he thought proper."[40]

Vice President, General Society of the Cincinnati

Founded on May 13, 1783, by former Continental Army officers, the Society of the Cincinnati is today the oldest patriotic organization in the United States.[41] It is led by a president general, a vice president general, a secretary general, and a treasurer general. Although the president general was traditionally elected and re-elected for life, in its later years, terms have been limited. The first president general was George Washington, who served until his death in 1799. He was succeeded by Alexander Hamilton, who was president general until he was killed in the famous duel with Aaron Burr in 1804. The last officer who served in the Continental Army during the American Revolutionary War was William Popham, who was president general until his death in 1847.

Interestingly, despite their association with the Conway Cabal, Horatio Gates and Thomas Mifflin were successive vice presidents general during George Washington's term as president general of the Society. Gates was in this second-most-important Society of the Cincinnati position from 1784 to 1787, and Mifflin replaced him in 1787 and served until 1799. Mifflin was succeeded by Alexander Hamilton, and, with the exception of vice president general Henry Knox, none of the dozens of president generals and vice presidents general up through the 21st century have been as famous as Hamilton.[42]

The Society of the Cincinnati set an example for future American patriotic organizations—most notably the American Legion and the Veterans of Foreign Wars. Begun at the end of World War I in 1919, the American Legion includes veterans of the U.S. Military. As of the 21st century, it has almost two million members. At least 11 U.S. presidents have been members: Wilson, Truman, Eisenhower, Kennedy, Lyndon Johnson, Nixon, Ford, Carter, Reagan, and both Bushes. The Veterans of Foreign Wars (VFW) is limited to veterans with "Honorable Service in a war, campaign, or expedition on foreign soil or in hostile waters." Numbering 1.5 million members (total of the VFW and its Auxiliary), it had at least four U.S. presidents as members: Truman, Eisenhower, Ford, and George H.W. Bush.

Pennsylvania Governor Election of 1796

As a Democrat-Republican, Thomas Mifflin won the 1796 Pennsylvania gubernatorial election with 96 percent of the vote.[43] In a second try at the governorship, Federalist candidate Frederick Muhlenberg only received 3 percent. A second Federalist candidate, Revolutionary

War hero Major General Anthony Wayne, received less than one-half of one percent.[44]

Pennsylvania Governor Thomas Mifflin was again tested as he dealt with enormous difficulties that arose during his final term in office. With his leadership skills, background experience, and common-sense approach, Mifflin led his citizens safely through each crisis. The first crisis was a health epidemic in 1797 that hit the city of Philadelphia and its surrounding areas. Mifflin recognized it and immediately issued quarantines. The second crisis was in 1798—an armed rebellion of Pennsylvanians who opposed high taxes. They revolted as they had done twenty years earlier against the British and their unfair taxation. Thomas Mifflin felt his duty was to his people—his priority was to keep his citizens as safe, as protected, and as calm as possible while staying true to the state and federal constitutions.

Yellow Fever, July 1797

In late July 1797, yellow fever again hit the city of Philadelphia. Richard Folwell's *Short history of the yellow fever, that broke out in the city of Philadelphia, in July 1797* mentions that the people of Philadelphia were aware of the danger earlier than they had been in 1793, and they were quicker to leave the city. This caused the death toll to be far less than the earlier epidemic.[45]

On August 11, 1797, Governor Mifflin issued a proclamation that ordered every ship arriving from the Caribbean islands, New Orleans, or any of the French, Dutch, or Spanish ports to be under quarantine for five days at the health office on State Island, or for a longer time if required by the resident doctors and officers of the health office. Four days later, he issued a second proclamation that included British ports.

Governor Mifflin released a letter addressed to Dr. John Redman, the President of the College of Physicians of Philadelphia:

> "The alarm that prevails, respecting the appearance of the Yellow Fever in the neighborhood of Penn Street, induces me to request that you will be so obliging as to obtain from your brethren of the college of Physicians, a statement of the facts that have occurred in the course of their practice, and an early opinion on the best mode of adverting the calamity that threatens."
>
> Apparently, this letter went out to the other colonies as the *Connecticut Courant* newspaper picked it up for its August 28th edition.[46]

Redman responded that "a malignant contagious fever has lately appeared in Penn-street, and its vicinity, of which ten or twelve persons have died." Author Folwell remarks in his 1798 account, *Short History of the Yellow Fever, That Broke out in the City of Philadelphia in July 1797,* that this was not as "exceedingly dismal" as in the fall of 1793.Then, according to Folwell, people would see carts with dead bodies speeding to Potter's field. He adds that the man who drove one cart was "frequently singing."[47]

Folwell points to the overcrowding conditions in Philadelphia as a contributing cause of the spread of yellow fever. He makes the comment that on a "continent twelve hundred leagues wide, and where land is so extremely plenty, contagion should be promoted by the narrowness of the streets." He contends that two or three hundred extra acres of ground, which were worth only 20 dollars an acre when the city streets were planned, would have saved over the years thousands of lives.[48] Folwell states that at the end of October, 1793, "some days of cold weather, or perhaps some natural cause beyond the reach of human conception, by degrees, abated its violence."[49]

Fries Rebellion, 1798

In 1798, an armed rebellion erupted in Pennsylvania's Bucks and Northampton counties against a Congressional tax law. U.S. President Adams sent a proclamation to Governor Mifflin, who, in turn, shared it with the state Assembly:

Message of the Governor of Pennsylvania, to the Two Houses of Assembly:

> GENTLEMEN:—It is announced, by proclamation issued by the President of the United States, dated the 12th inst., that combinations, to defeat the execution of the laws for the valuation of lands and dwelling houses within the United States, have existed in the counties of Northampton, Montgomery and Bucks, in the State of Pennsylvania: That in the judgment of the President it is necessary to call for the military force, in order to suppress the combinations aforesaid, and cause the laws aforesaid to be duly executed; and that the President has accordingly determined to do so, under the solemn conviction that the essential interest of the United States demands it.
>
> That I have received no communication from the President on this important occasion, yet it is my duty, as Executive Magistrate of Pennsylvania, to call your attention to the subject, that if any means ought to be taken on the part of the State to co-operate with the Federal government, they may be devised and authorized by the Legislature.[50]

In the 1790s, as a conflict between Britain and France heated up, the U.S. found itself in the middle. It had signed the Jay Treaty with Great Britain in 1794, and in response, French leaders permitted their vessels to seize U.S. merchant ships. The Federalists, who in general supported Britain, or remained neutral, were especially outraged. The Democratic-Republicans, who remembered French help during the American Revolutionary War, pushed for a peace treaty with France. The U.S. sent envoys to both France and Britain. Governor Thomas Mifflin hoped that amicable relations with France could be restored. His more pro–Britain opponents were agitating for war with France.

After France showed no inclination to reasonably negotiate with the Americans, the Adams administration continued to strengthen American defenses. A navy was created,[51] and the army was activated with retired president George Washington as its commander in chief. Although Mifflin had a longtime sympathy for France, he supported President John Adams' steps to beef up American military power.

Congress requested 80,000 militia troops from Pennsylvania, and Mifflin worked hard to meet that quota. Mifflin's son-in-law, Joseph Hopkinson, joined the patriotic sentiment with the release of his patriotic song "Hail! Columbia" to popular acclaim.

Before matters went too far, President Adams pushed hard for a negotiated a peace and Napoleon Bonaparte became the new leader of France. Thankfully, the threat of war vanished with the Treaty of Mortefontaine in 1800.

With the inauguration of Thomas McKean in December 1799, Thomas Mifflin's tenure as chief executive of the Commonwealth of Pennsylvania came to an end. He had served for two years as president of the Supreme Executive Council of Pennsylvania and nine years as governor, marking an 11-year term, longer than that of any subsequent Commonwealth of Pennsylvania governor even into the 21st century.

The Pennsylvania state constitution only allowed a maximum of three terms for a governor. Given the state of Thomas Mifflin's health in 1799, it is doubtful that he would have had the strength to campaign for a fourth term.

Thomas Mifflin's accomplishments were many, according to the Pennsylvania General Assembly's official biography of its former speaker. It states that Thomas Mifflin, "was considered responsible for diminishing Pennsylvania's debt after the Revolutionary War, instigating public works development, and laying the groundwork for a modern penal code in the Commonwealth. Mifflin also oversaw increased political regulation, especially of banking and of political parties."[52] There is no doubt that Pennsylvania benefited greatly when Thomas Mifflin was at its helm; there is no doubt that he worked tirelessly and was tremendously dedicated to the state that he loved.

Chapter Nineteen

Mifflin's Last Years

After Governor Thomas Mifflin completed three terms, he was ineligible to become governor again. Even though he was in poor health, Mifflin still believed that he should continue to work. He felt he had much to offer, and still desired to remain in public office. He ran for and won a seat in the Pennsylvania House of Representatives, where he was scheduled to represent Philadelphia County. In addition, when his third term as governor ended, he was honored by being appointed commanding general of the militia of the city and county of Philadelphia.[1]

The militia he was to command is continued by today's 111th Infantry and 103rd Engineer Battalion of the Pennsylvania Army National Guard.[2]

Mifflin's health worsened. On January 19, 1800, Governor McKean "visited Mifflin who had remained in Lancaster because of his election to the Assembly. After the visit, Governor McKean wrote to his wife: "General Mifflin is very ill.... I saw him today and stayed about an hour with him, he was delirious, totally debilitated and in my opinion cannot survive two days." McKean was correct in his judgement of Mifflin's physical condition; for on the following day Governor Mifflin, equally well known as General Mifflin, passed from time into eternity."[3] The *Lancaster Journal* printed the following obituary on January 22, 1800:

> Died in this Borough on Monday last at about 3 o'clock A.M. in the 57th year of his age Gen. THOMAS MIFFLIN,—a man who honorably waded thro' all the perils and dangers of the American Revolution, as a soldier, ably assisted in the first councils of the U. States—was 12 years Governor of Pennsylvania—and at his death a member of the State Legislature.
>
> His remains were this day interred in the burying ground of the German Lutheran Church. The following was the order of procession observed at the funeral: [the order of the procession is omitted].[4]

The name on the sign in front of this church reads: "The Lutheran Church of the Holy Trinity." The church is located only about 1,000 feet south of the site of the Lancaster Court House in which the Continental Congress met on September 27, 1777, after its members fled Philadelphia.[5]

The website of the Lutheran Historical Society of the Mid–Atlantic explains: "Although Mifflin came from a Quaker family, he was expelled from the Society of Friends because of his involvement in the military. Mifflin then embraced the Lutheran tradition."[6]

At the dedication in Lancaster, Pennsylvania, of the new Lutheran church on Trinity Sunday June 15, 1794, the new church was given the same name as the one it replaced: Holy Trinity Lutheran Church. A year and a half earlier, Philadelphia political leader Charles Biddle wrote a letter in which he listed 19 of the main contributors to the church building fund. It included Thomas Mifflin, who donated 3½ pounds, which is the equivalent of about 500 early 21st-century U.S. dollars.[7]

Financial Condition of the Signers of the U.S. Constitution

Many people during the revolution contributed generously to support the Patriot cause—some personally used their monies to fund military units—suppling them with food, clothing and arms. Other Patriots used their personal wealth to support this great movement that was constantly running out of money. After the war, there was a great deal of debt—both by government and by individuals. Some people were able to regain their wealth; others found their finances significantly diminished. Many of the once-wealthy found themselves speculating unwisely as they tried to recoup their wealth. Others found themselves in debtor's prison.

The financial condition of the signers of the U.S. Constitution reflected this as well. A young, well-educated Thomas Mifflin, who took a European tour after college, and was one of the wealthiest, most influential men in Philadelphia, confronted financial problems after the war. But he wasn't the only signer of the U.S. Constitution who experienced financial losses at the end of his life—others did, too. Three other signers were ruined by unwise land speculation. Two were members of the Pennsylvania delegation with Mifflin: Robert Morris (1734–1806), who at one time was believed to the richest man in America, spent three years in debtor's prison; and James Wilson (1742–1798) died virtually penniless. The third signer, Nathaniel Gorham (1738–1796) of Massachusetts, died in poverty.

In his autobiography, Charles Biddle, who served as the vice-president of the Supreme Executive Council of Pennsylvania during the first two years that Benjamin Franklin was its president, remarked about Mifflin's personal financial condition: "he was at that time [late 1780s–early 1790s] frequently embarrassed for money, of which he was extravagant and thoughtless. On these occasions he always applied to me."[8]

Thomas Mifflin was also not alone among Pennsylvania's revolutionary leaders who died in poverty. In an 1811 letter to 76-year-old John Adams, 65-year-old Benjamin Rush noted that "There was scarcely a single deceased person that was active in our Revolution that has not died poor in Pennsylvania. Witness Read, Mifflin, Morris, Wilson, and many Others of less note."[9] It is certainly a sad commentary that the bravest men who fought so valiantly against the greatest power in the world, and were victorious in their efforts, could not live out the remainder of their lives free of monetary worries.

Rawle writes about the end of Thomas Mifflin's life:

> Before his commission as governor expired, his fellow citizens, unwilling to part with him as a public man, again chose him a member of the state legislature; in which, however, he could not act, till his successor was installed in the office of governor. His last official communication in the latter character, was on the 7th of December, 1799. It was an eloquent valediction, and was respectfully and affectionately answered. He then took his seat in the house of representatives, but his shattered constitution disabled him from making in it that imposing figure which he had often done before. He died during a session of the house at Lancaster, on the 21st of January, 1800. Resolutions were passed, expressive of the high sense entertained of his merits and his services as a soldier and "a statesman;" providing for his interment at the public expense, and for the erection of a monument to his memory.

John Trumbull's painting of Thomas Mifflin, ca. 1790. Like Mifflin, Trumbull served as one of General George Washington's aides-de-camp during the Revolutionary War (courtesy Metropolitan Museum of Art).

Thus ended the chequered

life of Thomas Mifflin—brilliant in its outset—troubled and perplexed at a period more advanced—again distinguished, prosperous, and happy finally clouded by poverty, and oppressed by creditors. In patriotic principle never changing—in public action never faltering—in personal friendship sincerely warm—in relieving the distressed always active and humane—in his own affairs improvident-in the business of others scrupulously just.[10]

Chapter Twenty

Mifflin's Legacy

As we enter upon the celebration of the 250th anniversary of the American Revolutionary War, and the founding of the United States of America, we might ask: "What is the legacy of Thomas Mifflin?" What contributions did he make to the nation after holding high leadership positions in both the military and as a politician during the country's first quarter-century?

Before we answer, it might be beneficial to know how Thomas Mifflin was remembered almost 90 years after his death. The *Official Program of the Centennial Celebration of George Washington's Inauguration* includes a page on Mifflin that states: "He was not at all in sympathy with the methods of Washington, and entered the combination to supplant the Virginia statesman and soldier in favor of General Gates. The failure of this scheme brought those who had been concerned in it into something like general disrepute. But the hold which Mifflin had gained on the hearts of Pennsylvanians was not to be affected in that way."[1]

For information on how Thomas Mifflin was perceived in the mid–20th century, we can read an address delivered by Dr. H.M.J. Klein at the unveiling of a bronze memorial tablet at Trinity Lutheran Church in Lancaster, Pennsylvania, on September 29, 1937, on the occasion of the sesqui-centennial observance of the signing of the federal constitution.[2] Dr. H.M.J. Klein begins with:

> It was altogether a remarkable group of men that formed the Federal Constitutional Convention one hundred and fifty years ago. The eight delegates from Pennsylvania were among the most eminent and influential members of that distinguished body of statesmen. Benjamin Franklin, Thomas Mifflin, Robert Morris, George Clymer, Thomas Fitzsimons, Jared Ingersoll, James Wilson, Gouverneur Morris—these eight delegates of Pennsylvania signed the great document on September 17, 1787. We have come here today at the invitation of the Pennsylvania Constitution Commemoration Committee to honor one of these eight immortals who helped to construct the pattern of our national life.

Thomas Mifflin had a remarkably interesting career and deserves to be more widely known and recognized.

After mentioning several important facts of Mifflin's life, Dr. Klein brought up how Mifflin was one of the most active Pennsylvanians pushing for freedom:

> In the fall of 1776, General Mifflin travelled into the frontier counties of the State to rouse the people to the necessity of supporting the American cause with soldiers and supplies, for Philadelphia was threatened with British invasion. He spoke in school houses and taverns and at cross roads, appealing to the people of Pennsylvania to support the patriotic cause.

Dr. Klein proceeded to speak about the days after the British forced the patriot Congress from Philadelphia:

> There was confusion, criticism, discontent everywhere. The soldiers were half starving and freezing at Valley Forge. A great part of the criticism fell on the head of the quartermaster general, who became so weary of Congressional interference and unjust criticism that he resigned both as quartermaster and major general.

Dr. Klein then addresses the topic of the Conway Cabal in his talk. It's interesting to see how it was perceived by many in 1937:

> George Washington was equally the subject of criticism. He was accused of being too slow in his tactics, and when the victory of General Gates at Saratoga was announced, the Conway Cabal followed, in which a number of prominent military men were involved. Many of them felt that General Gates ought to replace General Washington. To what extent Thomas Mifflin was favorable to this movement is not so clear. But whatever his temporary attitude may have been, he remained the life-long friend of Washington, and said of him: "He was the best friend I ever had in my life."[3]

Dr. Klein concluded his talk with mention of the place he was giving it—the grave of Thomas Mifflin: "He was buried here in this little yard between the pavement and the front wall of Trinity Lutheran Church." By the instruction of Governor Thomas McKean, a marble slab was placed here 137 years ago bearing this inscription: "In perpetuation of the memory of Thomas Mifflin, Major General of the Revolutionary Army of the United States, and late Governor of the State of Pennsylvania. A distinguished Patriot and Zealous Friend of Liberty. Died January 19, 1800."

In the public arena, Mifflin was always consistent in two things: his patriotism and his desire to serve his fellow citizens well. Even his temporary opposition to General Washington was based upon his sincere belief—now proven quite wrong—that Washington's replacement would be best for the good of the country.[4]

Mifflin succeeded as a merchant and as a military leader, but it was in the realm of politics and government that he excelled. Few people of his time were so successful at all levels of government—local, state and federal. The main reason for this was his personal popularity among the residents of Philadelphia, the voters of Pennsylvania, and the citizens of the United States—as well as his fellow public servants. Rawle writes of Mifflin:

> In *person* he was remarkably handsome, though his stature did not exceed five feet eight inches. His frame was *athletic*, and seemed *capable* of bearing much fatigue. His manners were cheerful and affable. His elocution open, fluent, and distinct. [Alexander] Graydon,[5] who did not like [Mifflin], says that his manners were better adapted to *attract* popularity than to *preserve* it, and that he possessed in an eminent degree the talent of haranguing a multitude. He adds, that he was a man of "education, ready apprehension and brilliancy, and possessed a fortitude equal to any demands that might be made on it."[6]

Quartermaster Corps Website

In many ways, Thomas Mifflin was similar to 21st-century politicians who invoke both positive and negative feelings from their constituents. Fortunately for him, the former outweighed the latter as he racked up impressive majorities in each of his three state-wide campaigns for governor of the Commonwealth. In a review of Rossman's 1952 biography, Author J.H. Powell wrote: "If a substantial body of Mifflin papers existed, the biographer could show the General hard at work, and the mysteries of his personal life could be put in perspective."[7] However, in the 21st century such a body of papers still hasn't been found—and in all likelihood never will be.

In 1947, the Pennsylvania Historical & Museum Commission installed an historical marker at Shillington in Berks County, Pennsylvania. It states:

> Thomas Mifflin
> Member of the Continental Congress, a Revolutionary soldier, first Pennsylvania governor, 1790–99, lived at his estate Angelica from 1774 to 1794. The Berks County Farm and Home now occupies the site.[8]

The idea of memorializing historical figures through statues and markers often sparks debates and discussions about their legacies, values, and the historical context. In the case of Thomas Mifflin, it seems that opinions about him have varied over the years, with both positive and critical views expressed.

In 2017, a statue of Supreme Court Chief Justice Roger Taney, who was best known for his pro-slavery decisions before the American Civil War, was removed from the Maryland State House grounds. A few weeks later, political science Professor Mark Croatti proposed replacing the statue with one of Thomas Mifflin, who was the only person to serve as president of the United States Congress when it met in Annapolis, Maryland.

Croatti argued that the former location of the Taney statue "should be awarded to someone who acted with the highest of moral standards and who did not hide behind the Constitution, especially when it may have conflicted with his own sense of right and wrong."[9]

The following poem was written by a 19th-century relative of Mifflin—Pennsylvania poet and painter Lloyd Mifflin (1846–1921):

MAJOR GENERAL THOMAS MIFFLIN
1744–1800

Intrepid orator and statesman bold,
  At whose impetuous words and impassioned words
  Men dropped the plowshares and took up their swords
  To fight for Freedom, in the days of old—
Forgotten art thou in this lust for gold,
  Although thy strong and stirring life records
  Deeds that were noble. But this age rewards
  With calm neglect thy labors manifold.
Champion of Liberty and of the Right;
  Brother in perilous arms, to Washington;
  Thou zealous Ruler of a glorious State—
Is there no way thy service to requite?
  Sleep, Patriot, Sleep! nor wish to know thy fate—
  Th' ingratitude of Freedom for her son![10]

Born a century after Thomas Mifflin, Lloyd Mifflin accurately observes the 19th century—and 20th century—understanding of the earlier Mifflin. As an "orator and statesman" Thomas Mifflin knew few equals, and he was an undisputed "champion of liberty and of the right." Almost all historians have acknowledged the accuracy of these two statements.

What tarnished Mifflin's otherwise extraordinary reputation were two cases of poor judgment: his belief that Washington needed to be replaced by General Gates as commander in chief of the Continental Army, and his decision to resign as quartermaster general of the army in the fall of 1777—before the supply disaster of Valley Forge. There are reasons for these: Washington was losing battles while General Gates was proclaimed the victorious leader of the most important battle of the war—Saratoga—and Mifflin's illness contributed to his resignation as quartermaster general.

Twenty. Mifflin's Legacy

Perhaps the most important reason these decisions were enough to overshadow the memory of Mifflin was that they were by themselves so very important. Washington, more than any other person, was responsible for there actually being a nation called the United States of America, and Valley Forge is one of the most infamous cases of mismanagement in American military history. Did Mifflin know that Congress would not replace him as quartermaster general for months? No. Did he know how Washington would be seen as the great leader he turned out to be? No.

Only when we look at almost everything else in Thomas Mifflin's public service career, do we get a true understanding of the man.

This present biography of Thomas Mifflin portrays a man who always led with his convictions. He set himself a hazardous course when he stepped out of his safe, secure world to oppose British rule. He joined others who had the same dream of living in a free, independent nation. He joined the military and fought against the most powerful military force in the world, and in doing so, was banished from his religious community because of their pacifists' beliefs. Although considered young, Mifflin was quickly promoted in the Continental Army as he demonstrated his abilities and leadership skills. He showed bravery to the men that he led into battle, and was successful as a commander infusing them with an esprit de corps.

Mifflin followed orders when he accepted appointments as the Army's quartermaster. He again followed orders to use his affable personality and persuasive eloquence to gather new recruits for the Continental Army—even when events seemed doubtful of success. Mifflin believed in duty and hard work, and had a vision of making people's lives better. As a founder he served from the first days of the Continental Congress as a delegate (and later its president) to the signature of approval placed upon the U.S. Constitution 13 years later. In his role as president of Congress, he was the only delegate who placed his signature on the treaty that ended the American Revolutionary War. This Treaty of Paris formally recognized American independence and ceded most of the territory east of the Mississippi River that allowed for westward expansion. Mifflin would go on to work as a Pennsylvania statemen until the end of his life.

Thomas Mifflin's life and legacy contributed greatly to this country. His life was one that improved the quality of life for those he represented, and it was one that was well worth remembering.

Chapter Notes

Preface

1. Hubbard, Robert Ernest. *Major General Israel Putnam: Hero of the American Revolution*. McFarland, 2017
2. Hubbard, Robert Ernest. *General Rufus Putnam: George Washington's Chief Military Engineer and the "Father of Ohio."* McFarland, 2020.

Introduction

1. Rossman, Kenneth R. *Thomas Mifflin and the Politics of the American Revolution*. University of North Carolina Press, 1952. Kenneth R. Rossman (1911–1997) was a history professor at Doane College in Crete, Nebraska (renamed Doane University in 2016).
2. Tinkcom, Harry M. by Kenneth R. Rossman. *The Pennsylvania Magazine of History and Biography*, Apr. 1953, www.jstor.org/stable/20088463. Accessed 13 Dec. 2023.
3. The lack of physical documentation is similar to the case of Patrick Henry, who served with Mifflin in the Continental Congresses of 1774 and 1775. Henry was perhaps the greatest orator of the American Revolution and today is best known for his words "I know not what course others may take, but as for me, give me liberty or give me death!" However, he left no significant writings and many of his speeches were never written down.
4. This sentiment reminds me of my visit to Franklin D. Roosevelt's home in Hyde Park, New York, where everything from throughout the 32nd U.S. president's life had been carefully saved, preserved, and archived—a delight for any biographer.
5. Rawle, William. "Sketch of the Life of Thomas Mifflin." In *Memoirs of the Historical Society of Pennsylvania*, vol. 2, pt. 2. Carey, Lea & Carey, 1826, pp. 107–126.
6. Nash, Gary B., and Billy G. Smith. "The Population of Eighteenth-Century Philadelphia." *Pennsylvania Magazine of History and Biography*, 1 Jan. 1975, pp. 362–368, journals.psu.edu/pmhb/article/view/43167/42888. Accessed 13 Dec. 2023.
7. *Portrait and Biographical Record of Lehigh, Northampton and Carbon Counties, Pennsylvania*. Chicago, Pennsylvania Chapman Publishing Co., 1894.
8. Rawle. "Sketch of the Life of Thomas Mifflin." 123–124.
9. *Ibid.*, 108.

Chapter One

1. The other two drafters were Robert R. Livingston of New York and Roger Sherman of Connecticut. Lawyer Livingston (1746–1813) was a delegate to the Continental Congress from 1775 through 1777, and from 1779 to 1780. After his appointment as the first Chancellor of New York, he administered the first presidential oath of office—to George Washington on April 30, 1789. In 1801, as Minister to France, he and James Monroe negotiated the Louisiana Purchase. Years later, New York State chose a statue of Livingston to represent it in

the Hall of Statues in the United States Capitol—a statue of Livingston holding the Louisiana Purchase deed. Sherman (1721–1791) was the only Continental Congress delegate who signed all four of these founding documents: the Association of 1774, the Declaration of Independence, the Articles of Confederation, and the Constitution. He played an especially important role in the creation of the Declaration and the Constitution. Roger Sherman was chosen to represent Connecticut in the United States Capitol building's Hall of Statues.

2. Flexner, James. *Washington: The Indispensable Man*. Little, Brown & Company, 1974.

3. It wasn't until 1867 (92 years after the U.S. Declaration of Independence) that the British Parliament's "British North America Act" created "The Dominion of Canada." Full independence was not reached until the "Canada Act" of 1982 (also known as the "Constitution Act"). Approved by the British Parliament and Queen Elizabeth II, it made Canada "wholly independent."

4. Michals, Debra. "Mercy Otis Warren." *National Women's History Museum*, 2015, www.womenshistory.org/education-resources/biographies/mercy-otis-warren.

Chapter Two

1. On the day Mifflin was born, the old Julian calendar (established under Roman emperor Julius Caesar in 46 B.C.) was using the year "1743." In Britain's North America colonies, the year 1744 did not start until March. In most countries of Europe—the Roman Catholic ones—the Gregorian calendar (introduced by Pope Gregory XIII in 1582) was in use and they were already using "1744," since then each new year began on January 1st. It wasn't until 1752 that Great Britain and its colonies switched to the Gregorian calendar.

2. Census History Staff. "Population in the Colonial and Continental Periods." U.S. Census Bureau. 11.

3. *Ibid.*

4. World Bank. "Population, Total." *Worldbank.org*, World Bank Group, 2022, data.worldbank.org/indicator/SP.POP.TOTL.

5. Dr. H.M.J. Klein, at the unveiling of a bronze memorial tablet at Trinity Lutheran Churchyard, on the occasion of these squicentennial observance of the signing of the federal Constitution, September 29, 1937.

6. Montgomery, Thomas Harrison. *A History of the University of Pennsylvania: From Its Foundation to A. D. 1770; Including Biographical Sketches of the Trustees, Faculty, the First Alumni and Others*. G.W. Jacobs & Company, 1900. 216.

7. *Ibid.*

8. Judge Thomas Hopkinson's son Francis Hopkinson (1737–1791) was Joseph Hopkinson's father and a signer of the Declaration of Independence.

9. Montgomery, Thomas Harrison. *A History of the University of Pennsylvania*. 210–216.

10. Rawle. "Sketch of the Life of Thomas Mifflin." 108.

11. "1681-1776: The Quaker Province | PHMC > Pennsylvania History." *State.pa.us*, Pennsylvania Historical & Museum Commission, 26 Aug. 2015, www.phmc.state.pa.us/portal/communities/pa-history/1681-1776.html. Accessed 11 Dec. 2023.

12. "Population in the Colonial and Continental Periods." *www.census.gov*, U.S. Census Bureau, https://www.census.gov/history/pdf/colonialbostonpops.pdf. The U.S. Census bureau estimates there were 733,058 housing units in Philadelphia County, Pennsylvania in 2022. "U.S. Census Bureau QuickFacts: Philadelphia City, Pennsylvania." *www.census.gov*, U.S. Census Bureau, www.census.gov/quickfacts/fact/table/philadelphiacitypennsylvania.

13. Montgomery, Thomas Harrison. *A History of the University of Pennsylvania*. 347.

14. Montgomery, Thomas Harrison. *A History of the University of Pennsylvania*. 346–347.

15. "Hugh Williamson." *University Archives and Records Center*, archives.upenn.edu/exhibits/penn-people/biography/hugh-williamson. Accessed 2 Mar. 2024.

16. "Thomas Bond." *University Archives and Records Center*, archives.upenn.edu/

exhibits/penn-people/biography/thomas-bond/. Phineas Bond (1717–1773) practiced medicine in Philadelphia with his brother, Thomas Bond. He was on Philadelphia's Common Council from 1747 until his death. He was also active in the American Philosophical Society.

17. "The Early Years: The Charity School, Academy and College of Philadelphia." *University Archives and Records Center*, archives.upenn.edu/digitized-resources/docs-pubs/early-years-1972/. Accessed 12 Jan. 2024.

18. *Ibid.*

19. Franklin, Benjamin. *The Autobiography of Benjamin Franklin*. Henry Holt and Company, 1916, www.gutenberg.org/cache/epub/20203/pg20203-images.html. Accessed 15 Dec. 2023.

20. Risch, Erna. *Supplying Washington's Army*. Center of Military History, United States Army, 1981, history.army.mil/html/books/040/40-2/cmh-Pub_40-2.pdf. Accessed 10 Dec. 2023. 14.

21. "Portrait of Mr. and Mrs. Thomas Mifflin (Sarah Morris)." *Philamuseum.org*, www.philamuseum.org/collection/object/103026. Accessed 1 Jan. 2024.

22. The city of St. Louis, Missouri, was founded by French fur traders the day before Mifflin sailed.

23. Rossman. *Thomas Mifflin*. 8.

24. *Ibid.*

25. *Ibid.*

26. *A History of the Schuylkill Fishing Company of the State in Schuylkill ...* 1889.

27. Felten, Eric. "What America's Oldest Club May Quaff—WSJ." *WSJ*, www.wsj.com/articles/SB123758172905298941. Accessed 3 Mar. 2024.

28. Regan, Gary. *The Joy of Mixology, Revised and Updated Edition: The Consummate Guide to the Bartender's Craft*. Clarkson Potter, 2018.

29. "About the APS." *American Philosophical Society*, www.amphilsoc.org/about.

30. "History." *American Philosophical Society*, www.amphilsoc.org/about/history.

Chapter Three

1. Rawle. "Sketch of the Life of Thomas Mifflin." 108.

2. Rossman. *Thomas Mifflin*. 12.

3. Rawle. "Sketch of the Life of Thomas Mifflin." 109.

4. *Ibid.*

5. Rossman. *Thomas Mifflin*. 11.

6. William Spohn Baker. *Washington After the Revolution*. J. B. Lippincott Company, 1898.

7. Trumbull was Speaker from October 24, 1791, to March 4, 1793.

8. Baker. *Washington After the Revolution*. 233.

9. *Colonial and Revolutionary Families of Pennsylvania. Genealogical and Personal Memoirs*. Editor, Wilfred Jordan. Vol. IV. Pt. 1. Lewis Historical Publishing Company, 1932. 17–18.

10. A name composed of an identical (or nearly identical) first name and family name, is called a "reduplicated name." Interestingly, many years after Sarah's father died, another, apparently unrelated, man with the same name became famous in the United States: Nineteenth-century stage actor Morris W. Morris (1845–1906), who went by the stage name Lewis Morrison. Jamaican-born of black and Jewish ancestry, he was the grandfather of American movie actresses Constance and Joan Bennett.

11. In addition to being an expert in 18th and 19th century American portraiture, Charles Henry Hart was a lawyer and director of the Pennsylvania Academy of the Fine Arts (1885–1904).

12. It might be noted that both Thomas and Sarah were raised in Quaker homes and that could well account for the simplicity of their appearance.

13. Frederic Fairchild Sherman. *Art in America an Illustrated Magazine*. Vol. V, 1917. "A Finding Aid to the Charles Henry Hart Papers, 1774–1930, Bulk 1888–1918 | Archives of American Art, Smithsonian Institution." www.aaa.si.edu, www.aaa.si.edu/collections/charles-henry-hart-papers-9656. Accessed 1 Jan. 2024.

14. "Emily Mifflin Hopkinson (1774–1850)." *www.findagrave.com*, www.findagrave.com/memorial/47669656/emily-hopkinson. Accessed 16 Jan. 2024.

15. *Ibid.*

Chapter Four

1. "A Brief History of Newport." *Newport Historical Society*, newporthistory.org/about/newport-history/.
2. Ibid.
3. "1773 July 16." *Founders Online*, National Archives, https://founders.archives.gov/documents/Adams/01-02-02-0003-0006-0001.
4. "From John Adams to Hezekiah Niles, 13 February 1818," *Founders Online*, National Archives, https://founders.archives.gov/documents/Adams/99-02-02-6854. At the time of this letter, Hezekiah Niles (1777–1839) was a 40-year-old editor of a Maryland-based news magazine, which he founded. He used his publication to argue for many causes including the support of American manufacturing and the fight against slavery and anti-Semitism. Born in the same month that the Battle of Saratoga took place, Niles was raised as a Quaker. His father temporarily left the church to fight against the British in the Revolutionary War.
5. Joseph Galloway (1731–August 29, 1803), about 43 years old.
6. Edward Biddle (1738–1779), about 36 years old.
7. Samuel Rhoads (1711–April 7, 1784), about 63 years old.
8. John Morton (1725–April 1, 1777), about 49 years old.
9. Charles Humphreys (September 19, 1714–March 11, 1786), 60 years old.
10. Rawle. "Sketch of the Life of Thomas Mifflin." 109–110.
11. Ross (May 10, 1730–July 14, 1779) was an early support of American independence, signing the Declaration of Independence.
12. Dickinson (November 2, 1732–February 14, 1808) was one of the delegates who expected a break from Britain might be avoided and voted against the Declaration of Independence. Later, however, he became a brigadier general in the Pennsylvania militia.
13. Prowell, George Reeser. *Continental Congress at York, Pennsylvania, and York County in the Revolution*. The York Printing Company, 1914. 248.
14. "To Thomas Jefferson from Benjamin Rush, 4 January 1792." *Founders Online*, National Archives, https://founders.archives.gov/documents/Jefferson/01-23-02-0013.
15. Rossman. *Thomas Mifflin*. 197. Rush's autobiography was not published until many years after his 1813 death.
16. Mifflin, Martha J. *Sketch of Joseph Simon by Samuel Evans & Thomas Mifflin by Martha J. Mifflin: Paper Read Before the Lancaster County Historical Society on March 8, and April 7, 1899*. 175.
17. Eleven months later (April 18, 1775), Paul Revere would make his historic horseback ride in the Boston area to warn people that the British troops were marching towards them.
18. Harley, Lewis Reifsneider. *The Life of Charles Thomson*. George W. Jacobs & Co., 1900, www.google.com/books/edition/The_Life_of_Charles_Thomson/OlwSAAAAYAAJ?hl=en&gbpv=1&dq=The+Life+of+Charles+Thomson&printsec=frontcover. Accessed 13 Dec. 2023.
19. Mifflin. *Sketch of Joseph Simon*. 175.
20. Harley. *The Life of Charles Thomson*.
21. Harley. *The Life of Charles Thomson*. 73–73.
22. Ibid.
23. Mifflin. *Sketch of Joseph Simon*. 175.
24. "1681–1776: The Quaker Province | PHMC > Pennsylvania History." www.phmc.state.pa.us, www.phmc.state.pa.us/portal/communities/pa-history/1681-1776.html.
25. Philadelphia was the chosen location, as it would also be in 1776 for the adoption of the Declaration of Independence, as well as the drafting of the Articles of Confederation.
26. Johnson, Paul. *George Washington: The Founding Father*. Harper Perennial, 2009.
27. Adams, John, and Charles Francis Adams. *Familiar Letters of John Adams and His Wife Abigail Adams, during the Revolution*. HURD AND HOUGHTON, 1876, www.gutenberg.org/files/34123/34123-h/34123-h.htm. Accessed 11 Dec. 2023.
28. Wilson, Woodrow. *George Washington*. New York Harper, 1896.
29. Broadbrims was a nickname for Quaker men because of the

broad-brimmed hats that they often wore.

30. "John Adams to Abigail Adams, 7 October 1774," *Founders Online*, National Archives, https://founders.archives.gov/documents/Adams/04-01-02-0110.

31. "1774 Monday. Octr. 10th." *Founders Online*, National Archives, https://founders.archives.gov/documents/Adams/01-02-02-0004-0007-0011.

32. "Law Library Services—CT Judicial Branch." *www.jud.ct.gov*, www.jud.ct.gov/lawlib/history/sherman.htm. Connecticut's Roger Sherman is the only person to sign all of these documents.

33. "History." *www.pa.ng.mil*, www.pa.ng.mil/History/. Accessed 11 Dec. 2023.

34. Verenna, Thomas. "Explaining Pennsylvania's Militia." *Journal of the American Revolution*, 17 June 2014, allthingsliberty.com/2014/06/explaining-pennsylvanias-militia/. Accessed 16 Dec. 2023.

35. Rossman. *Thomas Mifflin*. 30.

36. *Bulletin of Friends' Historical Society of Philadelphia*. Vol. 16–18, Friends Historical Association, 1927.

37. Sharpless, Isaac. *A History of Quaker Government in Pennsylvania*. T.S. Leach & Company, 1890. In his 1890 work *A History of Quaker Government in Pennsylvania*, Isaac Sharpless stated that Thomas Mifflin in his career showed "but little trace of his Quaker education."

Chapter Five

1. National Park Service. "Timeline of the Revolution—American Revolution (U.S. National Park Service)." *www.nps.gov*, 4 Jan. 2021, www.nps.gov/subjects/americanrevolution/timeline.htm.

2. "Concord Bridge." *www.nationalguard.mil*, www.nationalguard.mil/Resources/Image-Gallery/Historical-Paintings/Heritage-Series/Concord-Bridge/.

3. Rawle. "Sketch of the Life of Thomas Mifflin." 110–111.

4. Many believed this proverb originated from Shakespeare's play *Hamlet*. In it, Polonius explains to his son Laertes that "apparel oft proclaims the man."

5. Rawle. "Sketch of the Life of Thomas Mifflin." 111.

6. "Letter from John Adams to Abigail Adams, 29 May 1775." *Masshist.org*, 2024, www.masshist.org/digitaladams/archive/doc?id=L17750529ja. Accessed 1 Jan. 2024.

7. "Collections of the New York Historical Society for the Year 1886." The New York Historical Society, 1887. 68.

8. "Collections of the New York Historical Society for the Year 1886." 78.

9. Rawle. "Sketch of the Life of Thomas Mifflin." 111. Thomas Craig rose from being a lieutenant in the Pennsylvania militia in 1771 to colonel of the Third Pennsylvania Regiment of the Continental Army in 1777. He saw action at the battles of Brandywine and Germantown. At the battle of Monmouth, "his regiment was conspicuous for gallantry and was in the thickest of the fight." After the war, Craig became a judge and "for several years" he was major-general of the Seventh Division Pennsylvania Militia. He died in 1832 at age 92. It was said that he was "a man fitted to lead an army against a powerful foe." *Portrait and Biographical Record of Lehigh, Northampton and Carbon Counties, Pennsylvania*. Pennsylvania Chapman Publishing Co., 1894. 123.

10. Rawle. "Sketch of the Life of Thomas Mifflin." 111–112.

11. The resolution was issued on July 19, 1775.

12. "Quartermaster's Department—the Army of the U.S. Historical Sketches of Staff and Line with Portraits of Generals-In-Chief | U.S. Army Center of Military History." *history.army.mil*, history.army.mil/books/r&h/R&H-QM.htm.

13. During the Revolution, Washington was to have a total of twenty-eight aides and military secretaries—from Mifflin, who was hired on July 4, 1775, and served for only 41 days before he was promoted—to Hodijah Baylies who served from May 13, 1782, until December 23, 1783. Before joining Washington's staff, Massachusetts native Baylies had been an aide to General Benjamin Lincoln. He was taken prisoner by the British when Lincoln surrendered Charleston, South Carolina, on May 12,

1780. After the war, Baylies married Lincoln's daughter and had a long career in industry and local government. When he died in 1843 at age 86, he was one of the last surviving field officers of the Continental Army.
14. *Journals of Congress:* Containing the Proceedings from January 1, 1776, to January 1, 1777. Vol. II. Yorktown, Pennsylvania, 1778. *Magazine of American History.* Vol. 7, A.S. Barnes & Company, 1881.
15. Risch. *Supplying Washington's Army.*
16. Hubbard. *Major General Israel Putnam.*
17. Almost 50 years old at the time the Revolutionary War began, James Warren was one of Massachusetts' strongest supporters of the Patriot cause. During the war, he was Paymaster General of the Continental Army and later a member of the Navy Board. His wife, author Mercy Otis Warren, became even more famous than her husband, as an influential Patriot.
18. "From John Adams to James Warren, 21 June 1775." *Founders Online,* National Archives, https://founders.archives.gov/documents/Adams/06-03-02-0026.

Chapter Six

1. Risch. *Supplying Washington's Army.* 35.
2. "From George Washington to Richard Henry Lee, 29 August 1775." *Founders Online,* National Archives, https://founders.archives.gov/documents/Washington/03-01-02-0270.
3. "To George Washington from Richard Henry Lee, 26 September 1775." *Founders Online,* National Archives, https://founders.archives.gov/documents/Washington/03-02-02-0046.
4. Rossman. *Thomas Mifflin.* 47.
5. Risch. *Supplying Washington's Army.* 33.
6. "Enclosure II: Thomas Mifflin's Estimate of Quarter Master Expenses, 5 October 1775." *Founders Online,* National Archives, https://founders.archives.gov/documents/Washington/03-02-02-0140-0003.

7. Born on August 10, 1729, Howe lived until July 12, 1814.
8. Heath, William. *Memoirs of Major-General Heath: Containing anecdotes, details of skirmishes, battles, and other military events, during the American war.* Written by himself. Published according to act of Congress. 1798.
9. What the Americans Found on the Nancy. boston1775.blogspot.com/2007/11/what-americans-found-on-nancy.html. Accessed 3 Feb. 2024.
10. Hubbard. *Major General Israel Putnam.*
11. "Quartermaster's Department—the Army of the U.S. Historical Sketches of Staff and Line with Portraits of Generals-In-Chief | U.S. Army Center of Military History." *history.army.mil,* history.army.mil/books/r&h/R&H-QM.htm.

Chapter Seven

1. Hubbard. *General Rufus Putnam.* 45–48.
2. "Orders and Instructions for Colonel Thomas Mifflin, 24 March 1776." *Founders Online,* National Archives, https://founders.archives.gov/documents/Washington/03-03-02-0391.
3. *Ibid.*
4. *Ibid.*
5. Orders were sent from Cambridge on March 29, 1776.
6. Nelson, Paul David. *Anthony Wayne, Soldier of the Early Republic.* Indiana UP, 1985. 20.
7. "To George Washington from Samuel Adams, 15 May 1776." *Founders Online,* National Archives, https://founders.archives.gov/documents/Washington/03-04-02-0244.

Chapter Eight

1. Force, Peter. *American Archives: Fourth Series, Containing a Documentary History of the English Colonies in North America.* 1833. 1398.
2. "Who Coined the Phrase "United States of America"? You May Never Guess | New York Historical Society." *www.nyhistory.org,* www.nyhistory.org/

blogs/coined-phrase-united-states-america-may-never-guess. Accessed 16 Dec. 2023.

3. "From George Washington to John Hancock, 22 January 1777." *Founders Online*, National Archives, https://founders.archives.gov/documents/Washington/03-08-02-0135.

4. Landrigan, Leslie. "Stephen Moylan, the Irishman Who Coined 'United States of America.'" *New England Historical Society*, 23 Dec. 2021, newenglandhistoricalsociety.com/stephen-moylan-the-irishman-who-coined-united-states-of-america/. Accessed 1 Jan. 2024. After 1776, Moylan participated in the Battles of Princeton, Brandywine, Germantown, and Monmouth, and the Siege of Yorktown.

5. Naval History and Heritage Command. "General Mifflin." *Dictionary of American Naval Fighting Ships*, www.history.navy.mil/research/histories/ship-histories/danfs/g/general-mifflin.html#. Accessed 3 Mar. 2024.

6. The Continental Congress established the Continental Navy on October 13, 1775. It had a number of vessels named after current Army generals, such as: the USS *General Gates*, which was a captured British brigantine with 18 guns; the USS *Warren*, a 32-gun frigate named for Boston Patriot leader Joseph Warren who died at the Battle of Bunker Hill; and the USS *Washington*, another 32-gun frigate, named after the Commander in Chief.

7. Hutchinson had been a sergeant in a company of rangers, a lieutenant in a ranger company in 1757, a lieutenant at Lake George and Ticonderoga in 1758, and a captain when the British army beat the French at the Battle of the Plains of Abraham in 1759.

8. Sargent, Winthrop, and the Library of Congress. *Colonel Paul Dudley Sargent. Internet Archive*, [Philadelphia?, 1920], archive.org/details/colonelpauldudle01sarg/page/n5/mode/2up. Accessed 3 Mar. 2024.

9. Brownfeld, Peter Egill. "From Private to Colonel: Jewish Service in the Revolutionary War." *The American Council for Judaism*, 2006, www.acjna.org/acjna/articles_detail.aspx?id=405.

10. Howard Morley Sachar. *A History of the Jews in America*. Alfred A. Knopf, 1994.

11. "To George Washington from Brigadier General Thomas Mifflin, 2 July 1776," *Founders Online*, National Archives, https://founders.archives.gov/documents/Washington/03-05-02-0120.

12. Ibid.

13. "1681–1776: The Quaker Province | PHMC > Pennsylvania History."

14. The Rubicon was a river that Julius Caesar and his army crossed in January 49 BC as he was on his way to conquer Rome and become Emperor. Today, the word means "making an irrevocable decision" or "passing a point of no return."

15. "Thomas Mifflin." *Historical Papers and Addresses of the Lancaster County Historical Society*. Volumes 2–3. Lancaster County Historical Society, 1897. 176.

16. "To George Washington from Brigadier General Thomas Mifflin, 14 July 1776." *Founders Online*, National Archives, https://founders.archives.gov/documents/Washington/03-05-02-0220.

17. Cha Thomson Secy. Journals of Congress: Jan. 1, 1776, to Jan. 1, 1777 (1 prelim. leaf, 520 ... By United States. Continental Congress, Peter Smith, Hugh Hughes, Samuel Sitgreaves. This resolution also covered communications and the transportation of funds to and from Congress:

> That they shall have the Care of forwarding all dispatches from Congress to the Colonies and Armies and all Monies to be transmitted for the public Service by order of Congress; and of providing suitable Escorts and Guards for the safe Conveyance of such dispatches & Monies when it shall appear to them to be necessary-
>
> That they shall superintend the raising fitting out and dispatching all such Land Stores as may be ordered for the Service of the United Colonies-
>
> That they shall have the Care and direction of all Prisoners of War agreeable to the Orders & Regulations of Congress.
>
> That they shall keep and preserve in the said Office in regular Order, all original Letters & Papers which shall

come into the said Office by Order of Congress or otherwise and shall also cause all Draughts of Letters and dispatches to be made or transcribed in Books to be set apart for that purpose and shall cause fair Entries in like manner to be made and Registers preserved of all other Business which shall be transacted in the said Office.
The Members chose, Mr. J. Adams, Mr. Sherman, Mr. Harrison, Mr. Wilson and Mr. E. Rutledge-
The Ballots being taken
Richard Peters Esquire was elected Secretary of the Board of War and Ordinance.

18. "The Board of War to George Washington, 21 June 1776." *Founders Online*, National Archives, https://founders.archives.gov/documents/Adams/06-04-02-0127.
19. "From John Adams to Nathanael Greene, 22 June 1776." *Founders Online*, National Archives, https://founders.archives.gov/documents/Adams/06-04-02-0129.
20. "John Adams to Abigail Adams, 26 June 1776." *Founders Online*, National Archives, https://founders.archives.gov/documents/Adams/04-02-02-0013.
21. "From George Washington to John Hancock, 13 June 1776." *Founders Online*, National Archives, https://founders.archives.gov/documents/Washington/03-04-02-0402.
22. Haas, Bernard D. *Charles Carroll of Carrollton: A Member of the Continental Congress, 1776–1778*. Feb. 1948. 25–26. ecommons.luc.edu/cgi/viewcontent.cgi?article=1199&context=luc_theses. Accessed 14 Dec. 2023.
23. Rawle. "Sketch of the Life of Thomas Mifflin." 112–113.
24. "From John Adams to Nathanael Greene, 4 August 1776." *Founders Online*, National Archives, https://founders.archives.gov/documents/Adams/06-04-02-0193.
25. Adams, John. *The Works of John Adams, Second President of the United States*. Charles C. Little and James Brown, 1851. 49–50.
26. Rawle. "Sketch of the Life of Thomas Mifflin." 112–113.
27. Miller, Richard. *Cyclopædia of Commercial and Business Anecdotes; Comprising Interesting Reminiscences and Facts. ... Embellished with Portraits, Etc*. Appleton and Company, 1864. 759. books.google.com/books?id=t3sPAAAAYAAJ&printsec=-frontcover&source=gbs_ge_summary_r&cad=0#v=onepage&q&f=false. Accessed 11 Dec. 2023.
28. *Ibid.*
29. Samuel Wheeler (1742–1820) also was known for the time he welded bars of iron to fashion a cannon that was used at the Battle of Brandywine. Lighter than the usual cannon, it is said to have been captured by the British, and later exhibited at the Tower of London. It's also believed to be a model for Napoleon Bonaparte's innovative artillery. After the war, Wheeler was elected to the Pennsylvania House of Representatives, became a justice of the peace, and was a member of the American Philosophical Society.
30. "From John Adams to Joseph Ward, 20 August 1776." *Founders Online*, National Archives, https://founders.archives.gov/documents/Adams/06-04-02-0221.
31. After the Battle of Long Island, Scammell served in various campaigns and eventually became Washington's Adjutant General. Following the execution of Benedict Arnold's co-conspirator, British Major John André, Scammell requested permission to resign due to the emotional toll. In 1781, Scammell was mortally wounded at the Siege of Yorktown.
32. Fleming, Thomas. *1776*. Createspace Independent Publishing Platform, 18 Oct. 2016. After the landing of the British at Manhattan's Kip's Bay days later, Smallwood (1732–1792) was wounded at the Battle of White Plains (1776) and participated in the Battles of Germantown (1777), and Camden (1780). He was promoted to major general in the Continental Army in 1780. After the war, Smallwood served a term as governor of Maryland.
33. Putnam, Rufus, and Rowena Buell. *The Memoirs of Rufus Putnam and Certain Official Papers and Correspondence, Published by the National Society of the Colonial Dames of America in the State of Ohio*. Houghton, Mifflin, 1903. 60.

34. Hubbard. *General Rufus Putnam.*
35. *Ibid.*
36. "From John Jay to Edward Rutledge, 11 October 1776." *Founders Online,* National Archives, https://founders.archives.gov/documents/Jay/01-01-02-0185.
37. Force. *American Archives,* 5th ser., 2:1011–14. Fifth Series. Volume 2 (Vol. 8 of 9).
38. Collections of the New York Historical Society: The John Watts De Peyster publication fund series. Volume 11. The Society, 1879—New York (State).

Chapter Nine

1. Force, Peter, and Matthew St. Clair Clarke. *American Archives.* Vol. II. M. St. Clair Clarke, 1848. 1298–1299.
2. Joseph E. Johnston (1807–1891), a U.S. Army BG from Virginia, served as Quartermaster General for ten months, resigning on April 22, 1861. He was the highest-ranking U.S. Army officer to join the Confederacy.
3. "To George Washington from Major General Nathanael Greene, 27 July 1780." *Founders Online,* National Archives, https://founders.archives.gov/documents/Washington/03-27-02-0267.
4. "1st Quartermaster Commandant—MG Thomas Mifflin—First Term." *U.S. Army Quartermaster Corps,* quartermaster.army.mil/bios/previous-qm-generals/quartermaster_general_bio-mifflin.html.
5. Rawle. "Sketch of the Life of Thomas Mifflin." 116–117.
6. Rossman. *Thomas Mifflin.* 158.
7. Peculation is the act of someone illegally taking or using money, especially public funds, that is entrusted to their care.
8. "To George Washington from Major General Thomas Mifflin, 9 March 1777." *Founders Online,* National Archives, https://founders.archives.gov/documents/Washington/03-08-02-0576.
9. "Thomas Jefferson to Walter Jones, 2 January 1814." *Founders Online,* National Archives, https://founders.archives.gov/documents/Jefferson/03-07-02-0052.
10. "From George Washington to Major General Thomas Mifflin, 18 March 1777." *Founders Online,* National Archives, https://founders.archives.gov/documents/Washington/03-08-02-0641.
11. Greene, George W. *Life of Nathanael Greene, Major-General in the Army of the Revolution.* Charles C. Little and James Brown, 1846. 81.
12. Reed, William Bradford. *Life and Correspondence of Joseph Reed. Volume 2.* Lindsay and Blakiston, 1847. 241–242. In the same letter, Nathanael Greene states: "I received a Resolution of Congress that the principal of the departments which handled public money, however diffuse, should be held responsible for all the subordinate agents. This appeared to me so unreasonable, as well as unjust, that the whole complexion of the business had something so cruel, and at the same time so personal in it, that I was determined to leave it be the consequence what it might."
13. "U.S. Army Quartermaster Corps & School | Fort Gregg-Adams, Virginia." *U.S. Army Quartermaster,* quartermaster.army.mil/bios/previous-qm-generals/quartermaster_general_bio-greene.htm. Accessed 1 Jan. 2024.
14. Prowell. *Continental Congress at York.* 248.
15. Rawle. "Sketch of the Life of Thomas Mifflin." 113.
16. "Instructions to Brigadier General Thomas Mifflin, 10 November 1776." *Founders Online,* National Archives, https://founders.archives.gov/documents/Washington/03-07-02-0097.
17. *Ibid.*
18. Benjamin Harrison and Francis Lightfoot Lee represented Virginia in Congress. James Wilson and Edward Rutledge were delegates from Pennsylvania and South Carolina, respectively. All four had signed the Declaration of Independence a few months earlier.
19. "To George Washington from the Board of War, 14 November 1776." *Founders Online,* National Archives, https://founders.archives.gov/documents/Washington/03-07-02-0110.
20. "To George Washington from Brigadier General Thomas Mifflin, 26 November 1776." *Founders Online,* National Archives, https://founders.archives.gov/documents/Washington/03-07-02-0156.

21. *Ibid.*
22. *Ibid.*
23. *Journals of Congress:* Containing the Proceedings from January 1, 1776, to January 1, 1777. Vol. II. Yorktown, Pennsylvania, 1778. 501–502.
24. Rawle. "Sketch of the Life of Thomas Mifflin." 113–114.
25. *Ibid.*
26. *Journals of the Continental Congress, 1774–1789 / Vol. IX: 1777.* Government Printing Office, 1907.
27. "To George Washington from Major General Israel Putnam, 12 December 1776." *Founders Online,* National Archives, https://founders.archives.gov/documents/Washington/03-07-02-0250.
28. "Letters of Delegates to Congress: Volume 5, August 16, 1776–December 31, 1776—Richard Henry Lee to Patrick Henry." *Library of Congress,* memory.loc.gov/cgi-bin/query/r?ammem/hlaw:@field(DOCID+@lit(dg005550)). Accessed 23 Feb. 2024.

Chapter Ten

1. Wright, Robert K., Jr., and Morris J. MacGregor, Jr. *Soldier-Statesmen of the Constitution.* Center of Military History, United States Army. 1987.
2. Rawle. "Sketch of the Life of Thomas Mifflin." 114.
3. "To George Washington from Brigadier General Thomas Mifflin, 28 December 1776." *Founders Online,* National Archives, https://founders.archives.gov/documents/Washington/03-07-02-0368.
4. Stryker, William S. *The Battles of Trenton and Princeton.* Houghton, Mifflin, 1898. 433.
5. Stryker. *The Battles of Trenton and Princeton.* 253.
6. Stryker. *The Battles of Trenton and Princeton.* Like Mifflin, John Cadwalader attended the College of Philadelphia and entered business in Philadelphia as a merchant with his brother. He became an active supporter of American independence like Mifflin but served as a militia general.
7. Stryker. *The Battles of Trenton and Princeton.* 429.
8. Major John Mifflin of Fifth Pennsylvania battalion.
9. Stryker. *The Battles of Trenton and Princeton.* 431.
10. Stryker. *The Battles of Trenton and Princeton.* 435–436.
11. A Scotland-born medical doctor, Hugh Mercer became a colonel during the French and Indian War and met life-long friend George Washington. In the early months of the American Revolution, Mercer rose from commander of Virginia Minute Men to a brigadier general in the Continental Army. World War II American General George S. Patton was a direct descendant of General Mercer's daughter Ann Mercer Patton.
12. Later, the College of New Jersey was renamed Princeton University. Nassau Hall was built two decades before the Battle of Princeton. Six years after the battle, it became the home of the Continental Congress for about five months.
13. Alfred Alexander Woodhull. *The Battle of Princeton.* 1913.
14. *Ibid.*; Wright, Robert K., Jr., and Morris J. MacGregor, Jr. *Soldier-Statesmen of the Constitution.* Center of Military History, United States Army. 1987.
15. Rossman. *Thomas Mifflin.* 78.
16. "31st Quartermaster General | LTG Edmund Gregory." *U.S. Army Quartermaster Corps,* quartermaster.army.mil/bios/previous-qm-generals/quartermaster_general_bio-gregory.html. Accessed 24 Feb. 2024. By the time of World War II, the responsibilities of the U.S. Army's Quartermaster General had grown substantially. Lieutenant General Edmund Gregory (1882–1961), who served in the position throughout that war, was responsible for "the development, procurement, distribution of billions of dollars' worth of equipment and supplies. He supervised the training of thousands of Quartermaster soldiers and controlled more than 90,000 military and civilian personnel. Over 900,000 personnel were employed by contractors under his supervision."
17. "From George Washington to Brigadier General Thomas Mifflin, 31 January 1777." *Founders Online,* National Archives, https://founders.archives.gov/documents/Washington/03-08-02-0215.
18. "To George Washington from Brigadier General Thomas Mifflin, 4 February 1777." *Founders Online,* National

Archives, https://founders.archives.gov/documents/Washington/03-08-02-0257.

19. "To George Washington from Brigadier General Thomas Mifflin, 13 February 1777." *Founders Online*, National Archives, https://founders.archives.gov/documents/Washington/03-08-02-0352.

20. "To George Washington from Brigadier General Thomas Mifflin, 4 February 1777."

21. "From George Washington to Brigadier General Thomas Mifflin, 14 February 1777." *Founders Online*, National Archives, https://founders.archives.gov/documents/Washington/03-08-02-0360.

22. Rawle. "Sketch of the Life of Thomas Mifflin." 114.

23. Even though Washington agreed with Arnold that he should have been promoted, Arnold's anger festered, until three years later he attempted to hand over the fort at West Point, New York, to the British. After his plans were revealed, Arnold eluded capture, joined and fought with the British against the Americans, and became the most famous traitor in the history of the United States.

24. From George Washington to Brigadier General Benedict Arnold, 3 March 1777." *Founders Online*, National Archives, https://founders.archives.gov/documents/Washington/03-08-02-0514.

25. "To George Washington from Brigadier General Benedict Arnold, 11 March 1777." *Founders Online*, National Archives, https://founders.archives.gov/documents/Washington/03-08-02-0584.

26. "To George Washington from Brigadier General Benedict Arnold, 26 March 1777." *Founders Online*, National Archives, https://founders.archives.gov/documents/Washington/03-08-02-0688.

27. Connecticut's two Continental Army major generals at the time were Israel Putnam, who was one of the first four major generals appointed (1775), and Joseph Spencer who was promoted to major general in 1776. The home states of the five men promoted over Benedict Arnold at the time were: Mifflin and St. Clair from Pennsylvania, Lincoln from Massachusetts, Stirling from New York, and Stephen from Virginia.

28. "From George Washington to Major General Benedict Arnold, 2 April 1777." *Founders Online*, National Archives, https://founders.archives.gov/documents/Washington/03-09-02-0044.

29. "From George Washington to Major General Benedict Arnold, 8 May 1777." *Founders Online*, National Archives, https://founders.archives.gov/documents/Washington/03-09-02-0357.

30. "From George Washington to John Hancock, 26 January 1777." *Founders Online*, National Archives, https://founders.archives.gov/documents/Washington/03-08-02-0167.

31. "From George Washington to Captain Edward Snickers, 19 January 1777." *Founders Online*, National Archives, https://founders.archives.gov/documents/Washington/03-08-02-0116.

32. "From George Washington to John Hancock, 26 January 1777."

33. "From George Washington to Major General Thomas Mifflin, 13 March 1777." *Founders Online*, National Archives, https://founders.archives.gov/documents/Washington/03-08-02-0601.

34. "To George Washington from Major General Thomas Mifflin, 17 March 1777." *Founders Online*, National Archives, https://founders.archives.gov/documents/Washington/03-08-02-0635.

35. "From George Washington to Major General Thomas Mifflin, 19 March 1777." *Founders Online*, National Archives, https://founders.archives.gov/documents/Washington/03-08-02-0645.

Chapter Eleven

1. Hubbard. *General Rufus Putnam*.

2. "From George Washington to Major General Thomas Mifflin, 10–12 April 1777." *Founders Online*, National Archives, https://founders.archives.gov/documents/Washington/03-09-02-0120.

3. "To George Washington from Major General Thomas Mifflin, 13 May 1777." *Founders Online*, National Archives, https://founders.archives.gov/documents/Washington/03-09-02-0408.

4. "From George Washington to Major General Thomas Mifflin, 15 May 1777." *Founders Online*, National Archives, https://founders.archives.

gov/documents/Washington/03-09-02-0428.

5. "To George Washington from Major General Thomas Mifflin, 27 May 1777." *Founders Online,* National Archives, https://founders.archives.gov/documents/Washington/03-09-02-0537.

6. "From George Washington to Major General Thomas Mifflin, 28 May 1777." *Founders Online,* National Archives, https://founders.archives.gov/documents/Washington/03-09-02-0542.

7. This letter was sent from Washington's headquarters at Middlebrook, New Jersey. This letter was written soon after Washington made his headquarters there for the first time. Three more times during the Revolutionary War, he would call Middlebrook his headquarters: for four months in 1779, and for a few days in 1778 and in 1782. Middlebrook is part of Bound Brook, New Jersey.

8. At the time of this letter, Jacob Morris was about 22 years old. During the war he was at various times aide to Generals Charles Lee, Nathanael Greene, and Benedict Arnold, and he served at several battles including Princeton and Monmouth. In later life, he settled in New York State, and became a businessman and militia general. He died at age 88.

9. "From George Washington to Major General Thomas Mifflin, 29 May 1777." *Founders Online,* National Archives, https://founders.archives.gov/documents/Washington/03-09-02-0552.

10. "To George Washington from Major Jacob Morris, 10 April 1777." *Founders Online,* National Archives, https://founders.archives.gov/documents/Washington/03-09-02-0121. Mifflin followed up by hiring Henry Emanuel Lutterloh as his "deputy." Also working for Mifflin were "Wagon Master General" Joseph Thornsbury and "Commissary General for Forage" Clement Biddle.

11. "From George Washington to Major General Thomas Mifflin, 31 May 1777." *Founders Online,* National Archives, https://founders.archives.gov/documents/Washington/03-09-02-0569.

12. Skinners Corps consisted of loyalist troops raised by Tory Brigadier General Cortlandt Skinner; Rogers's Corps were loyalist "Queen's Rangers" who were organized by famed French and Indian War guerrilla fighter Robert Rogers. Mifflin's sometimes commander Israel Putnam fought under Rogers as a member of his Rogers's Rangers in the French and Indian War but fought against him in the Revolution when Rogers chose to fight with the British against the American colonists.

13. "From George Washington to Major General Thomas Mifflin, 10 June 1777." *Founders Online,* National Archives, https://founders.archives.gov/documents/Washington/03-09-02-0658.

14. "John Adams to Abigail Adams, 14 June 1777." *Founders Online,* National Archives, https://founders.archives.gov/documents/Adams/04-02-02-0205.

15. Lloyd, June. "Colonel Jonathan Mifflin, Revolutionary War Patriot and Master of Hybla at Wrightsville." *York Daily Record,* 16 Dec. 2016, www.ydr.com/story/news/history/blogs/universal-york/2016/12/06/colonel-jonathan-mifflin-revolutionary-war-patriot-and-master-of-hybla-at-wrightsville/95089776/. Accessed 7 Jan. 2024. Jonathan Mifflin (1753–1840), who participated in several battles during the war, resigned from the Deputy Quartermaster General position on December 31, 1777. He was also a private in the Philadelphia City Cavalry. A businessman after the war, Mifflin and his wife Susannah Mifflin (1764–1821) and their son Samuel Mifflin (1805–1885) were dedicated opponents of slavery who used their large stone house at Wrightsville as an Underground Railroad station for enslaved people who were escaping to free states.

On March 4, 1831, 80-year-old Jonathan Mifflin was put on the pension rolls for his Revolutionary War service. His annual allowance was $425. Prowell, George Reeser. *Continental Congress at York, Pennsylvania and York County in the Revolution.* The York Printing Company, 1914. 286.

16. "To George Washington from Major General Thomas Mifflin, 27 July 1777." *Founders Online,* National Archives, https://founders.archives.gov/documents/Washington/03-10-02-0431.

17. "From George Washington to

Major General Thomas Mifflin, 28 July 1777." *Founders Online,* National Archives, https://founders.archives.gov/documents/Washington/03-10-02-0442.

Chapter Twelve

1. Monroe was General William Alexander's nineteen-year-old aide-de-camp at the time he was at Valley Forge.
2. Marshall was 22 years old when stationed at Valley Forge.
3. Tinkcom. *The Pennsylvania Magazine.*
4. "To George Washington from Richard Henry Lee, 20 October 1777." *Founders Online,* National Archives, https://founders.archives.gov/documents/Washington/03-11-02-0573.
5. "Lee Letter: N380." *Lee Family Digital Archive,* 2024, leefamilyarchive.org/papers/letters/transcripts-gw%20delegates/DIV0380.html. Accessed 15 Feb. 2024.
6. Pickering (1745–1829) later served as U.S. Secretary of State under Presidents Washington and Adams.
7. Harrison (1745–1790) was George Washington's military secretary during the American Revolutionary War.
8. *Journals of the Continental Congress, 1774–1789 / Vol. IX: 1777.* 959.
9. Procknow, Gene. "Thomas Mifflin: Revolutionary Enigma." *Researching the American Revolution,* 27 Jan. 2018, researchingtheamericanrevolution.com/2018/01/27/thomas-mifflin-revolutionary-enigma/. Accessed 13 Dec. 2023.
10. John Dickinson was famous for his "Letters from a Farmer in Pennsylvania," which questioned the British parliament's right to levy taxes on its North American colonies.
11. *Journals of the Continental Congress, 1774–1789.* 959.
12. Dorwart, Jeffery M. *Fort Mifflin of Philadelphia: An Illustrated History.* Google Books, University of Pennsylvania Press, 1 May 1998, www.google.com/books/edition/Fort_Mifflin_of_Philadelphia/TsnZ_jlDWvMC?hl=en&gbpv=1&dq=governor+mifflin&pg=PA73&printsec=frontcover. Accessed 10 Dec. 2023.
13. It was not officially given the name Fort Mifflin until 1795.
14. Fort Mercer was located in the state of New Jersey along the east shore of the Delaware River south of Philadelphia. The fort was named for Brigadier General Hugh Mercer who was mortally wounded at the Battle of Princeton. Today, a park and museum occupy the site.
15. Lydia Darragh was born in 1729 and died in Philadelphia in 1789.
16. *Portrait and Biographical Record of Lehigh, Northampton and Carbon Counties, Pennsylvania.* Chicago, Pennsylvania Chapman Publishing Co., 1894.
17. "Circular to the States, 29 December 1777." *Founders Online,* National Archives, https://founders.archives.gov/documents/Washington/03-13-02-0037.

Chapter Thirteen

1. Rawle. "Sketch of the Life of Thomas Mifflin." 124–126.
2. *Ibid.*
3. *Ibid.*
4. *Ibid.*
5. *Ibid.*
6. Procknow. "Thomas Mifflin."
7. Heitman, Francis Bernard. *Historical Register of Officers of the Continental Army During the War of the Revolution, April, 1775, to December, 1783.* 1892. On December 13, 1777, when Conway was appointed Inspector General of the Army, it was with the rank of major general. He resigned a few months later—on April 28, 1778.
8. Zellers-Frederick, Andrew A. "General Thomas Conway: Cabal Conspirator or Career Climber?" *Journal of the American Revolution,* 29 Oct. 2018, allthingsliberty.com/2018/10/general-thomas-conway-cabal-conspirator-or-career-climber/. Accessed 13 Dec. 2023.
9. "To John Adams from Benjamin Rush, 21 October 1777." *Founders Online,* National Archives, https://founders.archives.gov/documents/Adams/06-05-02-0187.
10. Lender, Mark Edward. *Cabal! The Plot Against General Washington.* Westholme Publishing, 2019. 130–131.
11. "To George Washington from

Richard Henry Lee, 20–22 November 1777."

12. *Ibid.*; "Lee Letter: N380." *Lee Family Digital Archive*, 2024, leefamilyarchive.org/papers/letters/transcripts-gw%20delegates/DIV0380.html.

13. "Secretaries of War & Secretaries of the Army." *U.S. Army Center of Military History*, history.army.mil/books/swsa/SWSA-Fm.htm. Accessed 8 Feb. 2024.

14. Rawle. "Sketch of the Life of Thomas Mifflin." 114–115.

15. Rawle. "Sketch of the Life of Thomas Mifflin." 115.

16. Rawle. "Sketch of the Life of Thomas Mifflin." 115–116.

17. "To George Washington from Major General Lafayette, 30 December 1777." *Founders Online*, National Archives, https://founders.archives.gov/documents/Washington/03-13-02-0063.

18. *Ibid.*

19. "From George Washington to Richard Henry Lee, 16 October 1777." *Founders Online*, National Archives, https://founders.archives.gov/documents/Washington/03-11-02-0538.

20. "From George Washington to Richard Henry Lee, 28 October 1777." *Founders Online*, National Archives, https://founders.archives.gov/documents/Washington/03-12-02-0035.

21. "To George Washington from Major General Thomas Conway, 29 December 1777." *Founders Online*, National Archives, https://founders.archives.gov/documents/Washington/03-13-02-0040.

22. "From George Washington to Major General Horatio Gates, 4 January 1778." *Founders Online*, National Archives, founders.archives.gov/documents/Washington/03-13-02-0113.

23. "Collections of the New York Historical Society for the Year 1878." The New York Historical Society, 1879. 434–435.

24. "George Washington Is America's Favorite Founding Father—CBS News Poll." *CBS News*, 2 July 2021, www.cbsnews.com/news/george-washington-americas-favorite-founding-father-cbs-news-poll/.

25. "From George Washington to Patrick Henry, 28 March 1778." *Founders Online*, National Archives, https://founders.archives.gov/documents/Washington/03-14-02-0310.

26. *Ibid.*

27. "From George Washington to Major General Thomas Mifflin, 24 April 1778." *Founders Online*, National Archives, https://founders.archives.gov/documents/Washington/03-14-02-0560.

28. "From George Washington to Major General Horatio Gates, 24 April 1778," *Founders Online*, National Archives, https://founders.archives.gov/documents/Washington/03-14-02-0557.

29. Cadwalader was born in 1742 and died in 1786.

30. "John Cadwalader." *University Archives and Records Center*, archives.upenn.edu/exhibits/penn-people/biography/john-cadwalader/. Accessed 14 Dec. 2023.

31. "To George Washington from Thomas Conway, 23 July 1778." *Founders Online*, National Archives, https://founders.archives.gov/documents/Washington/03-16-02-0153.

32. After leaving the service, Hamilton became a New York delegate to the Continental Congress, and after George Washington won the presidency, the first treasury secretary of the United States.

33. Fleming, Thomas. *1776*. Mifflin at the time was recently retired as a major general and as the quartermaster general of the Continental Army. The following year, he was to be reelected as a Pennsylvania delegate to the Continental Congress.

34. Ten years later, President George Washington appointed James Wilson (1742–1798) to be one of the justices on the first U.S. Supreme Court.

35. Robert Morris lived from 1734 to 1806.

36. Westcott, Thompson. *The Historic Mansions and Buildings of Philadelphia: With Some Notice of Their Owners and Occupants*. W. H. Barr, 1894, books.google.com/books?id=5m1TAAAAMAAJ&printsec=frontcover&source=gbs_ViewAPI#v=onepage&q=false. Accessed 3 Mar. 2024.

37. Reed, William Bradford. *Life and Correspondence of Joseph Reed.* 426.

38. Westcott. *The Historic Mansions and Buildings of Philadelphia*.

39. Reed, William Bradford. *Life and Correspondence of Joseph Reed.* 426–427.
40. *Ibid.*
41. Reed was President of the Supreme Executive Council of Pennsylvania, at the time the equivalent of governor of Pennsylvania.
42. Reed, William Bradford. *Life and Correspondence of Joseph Reed.*
43. Alexander, John K. "The Fort Wilson Incident of 1779: A Case Study of the Revolutionary Crowd." *The William and Mary Quarterly*, Vol. 31, No. 4, 1974. 589–612. JSTOR, https://doi.org/10.2307/1921605. Accessed 29 Oct. 2023.
44. Reed, William Bradford. *Life and Correspondence of Joseph Reed.*
45. "To John Adams from Henry Laurens, 4 October 1779." *Founders Online*, National Archives, https://founders.archives.gov/documents/Adams/06-08-02-0130.
46. "From John Adams to Henry Laurens, 25 October 1779." *Founders Online*, National Archives, https://founders.archives.gov/documents/Adams/06-08-02-0158.

Chapter Fourteen

1. Rossman. *Thomas Mifflin.* 275.
2. Baker. *Washington After the Revolution.* 84.
3. *Ibid.* In 1789, Legaux received the honor of membership in the American Philosophical Society. In the 1790s he encountered financial difficulties, but didn't lose his vineyard.
4. Baker. *Washington After the Revolution.* 407. Biddle, at the same time, provides a description of the Washington he knew: "He [Washington] was a most elegant figure of a man, with so much dignity of manners that no person whatever could take any improper liberties with him. I have heard Mr. Robert Morris, who was as intimate with him as any man in America, say that he was the only man in whose presence he felt any awe. You would seldom see a frown or a smile on his countenance, his air was serious and reflecting, yet I have seen him in the theatre laugh heartily."
5. *Ibid.*

6. Rossman. *Thomas Mifflin.* 197.
7. Iwanicki, Edwin. *The Village of Falls of Schuylkill.* Pennsylvania Historical Salvage Council, 1967. 336.
8. Iwanicki. *The Village of Falls of Schuylkill.* 337.
9. "Fountain Park, Falls of Schuylkill, Philadelphia." Extract of a letter from one of the editors of the *New York Mirror*, dated Philadelphia, September, 1845.
10. *Ibid.*
11. Rossman. *Thomas Mifflin.* 174.

Chapter Fifteen

1. McKean was destined to succeed Thomas Mifflin as Pennsylvania governor in 1799.
2. Grainger, John D. *The Battle of Yorktown, 1781: A Reassessment.* Boydell Press, 2005. 67. Less than three weeks earlier, Cornwallis saw the French fleet at Yorktown and wrote to British General Clinton: "There are between thirty and forty sail within the capes, mostly ships of war and some of them very large."
3. "Report on Books for Congress, [23 January] 1783." *Founders Online*, National Archives, https://founders.archives.gov/documents/Madison/01-06-02-0031.
4. Office of the Historian. "U.S.-China Chronology—Countries—Office of the Historian." *U.S. Department of State*, 2019, history.state.gov/countries/issues/china-us-relations.
5. *Journals of the Continental Congress, 1774–1789 / Vol. IX: 1777.*
6. "The Ordinance of 1784." *U.S. House of Representatives: History, Art and Archives*, history.house.gov/Historical-Highlights/1700s/Ordinance-of-1784/. Accessed 10 Dec. 2023.
7. Scudder, Horace E. *George Washington: An Historical Biography.* Houghton Mifflin Company, 1889. 210–211.
8. "III. Washington's Address to Congress Resigning his Commission, [23 December 1783]." *Founders Online*, National Archives, https://founders.archives.gov/documents/Jefferson/01-06-02-0319-0004.
9. "To George Washington from United States Congress, 23 December 1783." *Founders Online*, National

Archives, https://founders.archives.gov/documents/Washington/99-01-02-12224.

10. In the later 1780s and early 1790s, Trumbull traveled through the North American states meeting with, and painting small portraits of, most of the important people of the American Revolution. He would later use these images when he created his large paintings of historic events.

11. Rawle. "Sketch of the Life of Thomas Mifflin." 117–118. Rawle had nothing but words of admiration for Washington as he finished his description of the Commander in Chief's resignation: "Foreigners have not yet ceased to extol the *magnanimity* of him who thus voluntarily retired, from the command of a victorious army, to the shades of private life, without any *distinction* above his fellow citizens; and of his merits in this respect, his *fellow citizens* were duly sensible. If, indeed, he had made an *attempt* to arrogate to himself any *inordinate power*, or *personal privilege*, the *genius* and *character* of our country would have *prevented* its success; but the purity of his mind forbade his forming even such *a wish*; his example was followed by his fellow soldiers, and fellow sufferers, and never was the dissolution of an army marked by more resignation and tranquility. The slight and temporary ebullition of June, 1783, deserves scarcely to be mentioned as an exception to the general demeanor of the common men."

12. Office of the Historian. "Milestones: 1750–1775—Office of the Historian." *Foreign Service Institute United States Department of State*, 2018, history.state.gov/milestones/1750-1775/treaty-of-paris. "The Treaty of Paris of 1763 ended the French and Indian War/Seven Years' War between Great Britain and France, as well as their respective allies. In the terms of the treaty, France gave up all its territories in mainland North America, effectively ending any foreign military threat to the British colonies there."

13. Office of the Historian. "Milestones: 1866–1898—Office of the Historian." Foreign Service Institute United States Department of State, history.state. gov/milestones/1866–1898/spanish-american-war#:~:text=The%20war%20officially%20ended%20four. "The war officially ended four months later, when the U.S. and Spanish governments signed the Treaty of Paris on December 10, 1898. Apart from guaranteeing the independence of Cuba, the treaty also forced Spain to cede Guam and Puerto Rico to the United States."; Egle, William Henry. *An Illustrated History of the Commonwealth of Pennsylvania: Civil, Political, and Military, from Its Earliest Settlement to the Present Time Including Historical Descriptions of Each County in the State, Their Towns, and Industrial Resources.* DeWitt C. Goodrich, 1876, www.google.com/books/edition/An_Illustrated_History_of_the_Commonweal/q3AyTE9UM60C?hl=en&gbpv=1&dq=%22thomas+mifflin%22&pg=PA213&printsec=frontcover. Accessed 14 Dec. 2023.

14. Born in Philadelphia in 1753, Josiah Harmar rose to the rank of colonel in the Continental Army. When he was chosen by Congress to carry the ratified treaty to Europe, he was 29 years old. Later appointed commander of the U.S. Army in Ohio, he ordered the construction of a fort across the Muskingum River from present-day Marietta, Ohio. Five years later, he was sent by Secretary of War Henry Knox to attack Indian villages in the Northwest.

15. Mifflin concluded the letter to the American Peace Commissioners with, "[Harmar] will have the Honor of delivering to you the Ratification; together with Copies of the Proclamation of Congress and of their Recommendation to the States conformably to the 5th. Article. I take the Liberty of recommending Colonel Harmar to you as a brave and deserving Officer and am, with the highest Respect & Esteem, Gentlemen, Your obedient, and most humble Servant. THOMAS MIFFLIN."

16. Rawle. "Sketch of the Life of Thomas Mifflin." 118–119.

17. "To George Washington from Thomas Mifflin, 31 May 1784." *Founders Online*, National Archives, https://founders.archives.gov/documents/Washington/04-01-02-0277.

18. Six years later, on December 4, 1792, Wynkoop (1732–1812) would be

elected the 37th Speaker of the Pennsylvania House of Representatives.

19. "Thomas Mifflin—PA House of Representatives." *The Official Website for the Pennsylvania General Assembly*, www.legis.state.pa.us/cfdocs/legis/SpeakerBios/SpeakerBio.cfm?id=110.

20. Rossman. *Thomas Mifflin*. 301.

21. Ibid.

22. Ibid.

23. Powell. *Kenneth R. Rossman*. Dr. John H. Powell (1914–1971) was the author of the acclaimed "Bring Out Your Dead: The Great Plague of Yellow Fever in Philadelphia in 1793."

24. Just 18 days before the battle, Greene had been appointed a major general in the Continental Army.

Chapter Sixteen

1. Werther, Richard J. "Analyzing the Founders: A Closer Look at the Signers of Four Founding Documents." Journal of the American Revolution, 24 Oct. 2017, allthingsliberty.com/2017/10/analyzing-founders-closer-look-signers-4-founding-documents/.

2. Roger Sherman of Connecticut was both a lawyer and a merchant.

3. Immediately after the Constitution's ratification in 1789, the Episcopal Church was formerly established to be the successor of the Church of England in the United States.

4. Wright and MacGregor, *Soldier-Statesmen of the Constitution*. vi.

5. Rawle. "Sketch of the Life of Thomas Mifflin." 119.

6. In later years, Blair (1732–1800) would help interpretation of the Constitution as one of the new nation's first U.S. Supreme Court justices.

7. *The Documentary History of the Ratification of the Constitution Digital Edition*, ed. John P. Kaminski, Gaspare J. Saladino, Richard Leffler, Charles H. Schoenleber and Margaret A. Hogan. University of Virginia Press, 2009. https://csac.history.wisc.edu/wp-content/uploads/sites/281/2017/07/anno-pennsylvania.pdf.

8. "To John Adams from Thomas Jefferson, 13 November 1787." *Founders Online*, National Archives, https://founders.archives.gov/documents/Adams/06-19-02-0151.

9. "From John Adams to Thomas Jefferson, 6 December 1787." *Founders Online*, National Archives, https://founders.archives.gov/documents/Adams/06-19-02-0159.

10. Bloom, Sol, and United States. *The Story of the Constitution*. United States Constitution Sesquicentennial Commission, 1937.

11. Since its passage, the Constitution has been amended only 27 times—and the first ten of those amendments (known as the Bill of Rights) were ratified less than four years after the Constitution.

12. Boone, born in 1734, was ten years older than Mifflin.

13. Rossman. *Thomas Mifflin*. 197. When Rossman wrote his Mifflin biography in the early 1950s, much of that land of the Angelica farm was occupied by the Berks County Almshouse and Hospital.

14. Penn (1760–1834) was a grandson of William Penn, the founder of the Province of Pennsylvania.

15. Penn, John. *Pennsylvania Magazine of History and Biography*. Vol. 3, No. 3. University of Pennsylvania Press, 1879. 284–295.

16. Today, the county boasts of two institutions of higher learning: The Geisinger-Lewistown Hospital School of Nursing and the Mifflin County Academy of Science and Technology. Both of these are in Lewistown.

17. "U.S. Census Bureau QuickFacts: Mifflin County, Pennsylvania." *U.S. Census Bureau*, www.census.gov/quickfacts/mifflincountypennsylvania.

18. "Mifflin County Historical Marker." *CeraNet Cloud Computing's Historical Marker Database*, www.hmdb.org/m.asp?m=24273. Accessed 4 Jan. 2024.

Chapter Seventeen

1. Rawle. "Sketch of the Life of Thomas Mifflin." 119–121.

2. Rawle. "Sketch of the Life of Thomas Mifflin." 122.

3. Rawle. "Sketch of the Life of Thomas Mifflin." 121–122.

4. Rawle. "Sketch of the Life of Thomas Mifflin." 122.
5. Smith, Horace Wemyss. *Life and Correspondence of the Rev. William Smith, D. D.* 1880. 324.
6. *Ibid.*
7. Smith. *Life and Correspondence of the Rev. William Smith, D. D.* 325.
8. *Ibid.*

Chapter Eighteen

1. A "commonwealth" is a political unit founded for the common good. Only three other states of the United States besides Pennsylvania have "Commonwealth" as part of their official names: Kentucky, Massachusetts, and Virginia.
2. Rossman. *Thomas Mifflin.* 204.
3. Westcott. *The Historic Mansions and Buildings of Philadelphia.*
4. "Pennsylvania 1790 Governor." *A New Nation Votes: American Election Returns 1787–1825.* 11 Jan. 2012, elections.lib.tufts.edu/catalog/k930bz14c. Accessed 15 Dec. 2023.
5. Egle. *Notes and Queries.* 491–492.
6. Egle. *Notes and Queries.* 492.
7. A Fast Day was an annual holiday in Massachusetts and several other states in the 17th through the 20th centuries. It was designed as a day of public fasting and prayer to avert plagues, crop failures, and other calamities. People were directed not to work, to limit eating, and to attend church services.
8. "From John Adams to Thomas Jefferson, 30 June 1813." *Founders Online,* National Archives, https://founders.archives.gov/documents/Adams/99-02-02-6084.
9. Klein, Theodore B. *The Canals of Pennsylvania and the System of Internal Improvements,* 1901. 5.
10. Landis, Charles I. *The First Long Turnpike in the United States.* New Era Printing Company, 1917. 219.
11. *Farm Prices in Two Centuries.* Government Printing Office, 1892.
12. Rossman. *Thomas Mifflin.* 210.
13. Rossman. *Thomas Mifflin.* 198.
14. "To George Washington from Joseph Hopkinson, 9 May 1798." *Founders Online,* National Archives, https://founders.archives.gov/documents/Washington/06-02-02-0191.
15. "From George Washington to Joseph Hopkinson, 27 May 1798." *Founders Online,* National Archives, https://founders.archives.gov/documents/Washington/06-02-02-0227.
16. "Hail Columbia." Library of Congress, 2002. www.loc.gov/item/ihas.200000008/.
17. A native of Trappe, Pennsylvania, a town about 35 miles northwest of Philadelphia, Muhlenberg received religious training in Germany, was ordained a Lutheran minister in 1770, and served congregations in Pennsylvania and New York. He later entered politics and served in the Pennsylvania legislature—including a stint as its speaker—was a member of the Continental Congress, and was elected in 1789 to represent Pennsylvania in the new U.S. Congress. In perhaps the most notable single action of his career, he was the first person to sign the U.S. Bill of Rights. Mullenberg died in 1801 at age 51 and is buried in Lancaster, Pennsylvania, in a cemetery less than a mile from Mifflin's burial place, which is at the Lutheran Church of the Holy Trinity.
18. After Muhlenberg, there would only be two other speakers of the U.S. House of Representatives who were representatives of Pennsylvania up through the 21st century. They were the 24th speaker, Galusha A. Grow (1823–1907), who was in the position during the first half of the American Civil War, and the 29th speaker Samuel J. Randall (1828–1890), who was speaker from 1876 to 1881.
19. "Pennsylvania 1793 Governor." *A New Nation Votes: American Election Returns 1787–1825,* 11 Jan. 2012, https://elections.lib.tufts.edu/catalog/0v838073v. Accessed 15 Dec. 2023.
20. Genêt's farm was in East Greenbush, New York.
21. Rossman. *Thomas Mifflin.* 221.
22. "To James Madison from Francis Corbin, 7 December 1791." *Founders Online,* National Archives, https://founders.archives.gov/documents/Madison/01-14-02-0125.
23. Hildreth, Richard. *Despotism in America: An Inquiry into the Nature, Results, and Legal Basis of the Slave-*

Notes—Chapter Eighteen

Holding System in the United States. Scholarly Publishing Office, University of Michigan Library, 1854. 268.

24. The Thirteenth Amendment to the U.S. Constitution reads: Section 1—Neither slavery nor involuntary servitude, except as a punishment for crime whereof the party shall have been duly convicted, shall exist within the United States, or any place subject to their jurisdiction, and section 2—Congress shall have power to enforce this article by appropriate legislation.

25. Mifflin, Warner. *Writings of Warner Mifflin.* Rutgers University Press, 21 May 2021.

26. McDowell, Michael R. (2013). "Warner Mifflin: A Founding Father of Abolitionism" Quaker Hill Quill—Quaker Hill Historic Preservation Foundation. 1.

27. McDowell. "Warner Mifflin." 4.

28. Patterson, K.D. "Yellow Fever Epidemics and Mortality in the United States, 1693–1905." *Social Science Medicine*, Vol 34, No. 8. Apr. 1992. 855–865, doi: 10.1016/0277-9536(92)90255-o. PMID: 1604377. https://pubmed.ncbi.nlm.nih.gov/1604377/.

29. Prinzi, Andrea. "History of Yellow Fever in the U.S." *American Society for Microbiology*, 17 May 2021, asm.org/Articles/2021/May/History-of-Yellow-Fever-in-the-U-S.

30. "Proclamation—Thanksgiving Day—1793, Pennsylvania." *WallBuilders*, 2017, wallbuilders.com/proclamation-thanksgiving-day-1793-pennsylvania/. Accessed 11 Dec. 2023.

31. Hogarth, Rana. "A Contemporary Black Perspective on the 1793 Yellow Fever Epidemic in Philadelphia." *American Journal of Public Health*, Vol. 109, No. 10, Oct. 2019. 1337–1338, https://www.ncbi.nlm.nih.gov/pmc/articles/PMC6727299/. Accessed 2 Apr. 2020.

32. *Ibid.*
33. *Ibid.*
34. *Ibid.*

35. Shenk, H.H. "The Myerstown Riot of 1793." *The Lebanon County Historical Society. Papers and Addresses and Acts and Proceedings and Biographical and Memorial Sketches*, Lebanon County Historical Society, 1919. 430–444.

36. The Six Nations were composed of the Mohawk, Cayuga, Seneca, Oneida, Onondaga and Tuscarora Native American nations.

37. Walking, bicycling, picnicking, swimming, boating, and fishing are popular at the Presque Isle State Park.

38. "Proclamation—Thanksgiving Day—1793, Pennsylvania." *WallBuilders*, 2017, wallbuilders.com/proclamation-thanksgiving-day-1793-pennsylvania/. Accessed 11 Dec. 2023.

39. Henry Lee (1756–1818) was governor of Virginia from 1791 to 1794. During the Revolutionary War, Lee had been one of Washington's top cavalry commanders, earning the nickname "Light-Horse" Harry Lee. American Civil War Confederate General Robert E. Lee was his son.

40. Rawle. "Sketch of the Life of Thomas Mifflin." 122–123.

41. "Our Story Introduction." *The Society of the Cincinnati*, www.societyofthecincinnati.org/our-story-introduction/.

42. "Officers, 1783–Present." *The Society of the Cincinnati*, www.societyofthecincinnati.org/officers-1783-present/. Accessed 5 Jan. 2024.

43. "Pennsylvania 1796 Governor. " *A New Nation Votes: American Election Returns 1787–1825*, 11 Jan. 2012, https://elections.lib.tufts.edu/catalog/9c67wm944. Accessed 15 Dec. 2023.

44. "WAYNE, Anthony 1745–1796." *U.S. House of Representatives: History, Art and Archives*, history.house.gov/People/Listing/W/WAYNE,-Anthony-(W000216)/. Accessed 11 Dec. 2023.

45. Folwell, Richard. *Short History of the Yellow Fever, That Broke out in the City of Philadelphia in July 1797*. Richard Folwell, 1798.

46. *Connecticut Courant*, August 28, 1797, 3.

47. Folwell. *Short History of the Yellow Fever.* 13–14.

48. Folwell. *Short History of the Yellow Fever.*

49. *Ibid.*

50. Davis, William. *The Fries Rebellion, 1798–99.* 1899, tile.loc.gov/storage-services/public/gdcmassbookdig/friesrebellion1700dav/friesrebellion1700dav.pdf. Accessed 12 Dec. 2023.

51. The Naval Act of 1794 authorized

the construction of the Navy's first six frigates.
52. "Thomas Mifflin—PA House of Representatives." *The Official Website for the Pennsylvania General Assembly*, www.legis.state.pa.us/cfdocs/legis/SpeakerBios/SpeakerBio.cfm?id=110.

Chapter Nineteen

1. Rossman. *Thomas Mifflin*. 306.
2. "Thomas Mifflin: Soldier-Statesmen of the Constitution. A Bicentennial Series." *Army Center of Military History*, 1987.
3. Heiges, George L. "The Evangelical Lutheran Church of the Holy Trinity Lancaster, Pennsylvania Part One—1730–1861."
4. *Ibid.*
5. They only used the building for one day, as the Pennsylvania state government needed to use it.
6. *The History of Trinity, Reading, Pa., 1751–1894*. Trinity Lutheran Church Congregation, 1894.
7. *The History of Trinity Lutheran Church, Reading, Pa.* 113.
8. Biddle, Charles. *Autobiography of Charles Biddle, Vice-President of the Supreme Executive Council of Pennsylvania. 1745–1821*. Privately printed. E. Claxton and Company, 1883. 246.
9. "To John Adams from Benjamin Rush, 19 August 1811." *Founders Online*, National Archives, https://founders.archives.gov/documents/Adams/99-02-02-5674.
10. Rawle. "Sketch of the Life of Thomas Mifflin." 123–124.

Chapter Twenty

1. Alden, John. *Souvenir and Official Programme of the Centennial Celebration of George Washington's Inauguration as First President of the United States*. Garnett & Gow, 1889. 96. The full text of the page on Mifflin reads:

> It relates that at: He was the son of a Quaker, who intended him for a mercantile career, but on the outbreak of the Revolution he insisted on taking up arms, and became one of the best-known men in the army as well as one of the bravest. At that time he had already achieved a considerable personal popularity in the politics of his native State. He was not at all in sympathy with the methods of Washington, and entered the combination to supplant the Virginia statesman and soldier in favor of General Gates. The failure of this scheme brought those who had been concerned in it into something like general disrepute. But the hold which Mifflin had gained on the hearts of Pennsylvanians was not to be affected in that way, and, in 1783, after the end of the war, he was elected to Congress. Elected to the presidency of that body it became his rather embarrassing duty to receive back, on behalf of the Confederation, the commission of Washington on the resignation of the latter as Commander in Chief. He took this occasion to show that he had been moved by no petty sentiment in the past, and replied to the few words of the Commander as follows: "We join you in commending the interests of our dearest country to the protection of Almighty God, beseeching Him to dispose the hearts and minds of its citizens to improve the opportunity afforded them of becoming a happy and respectable nation. And for you we address to Him our earnest prayers that a life so beloved may be fostered with all his care, that your days may be as happy as they have been illustrious, and that He will finally give you that reward which this world cannot give." After holding the office of Governor for nine years, Mifflin died in 1800.

2. Henry John Martin Klein, Ph.D. (1873–1965) was Professor of History and Archaeology at Franklin and Marshall College.
3. Klein includes the following text in his talk:

> While the British occupied Philadelphia General Mifflin removed his family to his farm at Angelica, near Reading, and he was chosen to

represent Berks County in the General Assembly. In 1785, General Mifflin was a member of the General Assembly from Philadelphia and was unanimously selected as speaker of the House.

In this same year, Mifflin was a member of the Board of Trustees of the newly established Franklin College in Lancaster.

He was governor of Pennsylvania for three terms of three years each, which was the limit under the Constitution of 1790. Governor Mifflin was greatly interested in the building of roads and in inland navigation. During the Insurrection in the western counties in 1794, he personally led the troops to Bedford, Pennsylvania, where they were joined by the militia of New Jersey, Maryland and Virginia, to form a national army—President Washington's first test of the strength of the new nation.

4. One notable case in the American Civil War of a highly placed general attempting to destroy the military career of another involved Henry Halleck and his efforts to damage U.S. Grant's reputation. The Civil War might have turned out quite differently had Grant been dismissed. In 1864, President Abraham Lincoln gave General Grant control of the Union Army. One difference between that situation and the Mifflin-Washington case: Halleck had a personal animosity towards Grant, while Mifflin thought (although mistakenly) that Washington's replacement by General Gates would be better for the Continental Army and the nation.

5. In his autobiographical book, *Memoirs of a Life Chiefly Passed in Pennsylvania Within the Last Sixty Years*, Alexander Graydon (1752–1818) covers his life from his youth to his service in public office including his time as an officer and prisoner of war in the American Revolutionary War.

6. Rawle. "Sketch of the Life of Thomas Mifflin." 124.

7. Powell, J.H. "Review of *Thomas Mifflin and the Politics of the American Revolution* by Kenneth R. Rossman." *The William and Mary Quarterly*, Vol. 10, No. 2, Apr. 1953. 294–297, https://www.jstor.org/stable/2936953. Accessed 13 Dec. 2023.

8. "Thomas Mifflin Historical Marker." *The Historical Marker Database*, www.hmdb.org/m.asp?m=84488. Accessed 8 Jan. 2024.

9. Croatti, Mark. "Mark Croatti: Give Taney's Spot to an Unprecedented President." *Capital Gazette*, 20 Sept. 2017, www.capitalgazette.com/2017/09/20/mark-croatti-give-taneys-spot-to-an-unprecedented-president/. Accessed 3 Jan. 2024.

10. *Historical Papers and Addresses of the Lancaster County Historical Society*, Volumes 2–3. Lancaster County Historical Society, 1897.

Bibliography

Adams, John. *The Works of John Adams, Second President of the United States.* Charles C. Little and James Brown, 1851.

Biddle, Charles. *Autobiography of Charles Biddle, Vice-President of the Supreme Executive Council of Pennsylvania.* Privately printed. Philadelphia: E. Claxton and Company. 1883.

Bloom, Sol, and United States. *The Story of the Constitution.* Washington, D.C.: United States Constitution Sesquicentennial Commission, 1937.

"A Brief History of Newport." *Newport Historical Society.* newporthistory.org/about/newport-history/.

Bulletin of Friends' Historical Society of Philadelphia. Vol. 16–18. Friends Historical Association, 1927.

Census History Staff. "Population in the Colonial and Continental Periods." U.S. Census Bureau. https://www.census.gov/history/pdf/colonialbostonpops.pdf.

"Collections of the New York Historical Society for the Year 1878." New York: The New York Historical Society, 1879.

Davis, William. *The Fries Rebellion, 1798–99.* 1899. tile.loc.gov/storage-services/public/gdcmassbookdig/friesrebellion1700dav/friesrebellion1700dav.pdf. Accessed December 12, 2023.

Dorwart, Jeffery M. *Fort Mifflin of Philadelphia: An Illustrated History.* Google Books, University of Pennsylvania Press, May 1, 1998. www.google.com/books/edition/Fort_Mifflin_of_Philadelphia/TsnZ_jlDWvMC?hl=en&gbpv=1&dq=governor+mifflin&pg=PA73&printsec=frontcover. Accessed 10 December 10, 2023.

"The Early Years: The Charity School, Academy and College of Philadelphia." 1972. *University Archives and Records Center.* archives.upenn.edu/digitized-resources/docs-pubs/early-years-1972/.

Egle, William Henry. *Notes and Queries: Chiefly Relating to Interior Pennsylvania.* 1891.

Fleming, Thomas. *1776.* Createspace Independent Publishing Platform. October 18, 2016.

Flexner, James. *Washington: The Indispensable Man.* New York: New American Library, 1984.

Folwell, Richard. *Short History of the Yellow Fever, That Broke Out in the City of Philadelphia in July 1797.* 2023. Philadelphia: Richard Folwell, 1798.

Force, Peter. *American Archives.* Vol. II. Washington, DC: M. St. Clair Clarke, 1848.

Franklin, Benjamin. *The Autobiography of Benjamin Franklin.* New York: Henry Holt and Company, 1916. www.gutenberg.org/cache/epub/20203/pg20203-images.html. Accessed December 15, 2023.

Freeman, Douglas Southall. *George Washington, a Biography.* Clifton, NJ: A.M. Kelley, 1975.

Grainger, John D. *The Battle of Yorktown, 1781: A Reassessment.* Woodbridge, UK: Boydell Press, 2005.

Greene, George W. *Life of Nathanael Greene, Major-General in the Army of the Revolution.* Boston: Charles C. Little and James Brown, 1846.

Bibliography

Haas, Bernard D. "Charles Carroll of Carrollton: A Member of the Continental Congress, 1776–1778." Master's thesis, Loyola University Chicago, February 1948, pp. 25–26. ecommons.luc.edu/cgi/viewcontent.cgi?article=1199&context=luc_theses. Accessed December 14, 2023.

"Hail Columbia." Library of Congress, Washington, DC, 2002. Manuscript/Mixed Material. www.loc.gov/item/ihas.200000008/.

Harley, Lewis Reifsneider. *The Life of Charles Thomson*. Philadelphia: George W. Jacobs & Co., 1900. www.google.com/books/edition/The_Life_of_Charles_Thomson/OlwSAAAAYAAJ?hl=en&gbpv=1&dq=The+Life+of+Charles+Thomson&printsec=frontcover. Accessed December13, 2023.

Heiges, George L. "The Evangelical Lutheran Church of the Holy Trinity Lancaster, Pennsylvania: Part One, 1730–1861." *Journal of the Lancaster County Historical Society*, vol. 83, no. 1 (1979): 2–71.

Hubbard, Robert Ernest. *General Rufus Putnam: George Washington's Chief Military Engineer and the "Father of Ohio."* Jefferson, NC: McFarland, 2020.

_____. *Major General Israel Putnam: Hero of the American Revolution*. Jefferson, NC: McFarland, 2017.

Iwanicki, Edwin. *The Village of Falls of Schuylkill*. Pennsylvania Historical Salvage Council, 1967.

"John Cadwalader." Penn Libraries: University Archives and Records Center, Penn People A-Z. archives.upenn.edu/exhibits/penn-people/biography/john-cadwalader/. Accessed December 14, 2023.

Journals of Congress: Containing the Proceedings from January 1, 1776, to January 1, 1777 / Vol. II. Yorktown, Pennsylvania, 1778.

Journals of the Continental Congress, 1774–1789 / Vol. IX: 1777. Washington, DC: Government Printing Office, 1907.

Landis, Charles I. *The First Long Turnpike in the United States*. Lancaster, PA: New Era Printing Company, 1917.

Lender, Mark Edward. *Cabal! The Plot against General Washington, The Conway Cabal Reconsidered*. Yardley, PA: Westholme Publishing, 2019.

Lengel, Edward G. *General George Washington: A Military Life*. New York: Random House, 2007.

"Letters of Delegates to Congress: Volume 5, August 16, 1776–December 31, 1776: Richard Henry Lee to Patrick Henry." Library of Congress. memory.loc.gov/cgi-bin/query/r?ammem/hlaw:@field(DOCID+@lit(dg005550)). Accessed February 23, 2024.

Long, O.F. "Quartermaster's Department: The Army of the U.S. Historical Sketches of Staff and Line with Portraits of Generals-In-Chief." U.S. Army Center of Military History. history.army.mil/books/r&h/R&H-QM.htm. Accessed December 13, 2023.

Lutheran Church: The History of Trinity, Reading, Pa., 1751–1894. Trinity Lutheran Church Congregation, 1894.

Magazine of American History. Vol. 7. A.S. Barnes & Company, 1881.

McCullough, David. *John Adams*. New York: Simon & Schuster Paperbacks, 2008.

_____. *1776*. New York: Simon & Schuster Paperbacks, 2006.

Mifflin, Martha J. *Sketch of Joseph Simon by Samuel Evans & Thomas Mifflin by Martha J. Mifflin:* Paper Read before the Lancaster County Historical Society on March 8, and April 7, 1899.

Mifflin, Warner. *Writings of Warner Mifflin*. New Brunswick, NJ: Rutgers University Press, 2021.

Montgomery, Thomas Harrison. *A History of the University of Pennsylvania: From Its Foundation to A.D. 1770; Including Biographical Sketches of the Trustees, Faculty, the First Alumni and Others*. Philadelphia: G.W. Jacobs & Company, 1900.

Nagy, John A. *George Washington's Secret Spy War: The Making of America's First Spymaster*. New York: St. Martin's Press, 2016.

Nash, Gary B., and Billy G. Smith. "The Population of Eighteenth-Century Philadelphia." *Pennsylvania Magazine of History and Biography*, January 1, 1975, pp. 362–368. journals.psu.edu/pmhb/article/view/43167/42888. Accessed December 13, 2023.

Penn, John. *Pennsylvania Magazine of History and Biography*, vol. 3, no. 3. University of Pennsylvania Press, 1879.

Portrait and Biographical Record of Lehigh, Northampton and Carbon Counties, Pennsylvania. Chicago: Pennsylvania Chapman Publishing Co., 1894.

Powell, J.H. Review of *Thomas Mifflin and the Politics of the American Revolution* by Kenneth R. Rossman. *The William and Mary Quarterly*, vol. 10, no. 2 (April 1953): 294–297. https://www.jstor.org/stable/2936953. Accessed December 13, 2023.

Prinzi, Andrea. "History of Yellow Fever in the U.S." *American Society for Microbiology*, May 17, 2021. asm.org/Articles/2021/May/History-of-Yellow-Fever-in-the-U-S.

Procknow, Gene. "Thomas Mifflin: Revolutionary Enigma." *Researching the American Revolution*, January 27, 2018. researchingtheamericanrevolution.com/2018/01/27/thomas-mifflin-revolutionary-enigma/. Accessed December 13, 2023.

Prowell, George Reeser. *Continental Congress at York, Pennsylvania and York County in the Revolution*. The York Printing Company, 1914.

Rawle, William. "Sketch of the Life of Thomas Mifflin." In *Memoirs of the Historical Society of Pennsylvania*, vol. 2, pt. 2. Philadelphia: Carey, Lea & Carey, 1826, pp. 107–126.

Reed, William Bradford. *Life and Correspondence of Joseph Reed*. Philadelphia: Lindsay and Blakiston, 1847.

Regan, Gary. *The Joy of Mixology, Revised and Updated Edition: The Consummate Guide to the Bartender's Craft*. New York: Clarkson Potter, 2018.

Risch, Erna. *Supplying Washington's Army*. Washington, DC: Center of Military History, United States Army, 1981. history.army.mil/html/books/040/40-2/cmhPub_40-2.pdf. Accessed December 10, 2023.

Rossman, Kenneth R. *Thomas Mifflin and the Politics of the American Revolution*. Chapel Hill: University of North Carolina Press, 1952.

Sachar, Howard Morley. *A History of the Jews in America*. New York: Alfred A. Knopf, 1994.

Scudder, Horace E. *George Washington: An Historical Biography*. Boston: Houghton, Mifflin Company, 1889.

"Selections from the Military Papers of John Cadwalader." *Pennsylvania Magazine of History and Biography*, vol. 32, no. 125 (1908).

Stryker, William S. *The Battles of Trenton and Princeton*. Boston: Houghton, Mifflin, 1898.

Tinkcom, Harry M. Review of *Thomas Mifflin and the Politics of the American Revolution* by Kenneth R. Rossman. *The Pennsylvania Magazine of History and Biography*, vol. 77, no. 2 (April 1953): 218–220. www.jstor.org/stable/20088463. Accessed December 13, 2023.

"U.S. Census Bureau QuickFacts: Mifflin County, Pennsylvania." U.S. Census Bureau. www.census.gov/quickfacts/mifflincountypennsylvania.

Verenna, Thomas. "Explaining Pennsylvania's Militia." *Journal of the American Revolution*, June 17, 2014. https://allthingsliberty.com/2014/06/explaining-pennsylvanias-militia/. Accessed December 16, 2023.

Werther, Richard J. "Analyzing the Founders: A Closer Look at the Signers of Four Founding Documents." *Journal of the American Revolution*, October 24, 2017. https://allthingsliberty.com/2017/10/analyzing-founders-closer-look-signers-4-founding-documents/.

Wilson, Woodrow. *George Washington*. New York: Harper, 1896.

Wright, Robert K., Jr., and Morris J. MacGregor, Jr. *Soldier-Statesmen of the Constitution*. Washington, DC: United States Army Center of Military History, 1987.

Zellers-Frederick, Andrew A. "General Thomas Conway: Cabal Conspirator or Career Climber?" *Journal of the American Revolution*, October 29, 2018. https://allthingsliberty.com/2018/10/general-thomas-conway-cabal-conspirator-or-career/.

Index

Numbers in **_bold italics_** indicate pages with photographs

Academy and Charitable School in the Province of Pennsylvania 16
Adams, Abigail 10, 26, **_27_**, 28, 34–35, 42, 102
Adams, John 5, 9–10, 19, 23, 26, **_27_**, 28, 34–35, 42, 46, 62, 64–67, 102, 117, 126, 132, 149, 164, 167–168, 185–186, 189, 203–204n17, 209n6
Adams, John Quincy 17
Adams, Samuel 9, 27, 30, 32, 37
African Americans 173–175, 178, 199n10
African Methodist Episcopal Church 175, 178
Alexander, William (Lord Stirling) 92–93, 104, 116, 120, 124–125, 207n27
Alison, Patrick 15
Allen, Richard 178
American Civil War 25, 38, 72, 93, 111–112, 118, 174–175, 193–194, 215n39, 217n4
American Legion 183
American Peace Commissioners 145, 212n15
American Philosophical Society 13–14, 19, 160, 198n16, 204n29, 211n3
Angelica (Mifflin farm) 134, 136, 154, 173, 193, 213n13, 216n3
Anglicans (Pennsylvania) 14
Armstrong, Gen. John 155
Armstrong, Joseph (Col.) 86
Arnold, Benedict 30, 92–95, 105, 137, 204n31, 207n23, 207n27, 208n8
Arnold, Henry H. "Hap" 93
Articles of Association 36–37
Articles of Confederation 38–39, 109, 138, 140, 149, 157, 197–198n1

Baptists 14
Berks County 134, 136, 137, 193, 213n13, 216–217n3
Berks County Farm and Home 193, 213n13
Biddle, Charles 133, 188
Biddle, Clement 97, 99–100, 103, 208n10, 211ch14n4
Biddle, Edward 30, 200n6
Bland, Theodorick 139
Blyth, Benjamin 27
Board of War 62–65, 71, 79, 99, 107–110, 117–119, 122–123
Bolívar, Simón 126
Bonaparte, Napoleon 186, 204n29
Boone, Daniel 154, 213n12
Boston (city) 11–12, 23, 26–30, 32–33, 40–**_45_**, 48–51, 53–54, 58, 99, 106, 127, 200n17, 203n6
Boston Massacre 28, 30
Boston Tea Party 28, 30
Brandywine Creek, Battle of 105
Brattle House (in Cambridge, Massachusetts) **_45_**
Breed's Hill Battle of, Bunker Hill, Battle of
Brooklyn, Battle of see Long Island, Battle of
Brown, William (Capt.) 86
Bunker Hill, Battle of 43–46, **_53_**, 62, 127, 203n6
Burd, James (Col.) 86
Burgoyne, Gen. John 54, 106, 115, 123
Burr, Aaron 25, 105, 183
Butler, Richard 155

Cadwalader, John 19, 85, 86, 87, 88, 128, 206n6

223

Index

Cambridge, Massachusetts 45, 48–49, 50–51, 202n5
Caribbean islands 12, 14, 18, 21, 46, 112, 145, 176, 184
Carroll, Charles 65
Carroll, Daniel 153
Cary, Richard 60
Chase, Jeremiah Townley 142
China, First American trade mission to 140–141
Christ Church (Philadelphia) 160
Clinton, Gen. George 68, 112, 173
Clinton, Gen. Henry 206, 123, 127
Clymer, George 60, 87, 149–150, 191
Cole, Philip (Col.) 86
Coleman, William 12–13, 16, 18
College of Philadelphia, Academy and College of Philadelphia 14–15, 29, 159–160, 206n6
Concord, Massachusetts 37, 40, 41, 44, 50
Congress of the Confederation 34, 38, 61, 118, 138–142, 163, 180
Congress's Committee of Safety 79
Constitutional Convention, Pennsylvania 147, 156–158
Constitutional Convention, United States 39, 147, 149–*152*, 156–157
Constitutional Convention, Virginia 56
Continental Congress 1, 3–6, 13, 27–31, 33–34, 36, 38, 41, 43–44, 47, 56–57, 60, 62, 69, 71, 73, 75–76, 80–81, 89, 92, 93, 95, 100, 105–106, 109, 116–118, 125, 132, 137, 139–143, 145, 147, 149, *152*, 157, 162, 175, 193, 197–198*ch*1*n*1, 203*n*6, 210*n*32, 214*n*17
Conway, Thomas 42, 107, 114–133, 209*ch*13*n*7
Conway Cabal 110, 114–133, 145–147, 183, 192
Cooke, William (Col.) 86
Copley, John Singleton 23–*24*, 25, 27
Cornwallis, Gen. Charles 211*n*2
court martial 73, 103
Cowpens, Battle of 137–138
Craig, Isaac (Capt.) 86
Craig, Thomas 7, 42, 112, 201*n*9
Crawford, James (Col.) 86
Croatti, Mark 194
Cumberland County (Pennsylvania) 136
Curie, Marie 20

Danbury (Connecticut) 99
Danvers (Massachusetts) 58
Darragh, Lydia 99, 112, 209*n*15
Davis, John 173–175

Deane, Elizabeth 42
Deane, Silas 42
Declaration of Independence 10, 36–37, 56, 60–61, 131, 145, 149, *152*, 198*n*8, 200*n*11
De Gaulle, Charles 126
De Haas, John Philip (Col.) 85
De Kalb, Gen. Johann 42, 106, 121, 123
Democrat-Republicans 171, 183
Dickinson, John 19, 31–33, 36, 42, 137, 149–150, 162, 200*n*12
Dorchester Heights 51
dueling 25, 128, 183
Duff, Thomas (Maj.) 86
Dunwoody, William 99

Edison, Thomas 20
Einstein, Albert 6, 20
Erie Triangle 180
Erwin, Arthur (Col.) 86

Falls of Schuylkill Estate 19, 35, *134*–136, 159, 211*ch*14*n*9
Federalists 5, 137, 157–158, 160–162, 164, 183, 186
Fellows, John 68
Fleming, Thomas 130, 204*n*32, 210*n*33
Folwell, Richard 184, 185
Forrest, Thomas 86
Fort Lee 70–72, 84
Fort Mifflin 110, *111*, 112, 209*n*13
Fort Ticonderoga (Fort Carillon) 50, 51, 203*n*7
Fort Washington 61, 70, 84, 115
Fort Wilson Riot 130–132
Fountain Green *134*–135
Franklin, Benjamin 6–7, 9–13, 16, 18–19, 22, 34, 37, 60, 100, 126, 128, 146, 149, 151, *153*, 156, 159–160, 189, 191
French and Indian War 9, 29, 37, 41, 45, *53*–54, 56, 58, 69, 90, 96, 145, 206*n*11, 208*n*12
French Revolution 124, 168, 172
Fugitive Slave Act of 1793 174
Fugitive Slave Act of 1850 175

Gage, Gen. Thomas 40
Galbraith, Bartram (Col.) 86
Gates, Gen. Horatio 52, 54–55, 66, 106, *110*, 114–118, 120, 122–127, 129, 183, 191–192, 194, 203*n*6, 216*n*1, 217*n*4
Geiger, Henry (Col.) 86
Genêt, Edmond-Charles 159, 167–168, 172–173, 214*n*20
Genêt Affair 159, 172–173
George III (English King) 17, 28–29, 33

Index

Germantown, Battle of 105, 115–116, 128, 204*n*32
Gloucester Fox Hunting Club 18
Glover, John 58
Gorham, Nathaniel 139, 150, 153, 188
Gradual Abolition Act of 1780 (Pennsylvania General Assembly) 14
Green, Timothy (Col.) 86
Greene, George Washington 76
Greene, Nathanael 13, 39, 54, 64–65, 70, 72, 76, *77*, 78, 94, 96, 105, 114–115, 117, 119, 129, 137, 148, 155, 205*n*12, 208*n*8, 213*n*24
Griffin, Cyrus 139

Haas, Bernard D. 65
Haig, Alexander 93
"Hail Columbia" 170–171
Hamilton, Alexander 9, 25, 129, 164, 173
Hancock, John 27, 30, 32, 57, 64, 79, 95, 139, 140, 145
Hanson, John 138
Harlem Heights 69
Harmar, Josiah 145–146, 212*n*14, 212*n*15
Harrison, Benjamin 62, 64, 79, 205*n*18
Harrison, Robert 107–108, 117, 122, 203–204*n*17, 209*ch*12*n*7
Hart, Charles Henry 23–25, 199*n*11
Hazen, Col. Moses 131
Heath, Gen. William 49, 51–52, 68
Henry, George (Capt.) 86
Henry, Patrick 9, 30–31, 40, 82, 126, 197*n*3
Hessians 69, 84, 102
Hildreth, Richard 174
Hoover, Herbert 171
Hopkins, Esek 141
Hopkinson, Emily Mifflin 13, 25, 169, *170*, 171
Hopkinson, Joseph 13, 25, 169–171, 186, 198*n*8
Hopkinson, Oliver 25
Howe, Gen. William 50–51, 70, 84, 88, 96, 103, 112, 175, 202*ch*6*n*7
Howell, David 142
Humpton, Richard (Col.) 85
Hunter, Samuel (Col.) 86
Huntington, Jedediah 124, 139
Hutchinson, Israel 58, 203*n*7

Independence Hall (Philadelphia) 13, *152*
Ingersoll, Jared 149, 191
Intolerable Acts 30, 36

Jay, John 17, 69
Jay Treaty (1794) 185–186
Jefferson, Thomas 9, 10, 17, 19, 31, 34, 59, 75, 126, 128, 140, 142, 149, 151, 160, 164, 167, 168, 173
Jewish residents (Pennsylvania) 58–59, 160, 199*n*10
Johnson, Paul 34
Johnson, Thomas 36
Jones, Absalom 178
Jones, Cadwalader 99
Juarez, Benito 126

Kenyatta, Jomo 126
King, Rufus 15
Kings Mountain, Battle of 138
Kip's Bay (battle) 69–70, 204n32
Klein, H.M.J. 191–192, 198*n*5, 216–217*n*3
Knox, Henry 51, 90, 105, 115, 118, 124, 154, 183, 212*n*14
Kościuszko, Thaddeus 105

Lafayette, Marquis de 19, 92, 106, 119–121, 129, 155
Lancaster Court House 188
Laurens, Henry 132
Lechmere's Point 42
Lee, Charles 62, 208*n*8
Lee, Francis Lightfoot 79, 205*n*18
Lee, John (Capt.) 86
Lee, Richard Henry 47–48, 82, 107–110, 118, 121, 139
Lender, Mark Edward 117
Lexington, Battle of 40–41, 43, 44, 50, 58
Library Company (Philadelphia) 12
Library of Congress 27, 43, 45, 134, 140, 152
Lincoln, Abraham 93, 171, 217*n*4
Lincoln, Benjamin 92–93, 104, 118, 201*n*13, 207*n*27
Long Island, Battle of 56, 58–59, 67–68, 115, 129, 148, 204*n*31
Louis XV 18
Louis XVI (King of France) 172
Lutheran Church of the Holy Trinity (Lancaster, Pennsylvania) 187, 214*n*17, 216*ch*19*n*3
Lutheran Historical Society of the Mid-Atlantic 188
Lutter, Henry Emanuel 100, 103, 208*n*10

Madison, Dolley 10
Madison, James 9, 19, 34, 59, 126, 139, 149–150, 164
Magaw, Robert 58–60

Manhattan Island 68, 69, 98, 204*n*32
Manwood, Charles 88
Marshall, John 9, 19, 105, 209*ch*12*n*2
Maryland State House 142, 194
Matlock, Timothy (Col.) 86
Maxwell, William 124
McClellan, George B. 93
McDougall, Alexander 68
McDowell, Michael R. 175
McIntosh, Lachlan 124
McKean, Thomas 138, 155, 156–157, 159, 162–163, 186–187, 192, 211*ch*15*n*1
Mead, Margaret 20
Meade, George 93
Meigs, Montgomery C. 72
Mercer, Hugh 88–*89*, 111, 155, 206*n*11, 209*n*14
Middleton, Henry 140
Mifflin, Elizabeth (Bagnell) (mother) 12, 170
Mifflin, Emily (daughter) *see* Hopkinson, Emily Mifflin
Mifflin, Frances (daughter) 25
Mifflin, George (brother) 18
Mifflin, John (father) 12, 21
Mifflin, John Fishbourne (half-brother) 13
Mifflin, Jonathan (cousin) 66, 103, 208*n*15
Mifflin, Lloyd 194
Mifflin, Martha J. 32
Mifflin, Sarah Morris (wife) 23–*24*, 25–27, 136, 169–170, 199*n*10, 199*n*12
Mifflin, Thomas: American Philosophical Society 14, 19; Battle of Princeton 88; Battle of Trenton 84; birth 6, 11, 198*ch*2*n*1; Board of War appointment 108; childhood 11–14; Constitutional Convention delegate 147; Continental Congress member 34, 210*n*33; Continental Congress president 3, 140, *142*, 212*n*15; Conway Cabal 110, 114–133, 145–147, 183, 192, 216*ch*20*n*1; country home at the Falls of Schuylkill 134; daughters born 25; death 182–185; education 13–16; European tour 16–19, 199*n*22; Fries Rebellion 185; governor of Pennsylvania 3, 5, 23, 31, 43, 133–134, 139, 147, 155, 157–190, 216–217*ch*20*n*3; Lutheran Church 150, 172, 187–188, 192; marriage 12, 24; military aide to Washington 6, 201*n*13; Newport (RI) trip 26; Pennsylvania Provincial Assembly 22; Philadelphia warden 22; physical appearance 193; portraits *4*, *24*,

37, *54*, 89, *142*, *189*; president of the Pennsylvania Constitutional Convention 147, 156–158, 162; promoted to brigadier general 53; promoted to major general 71; Quakers 12–14, 26, 29, 39, 172, 175, 199*n*12, 201*n*37; Quartermaster General appointment 47, 208*n*10, 210*n*33; requests extradition of Virginia slave kidnappers 173; Society of the Cincinnati Vice President General 183; Supreme Executive Council of Pennsylvania President 156, 186; Washington's Resignation accepted *142*; Whiskey Rebellion suppressed 67, 181–182
Mifflin, Warner 175
Mifflin County (Pennsylvania) 155, 163, 213*n*16
Mifflin Hall (Headquarters Building for the Quartermaster School) 72
Mississippi (river) 142, 175, 195
M'Lane, Allen 131–132
Monmouth, Battle of 128, 201*n*9, 203*n*4, 208*n*8
Monroe, James 34, 105, 197*ch*1*n*1
Moores Creek Bridge, Battle of 50–51
Morgan, Daniel 137–138
Morris, Gouverneur 101, 149, 191
Morris, Jacob 101, 208*n*8, 208*n*10
Morris, Lewis 101, 199*n*10
Morris, Samuel 86
Moylan, Stephen 57, 61, 65, 69, 71, 72, 90, 203*n*4
Muhlenberg, Frederick 171–172, 183, 214*n*17, 214*n*18
Myerstown, Pennsylvania Riot 178–179, 215*n*35

Nassau Hall (Princeton University) 89
National Whistleblower Day 141
Native Americans 44–46, 172–173, 180–181, 212*n*14, 215*n*36
New Haven, Connecticut 99
New Orleans 176, 184
New York (city) 1, 6, 12, 51–54, 56–57, 59–60, 67–70, 78, 84, 104
Newport, Rhode Island 26, 70
Nicholas, Samuel (Maj.) 86
nicknames 14, 39, 77, 215*n*39

Ordinance of 1784 140–142
Ordinance of 1787 142

Packer, William F. 147
Paine, Thomas 13, 126
Pasteur, Louis 20

Paterson, John 124
Peale, Charles Willson **43**
Penn, John 154, 213*n*14
Penn, William 14, 213*n*14
Pennsylvania Army National Guard 38, 187
Pennsylvania Board of War 99
Pennsylvania Constitution of 1790 147, 156–158, 162
Pennsylvania Gazette 15, 151
Pennsylvania General Assembly 14, 137, 146–147, 182, 186
Pennsylvania Governor Election of 1790 162–168
Pennsylvania Governor Election of 1793 171–172
Pennsylvania Governor Election of 1796 183–184
Pennsylvania House of Representatives 163, 164, 165, 187, 204*n*29, 212*n*18
Pennsylvania Provincial Assembly 22, 29, 133
Penrose, Joseph (Col.) 85
Percival, Thomas 128
Peters, Richard 117, 203–204*n*17
Philadelphia and Lancaster Turnpike 169
Philadelphia Associators 37–38, 84, 86
Philadelphia Dancing Assembly 23
Philadelphia, Port of 31, 163, 173
Phile, Philip 170
Pickering, Timothy 72–73, 107–108, 117, 122, 209*ch*12*n*6
Piper, John 86
Plains of Abraham, Battle of 203*n*7
Poor, Enoch 124
Popham, William 183
Porter, Thomas (Col.) 86
Potter, James 86, 155
Powell, J.H. 147, 193, 213*n*23
Prescott, Col. William 45
Presque Isle 180–181, 215*n*37
Princeton, Battle of 88, **89**, 90, 100, 128, 206*n*12, 209*n*14
Procknow, Gene 109, 115
Putnam, Israel 1, 45, 50, 52, **53**, 54, 56, 62, 68–70, 80–82, 87, 98–99, 104, 207*n*27
Putnam, Rufus 1, 51, 68–69, 98

Quakers 12–14, 26, 29, 39, **77**, 112, 132, 168, 172, 175
Quartermaster General 3, 38, 43–44, 47–51, 57, 60, 61, 69, 71–79, 90–91, 95–96, 99, 100, 103, 107–108, 129, 192, 194–195, 205*n*2, 206*n*16

Quebec 203*n*7
Queen's Rangers 208*n*12

Randolph, Beverly 174
Rawle, William 148, 150, 157–159, 169, 182, 189, 193, 201*n*9, 212*n*11–15
Read, Thomas 86
Redman, John 184–185
Reed, Joseph 32–33, 42, 44, 48, 57, 76, 211*n*41
Revere, Paul 32, 40, 200*n*17
Ritner, Joseph 147
Rodney, Thomas (Capt.) 86
Rogers, Robert 102, 208*n*12
Roman Catholics 14, 57
Roosevelt, Franklin 197*n*4
Ross, George (Col.) 86
Rossman, Kenneth 3, 5, 18, 22, 23, 48, 73, 89, 107, 133, 147, 170, 173, 193, 200*n*15, 213*ch*15*n*20, 213*ch*15*n*23, 213*ch*16*n*13
Rush, Benjamin 31–32, 60, 117, 126–127, 176–178, 189, 200*n*15
Rutherford, Thomas 96–97
Rutledge, Edward 36, 62, 64, 69, 79, 203–204*n*17, 205*n*18
Rutledge, John 36, 149

Sachar, Howard M. 59
St. Clair, Arthur 92–93, 139, 158, 162–163, 207*n*27
Salomon, Haym 59
San Martín, José de 126
Saratoga, Battle of 54, 106–107, 110, 115, 117–118, 126, 137–138, 194, 200*n*4
Sargent, Paul 58
Scammell, Alexander 68, 204*n*31
Schuyler, Philip 62, 71
Schuylkill Fishing Company 19
Scott, Charles 124
Scudder, Horace Elisha 142–143
Second Continental Congress 3, 34, 38, 48, 60, 73, 109, **152**
Sedgwick, John 148
Shaw, Samuel 141
Shays, Daniel 181
Shays' Rebellion 181
Sherman, Roger 36, 62, 64, 149, 197–198*n*1, 201*n*32, 203–204*n*17
Shippen, William (Capt.) 86
Six Nations of the Iroquois Confederacy 180, 215*n*36
Smallwood, William 68–70, 204*n*32
Smallwood's Maryland regiment 68
Smith, William Rev. 159–160
Snickers, Edward 74, 95–97

Snyder, Simon 147, 155
Society of the Cincinnati 183
Sons of Liberty 30, 59
Spanish flu of 1918 176
Spencer, Gen. Joseph 68, 207n27
Stamp Act 30
"The Star-Spangled Banner" 171
Stark, John 45
Stephen, Adam 92
Stroud, Jacob (Col.) 86
Sullivan, John 51–62, 101, 104, 155
Sun, Yat-sen 126
Supreme Executive Council of Pennsylvania 146, 156, 160, 163, 186, 188, 211n41

Taney, Roger 193–194
Tarleton, Banastre 137–138
Taylor, George (Col.) 86
Thomson, Charles 4, 32, 33, 36
Throg's Neck (in Bronx, New York) 70
Tilghman, Tench 85, 125
Tinkcom, Harry M. 107
Tories 29, *45*, 61, 66, 131, 208n12
Toulon, Battle of 11
Treaty of Paris (1763) 145, 212n12
Treaty of Paris (1783) 145, 195
Treaty of Paris (1799) 145, 212n13
Trenton, Battle of 38, 58, 84–87, 102, 130, 206n6
Truman, Harry S. 118, 183
Trumbull, John (Painter) 54, *89*, *142*, 144, 189, 212n10
Trumbull, Jonathan, Jr. 23
Trumbull, Joseph 117
Tryon, William 99

U.S. Army Quartermaster Corps and Quartermaster School 72, 193, 206n16
United States Constitution 3, 9–10, 15, 37, 39, 56–57, 60, 84, 101, 109, 118, 139, 144, 147, 149–*152*, *153*–154, 156–158, 161, 163, 166–167, 174–175, 178–179, 182, 184, 188–189, 191, 194–195, 197–198ch1n1, 198ch2n5, 213n11, 215n24
United States House of Representatives 23, 139, 150, 171, 172, 214n18
U.S. Supreme Court 9, 15, 17, 105, 160, 167, 193, 210n34, 213n6

Valley Forge 77, 105–109, 111–113, 119, 126, 147, 192, 194–195, 209ch12n1, 209ch12n2
Varnum, James 124
Veterans of Foreign Wars 183
Virginia House of Delegates 174
Von Steuben, Baron 42, 59, 105

Walton, George 87
Ward, Artemas 62, 67
Warren, James 46, 202n17
Warren, Joseph 155, 203n6
Warren, Mercy Otis 10, 202n17
Washington, George 6, 7, 9–10, 15, 19, 23, 34, 37, 41, *43*–44, 46, 51, 60, 74, 76, 88, 92, 95, 105, 115, 118, 126–129, 133, 139, *142*, 144, 148–150, *153*, 165, 172, 174–176, 186, 189, 191, 197ch1n1, 201n13, 203n21, 204n31, 206n11, 207n23, 208n7, 209ch12n7, 210n32, 210n34, 211n4, 212n11, 216ch20n1, 216ch20n3, 217n4
Washington, Martha 23
Waxhaws, Battle of 137
Wayne, Anthony 54, 105, 115, 155, 184, 202n6
Weedon, George 124
West, Benjamin 17
West Point Chain 66–67
Wheeler, Samuel 66–67, 204n29
Whiskey Rebellion 133, 181
White Plains, Battle of 58, 70, 129, 204n32
Wilkinson, James 114–116, 125
William Brattle House *45*
Williamson, Hugh 15, 139
Willing, Thomas 159–160
Wilson, James 5, 60, 62, 64, 79, 130, 149, 182, 188, 191, 205n18, 210n34
Wilson, Woodrow 35
Woodhull, Alfred Alexander 89
Wooster, David 99
Wynkoop, Gerardus II 146, 212n18

Yale University Art Gallery 54, 77, 89, 110
Yellow Fever epidemics 175–178, 184–185, 213n23
Yorktown, Battle of 72, 129, 139, 148, 203n4, 204n31, 211ch15n2

www.ingramcontent.com/pod-product-compliance
Lightning Source LLC
Chambersburg PA
CBHW032040300426
44117CB00009B/1126